ISLAM a code of social life

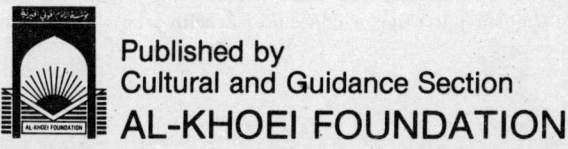

Published by
Cultural and Guidance Section
AL-KHOEI FOUNDATION

ISLAM – A CODE OF SOCIAL LIFE
Persian Title : *Islam dar Qalb-i-Ijtima'*
&
Arabic Title : *Tuhaful Uqūl 'An Āle Rasūl*

First Published in Pakistan in 1980 by
ISLAMIC SEMINARY PUBLICATION
A Publishing Division of
ISLAMIC SEMINARY PAKISTAN
P.O. BOX 5425 KARACHI-74000
This impression 1997

ISBN 0-941724-14-X
Copyright © Islamic Seminary Pakistan
All rights reserved

Mailing Address

The General Secretary,
Al-Khoei Foundation,
Chevening Road,
London NW6,
ENGLAND

Conditions for Sale

This book or any part thereof is sold subject to the condition that it shall not by way of any trade or otherwise circulated in any form of binding or cover other than what it is published in, without a similar condition including this condition being imposed on the subsequent purchaser or donee, except with prior written permission of the copyright owner.

بِسْمِ اللهِ الرَّحْمٰنِ الرَّحِيمِ

اَلْحَمْدُ لِلّٰهِ الَّذِي عَلَّمَ بِالْقَلَمِ
عَلَّمَ الْإِنْسَانَ مَا لَمْ يَعْلَمْ
وَصَلَّى اللهُ عَلَى مُحَمَّدٍ وَآلِهِ وَسَلَّمْ

IMAM KHOEI

CONTENTS

PART – I

	Page
Foreword	9
Campaign against Ignorance	16
Dispute is Forbidden	22
Social Responsibilities	24
Education and Training of Child	27
Duties of the Children	32
Service to Humanity	35
Good Deeds	39
Helping the Oppressed	41
Mutual Co-operation amongst Muslims	43
Behaviour towards the Servants	46
Zakat — The Share of the Needy	48
The Financial Rights	52
Charity in the Cause of Allah	54
Do not let them feel Inferior or Humiliated	56
Moderation	58
Granting a Loan	59

Forgiveness and Toleration	64
Hypocrisy and Double-dealing	66
Mutual Trust	69
Truthfulness	71
Trustworthiness	74
Visiting the Sick	76
Sympathy with the Bereaved	78
Friendship	80
The Decencies	83
Redeeming the Promise	85
Consultation	87
During Journey	90
Jihad	95
In the Battlefield	98
On the Seat of Justice	101
Work and Effort	105
Farming, Animal Husbandry and Trade	107
What the Businessmen should Know	110
Formation of a Family	116
What Married Couples should Know	120
Cleanliness and Purity	125
The Dress We should Wear	130
Relation of Kinsmanship	134
Hospitality	136
Showing Love to Orphans	140
Respect for the Dead	142
Protection of Animals	145

PART — II

A Few Words	150
Desire — Gift — Goodness	152
Sincerity — Good morals — Management of the Household — Perseverance — Prodigality	153
Moderation — Friendship — Honesty	154
Equity — Charity in the Path of Allah — Faith	155
Parsimony — Mistrust — Brotherhood	156
Forbearance — Goodness — Rebellion	157
The Helpless — Independence and Poverty	158
Regret — Resignation and Fortitude — Piety	159
Pride — Laziness — Humility	160
Wealth — Pepentance	161
Trust in Allah — Calumny	162
Peeping at the Sins of Others — Jihad — Flattery Love for Worldly Passions — Jealousy	163
Truth — Wisdom	164
Modesty — Deceit — Intellect — Humility	165
Sincerity — Cheerfulness — Dishonesty	166
Goodness — Using Abusive Language Remembering Allah — Friendship	167
Leniency — Hypocrisy — Piety	168

Generosity — Salutation — Ill-nature 169
Evil Deeds — Thanksgiving — Patience 170
Truth — Observation of relationship 171
Feast — Covetousness — Oppression 172
Welfare — Self-conceit — Justice 173
Honour — Forgiviness 174
Forgivness and Remission — Knowledge and Learning 175
Table Manners — Vanity 176
Anger — Negligence — Working for sustenance 177
Backbiting — Corruption — Wickedness
Hard-heartedness 178
Retaliation — Contentment — Falsehood
Lawful Earning — Curbing one's anger 179
Ingratitude — Begging — Obstinacy — Manliness 180
To brush the teeth — Consultation
Knowledge — Deceit 181
Hypocrisy — Tale-bearing — Deceit and fraud
Keeping one's promise 182
Gift — Neighbour — Despair 183

APPENDIX

Contributors 185
Bibliography 186
Arabic Text 194

(viii)

FOREWORD

In the Name of Allah, the Beneficent, the Merciful

It is true that whatever the difficulties may be, they can be solved with resolute courage, firm determination and steady efforts. Our social problems are not a few in number; they are too many and each one of them has to be tackled in right earnest.

We have powerful and relentless enemies who are keen to suck even the last drop of our blood. If they want to see us alive it is for the reason that we should serve their interests.

We have also amongst us some foolish friends, who miss no opportunity to create dissensions and dispersion. It so appears that they have been created only to cause conflicts among the people and to sow the seeds of dispersion and disunity. In fact these people are unpaid agents of our enemies and they provide an effective assistance to them to let them succeed in their nefarious designs.

When the intelligentsia have not yet succeeded in filling even one fissure of disunity among our rank and file, one of these lunatics comes round and throws a fresh stone in the well so as to create fresh ripples of dissension and dispersion!

We do not know why the temperament of our society, too, is much more prepared to accept the material which leads to differences and disputes as compared with the programmes which end in unity, fraternity, friendliness and brotherly feelings. At times we find that if ten persons participate in a maeeting they suggest ten different views, ten ways of thinking and consequently ten contradictory schemes and programmes.

Able-minded and influential people in our society usually harp on their own worthless ideas and the spirit of co-operation and collective efforts are hardly found in them. Everyone of them is like an individual piece of a cloud which passes on, drizzles and vanishes. It is quite evident that the edifice of our society cannot be built up in this slip-shod manner.

This spirit of diversity and dispersion has taken roots in all sections of our society like a malignant tumor and it is for this very reason that collective efforts are not usually made, so much so that even the economy of our country is not supported by the real sense of co-operative spirit. Those concerns which are run on partnership basis are in a state of disarray much like the unstable atoms of uranium; and those which are stable and flourishing are in fact one man's show with only the name and structure of partnership-based enterprise.

The present-day world complexion is such that individuals to whatever extent they may be competent, skilled and intelligent, are bound to face defeat as the world today is the world of collective bodies, union and organizations and not of individuals.

Now the question arises as to why we are in this deplorable condition. Have we not yet realized that nothing can be achieved through dissensions or by individual activities?

Maybe we have received a wrong guidance which has prompted different sections of our society towards individual activities instead of collective performance. Or perhaps we have not as yet acquired sufficient moral strength, spirit of self-sacrifice, tolerance, broad mindedness and high qualities of character, which are essential for nurturing a collective system of social activities.

These are the questions whose replies are unfortunately beyond the scope of the task undertaken by us. However, it is our duty to acquaint the Muslims with those problems and to seek solutions for them.

For quite some time there has appeared in our society

class distinction, which has divided it into two divergent groups. One group consists of enlightened individuals and the other of those, who cling to old ideas.

The second group considers the first to consist of persons who are new-comers, raw and immature, superficial and brainless, unrestrained and careless, whereas the first group considers the second to be stubborn, fanatical, static and ignorant. Thus they are engaged in constant state of confrontation.

It is a fact that our age is an age of revolutionary changes and our society is entering a new historical phase. In other words we are leaving behind the times of oil lamps and are entering the era of electricity, atom and rockets. And the conflict between the newer elements and those of the past age is a natural phenomenon in every transitional period. However, we do not consider it necessary that we should give up everything for fear of these conflicts. The best thing would be that we should profit from this contrariness and competition in such a manner that we should adopt whatever is beneficial and useful under the new circumstances and discard all that entails deviation, misfortune and backwardness.

Ours is a strange country. It consists of areas with different dialects, different races, different customs and traditions and different climates. For example, there is no common factor which may unify the residents of northern areas with those of the southern areas except, one factor. Yes! The only factor which unifies all these people with different languages, races and geographical zones is Islam which is the religion of an absolute majority constituting the country's population. It is only this common factor which can serve as a symbol of unity, fraternity and solidarity amongst the people.

Now, please ponder over this point! In this world which is spending huge sums of money to create artificial and unstable common values, under one or the other group formation or party affiliation, how immensely valuable is the existence of Islam — a really strong and stable common value which can bring all of us on one common platform.

However, it may be stated with great regret that this common value is also being neglected like other resources of the Muslim Ummah. Not only that it is not being utilized beneficially but we ourselves are also creating means to weaken it!

What should we do, so that we may derive maximum possible benefit from this common value (Islam) which once had made Muslims to reach the height of glory, and splendour under the glow of its radiant light.

There is certainly no better way than presenting Islam, in its true perspective and without any pretentions and ostentations, to the masses. This is the best and the most effective means of attracting people's attention to this Divine religion. If some thoughts and beliefs need to be presented in an exaggerated manner with apparent praise and commendation, Islam does not need any such instruments of glorification and ornamentations, because its teachings and guidance are so genuine that they appeal to the mind and touch the soul. Hence it is vitally important that Islam should be presented in its pristine purity, so that its blessings could be derived easily by the people.

In the modern times the hearts of some of our educated young men have turned away from Islam. We feel that it is only because they have not been informed of the realities of this sacred religion.

Well-informed sources say: "At present more readiness is observed in the western world for embracing Islam and it can be said that the civilized world is on the cross-road either to accept Islam or to go atheist. There is no third way".

However, notwithstanding all these possibilities, Islam is not making appropriate headway in this sensitive part of the world. Why? It is because it has not been properly introduced to the western countries.

We believe that one of the reasons for deep penetration and expansion of Islam in so short a time in the bygone days, that it stormed the old world and established a new world with a new zest of life, wisdom, virtues and blessings, was that it was presented to the people in its right perspespective on realistic grounds.

It is this very thing which can provide an atmosphere of honesty, resolution, truth and goodness to a world which is burning in the fire of corruption, strife, dispersion, nerve wars, armed conflicts, racial discrimination, mischief and imperialistic designs.

Thus it should be admitted once again that the most effective method of introducing Islam to the outside world is to present its teachings in pure and simple manner.

It is a matter of great regret that some persons residing at distanct places think that Islam is confined to prayers, fasting and performing Hajj of the Holy Ka'bah. Some, who do not perhaps know even this much, believe Islam to consist of lamentation at the time of commemorating the tragedy of Karbala. It may be admitted that the behaviour of some followers of Islam who have practically dissociated themselves from all social activities also lends support to this misunderstanding.

It should also be admitted that our organizations imparting religious instruction are not yet so well-equipped that they should make at least those people, who live in our own environments, understand Islam in its original form.

Books on 'Islamic Studies' are, no doubt, included in the syllabus of our schools. However, that too is nothing more than a dry, insipid, difficult and intricate set of teachings which, instead of acquainting our young ones with the true spirit and the realities of Islam, distracts them from Islam and makes them weary and disgusted.

Our people who have visited the West also have some queer ideas about Islam. Whatever they have seen of the practices and religious ceremonies of the Christians is declared by them to be a pattern for Islam viz. they consider the extensive teachings of Islam to be at par with the insipid ceremonials and brief worship of the Christians performed once in a week in the church accompanied with music which have very little social value. On the contrary Islam is the religion of life and contains the most sublime rules and regulations for a prosperous life.

Islam possesses such an extensive, self-contained and rich programme that it specifies the itinerary of human prosperity from cradle to grave, from the confines of the house to the theatre of war and from business institutions to the seat of justice.

At the same time, in view of the stimulating strength inherent in this religion, it conforms to the conditions of space age and satisfies the needs of man in different matters. Not only that Islam lays down man's obligations towards animal care, too, of which the modern civilization is bragging too much under the slogans: "Prevention of cruelties to animals' and 'Preservation of wild life'.

The object of compilation of this book is to present to the readers the text of the sublime Islamic laws without any ornamentation or embellishment. To achieve this end more than 1900 verses of the Holy Qur'an and traditions were collected and out of them 582, which were found to be more interesting, simple and clear, have been selected and incorporated in this book. Here we should like to invite the attention of the readers to the following points:

(i) As stated above 582 verses of the Holy Qur'an and traditions of the Prophet of Islam and his progeny have been selected out of more than 1900. The task of collecting the traditions from scores of relevant authentic books was performed by as many as 30 scholars whose names are mentioned in Appendix-I.

(ii) The texts of the traditions have been compared with their original sources.

(iii) In order to present the original text of Islamic rules and regulations the following method has been adopted.

(a) English translation of the verses and traditions has been given in the book itself.

(b) References of the verses and traditions have been given in Appendix-II.

(c) Complete Arabic texts of the verses and traditions have been quoted in Appendix-III. This is for the benefit of those who wish to study the original Arabic texts or to conduct further research on the subject.

In some cases only short sentences have been added to elucidate the meanings of some traditions and to show their relationship with one another. At the same time care has been taken to record such sentences separately so that they do not mingle up with the translation of the traditions.

(iv) Care has been taken to give simple and intelligible translation instead of word-for-word translation which is often difficult to understand.

It appears necessary to mention here that in this book only some rules and regulations pertaining to social life have been collected as many books would be required to be prepared to deal with all of them.

We hope that the book in hand will enable different sections of the society and especially the educated young men and women, to observe new horizons of the social laws of Islam and will induce them to recognize Islam as a meaningful Code of Life.

The Publishers

Campaign against Ignorance

The first and foremost condition for the vitality of a nation is acquisition of knowledge. It is for this reason that in the term of modern writers the nations which are advanced in the matter of knowledge and culture are called 'live' and on the contrary the backward communities are styled as 'dead' and 'uncultured'. Roots of this interpretation can be observed in the light of the sayings of the pioneer leaders of Islam. The Holy Prophet, peace be on him and his progeny, says: "Learned discussions enliven the dead hearts provided they lead to Allah and His commands".[1]

A person who dies while acquiring knowledge with the purpose of enlivening the Muslims will be one degree below the prophets in Paradise.[2]

In view of this, Islam has encouraged the people soundly to acquire knowledge and wisdom. As a matter of fact it has made it obligatory for them. The Holy Prophet, peace be on him and his progeny, says: "It is obligatory for every Muslim to acquire knowledge. Allah likes those who seek knowledge".[3] "It is obligatory for every Muslim to acquire knowledge. Acquire it from its proper place and impart it to the one who deserves it, because imparting knowledge for the sake of Allah is virtue; seeking it is worship; having discussion on it is like praising and gloifying Allah; acting on it is like proceeding on to Jihad in the cause of Allah; teaching it to an ignorant person is like giving alms, and passing it on to learned persons is the source of coming in close proximity of Allah".[4] "A person who seeks knowledge is like the one, who observes fast during day time and prays during night. It is better for a man to acquire a part of knowledge than to possess a mountain of gold as big as Abu Qubays and distribute it in the way of Allah".[5]

And after all the Holy Qur'an says: *"Whoever is given wisdom and knowledge is blessed with bounties in good abundance".*[6]

Imam Sajjad, peace be on him, says: "If people had known the advantages of acquiring knowledge they would have acquired it even if it had necessitated the shedding of their hearts' blood or their going down into the deep seas".[7]

Islam attaches so much importance to the acquisition of knowledge that it has declared the path of knowledge and wisdom to be the path leading to Paradise. The Holy Prophet, peace be on him and his progeny, says: "Allah opens the path of Paradise to one who takes a step on the path of acquisition of knowledge."[8]

Islam considers knowledge to be one of the best legacies which man leaves behind. The Holy Prophet, peace be on him and his progeny, says: "The best monuments and legacies which a man leaves behind are a dutiful son, useful buildings, knowledge and wisdom, which benefit the people after him".[9]

Islam has introduced knowledge and wisdom as a means of deliverance from the Fire of Hell. No doubt, a true scholar cannot deviate or diverge from the right path and cannot fall a prey to the Flames of Hell. On the other hand his knowledge and wisdom lead him to Paradise.

The Holy Prophet, peace be on him and his progeny, says: "One who wishes to see those who are safe from the Fire of Hell should look at the seekers of knowledge".[10]

Islam has not prescribed any limits for the acquisition of knowledge and wisdom.

The Holy Prophet, peace be on him and his progeny, says: "Acquire knowledge even if it be in China".[11] (i.e. there is no restriction of place and distance).

Islam has condemned bashfulness in the matter of acquisition of knowledge at any age or in any situation. Imam Ali, peace be on him, says: "Do not feel shy of learning what you do not know."[12]

It must, however, be remembered that the pioneers of Islam have always approved of that knowledge only which is accompanied with action and have commended only that wisdom which is associated with lofty character. Imam Ali, peace be on him, says: "O People! Remember that the excellence of your faith lies in acquiring knowledge and acting upon it. It is more essential for you to crave for knowledge than for riches".[13] And Imam Ja'far Sadiq, peace be on him, says: "Knowledge and action are associated with each other because whoever possesses knowledge acts upon it (as the real sign of knowledge is action) and the knowledge and wisdom of the one who puts them into practice remains unimpaired. Knowledge is a Divine voice which invites its bearer to act upon it. If he accepts its invitation and acts (according to his knowledge) his knowledge lasts, but if he does not give a positive response to it, it forsakes him".[14]

Islam always commends only that knowledge, which is for the sake of Allah. Imam Ja'far Sadiq, peace be on him, says: "A person who learns a tradition for worldly gains does not benefit from it in the Hereafter, and if he learns it for his betterment in the next world, Allah blesses him in this world as well as in the Hereafter".[15]

Islam has prescribed precise duties for the teacher and the pupil with regard to each other. The gist of it can be found in the following narrative:

Imam Ja'far Sadiq, peace be on him, says: "Your teacher has the right over you that you should honour him and pay him respect in different assemblies. You should be very attentive to his words. You should not raise your voice above his. If anybody asks him a question, you should not give its reply. You should not converse with others in his presence and you should allow the people to benefit from his knowledge. You should not speak ill of anyone before him. If anybody speaks ill of him in your presence, you should defend him. You should conceal his shortcomings and bring his virtues to light. You should not associate with his enemies and should not dispute with his friends. If you act on these lines the angels of Allah will testify that you have paid attention to him and have acquired knowledge for the sake of Allah and not to attract the attention of the people. And the right of your pupils on you is that you should realize that in granting you knowledge and opening its path for you, Allah has appointed you to be their guardian. In case, therefore, you teach them properly and do not frighten them and are not furious with them, Allah will, through His kindness, increase your knowledge. But if you drive the people away from knowledge and, as and when they approach you for it, you frighten them and get annoyed with them, it will be only appropriate that Almighty Allah may take away the light of knowledge from you and may degrade you in the eyes of the people."[16]

One of the real targets of Islam is the establishment of a perfect social and political system and the creation of environments in which people should live as humans, and refrain from octs of barbarity and savagery.

There are some pre-requisites for the achievement of this end and at the top of them is the existence of able, learned and faithful persons, who should invite the society to virtuous deeds and to the worship of Allah. Hence Islam attaches extraordinary importance to the scholars and leaders of this ideal society. The Holy Prophet, peace be on him and his progeny, has given them the status of the prophets.[17]

The Holy Qur'an considers the difference and the long distance between the learned persons and the ignorant ones to be an established fact and calls human conscience and intellect to witness it. It says: *"Say: Are the learned and the ignorant at par with each other? (Never). Only the wise persons take heed."*[18]

The Holy Qur'an further says: *"Allah elevates to high positions from amongst you those who are faithful and those, who have acquired knowledge."*[19]

Imam Ali, peace be on him, says: "The learned men and scholars will continue to exist till the world lasts. Although their bodies may be hidden from the eyes their impressions will for ever remain imprinted on the hearts of the people."[20]

Islam insists particularly that the shcolars should be accorded more respect than the devout and the pious, because the latter are mindful of themselves only but the former take care of others also.

The Holy Prophet, peace be on him and his progeny, says: "Sleep of a scholar is superior to one thousand rak'ats of prayers offered by a devout person."[21]

"A scholar (although he may not offer prayers other than the obligatory ones) is like a person, who always observes fast and offers prayers, and he is like a *mujahid* who sacrifices his life in the cause of Allah. As and when a scholar dies a breach takes place in Islam and it cannot be filled till the Day of Judgement."[22]

It is on this very account that the prayers offered by a scholar are many times superior to those offered by other persons because it is a good deed based on knowledge.

Imam Ali, peace be on him, says: "Two *rak'ats* of prayers offered by a scholar are better than seventy *rak'ats* of prayers offered by an ignorant person."[23]

Islam also encourages people to associate with learned persons because this affords opportunities for profiting from their knowledge.

The Holy Prophet, peace be on him and his progeny, says: "Having the company of learned scholars is (Allah's) worship.[24] "Looking at their faces is (also) worship".[25]

Luqman, the sage, says to his son: "My son! Associate with the scholars and always sit with them, because Allah enlivens the hearts with the light of knowledge."[26]

This matter is so extensive and important that according to the religious leaders, the Pleasure and Wrath of Allah depend on the pleasure and wrath of a scholar.

Imam Ja'far Sadiq, peace be on him, says: "On the Day of

Judgement Allah will be pleased with a person who honours and respects a Muslim scholar; and He will be annoyed with one who insults a Muslim scholar".[27]

Islam attaches great importance to the aged and the elders of every group and community and looks at them with due respect.

Imam Ja'far Sadiq, peace be on him, says: "Respect to the aged persons is a sign of respect to Allah."[28] "One who does not show respect to the aged is not one of us."[29]

The Holy Prophet, peace be on him and his progeny, says: "As and when the elder of a community or a nation meets you, honour him and respect him."[30]

* * * * *

Dispute is Forbidden

It is true that debates and discussions are the key to the solution of difficulties. However, this is so only if discussion is pursued on the basis of search for truth and discovery of facts. In case one or both the two parties commence dispute and contention to assert superiority over the other and to support their own points of view, the result will be nothing except malice, discord, enmity and concealment of truth.

Islam condemns dispute and contention in worldly affairs as well as in academic discussions and considers it to be the cause of hostility.

Imam Ali, peace be on him, says: "Refrain from dispute and controversy because it offends two brothers in faith and creates mutual enmity."[31]

Imam Ja'far Sadiq, peace be on him, says: "Refrain from contention in your discourse because it creates anger and exposes one's secrets."[32] He also says: "One who disputes with others loses manliness."[33]

Imam Ali, peace be on him, says: "Whoever loves self-respect avoids dispute".[34]

Imam Ja'far Sadiq, peace be on him, says: "Refrain from dispute because it occupies one's intellect and places discord and enmity in its place and creates jealousy and hatred."[35]

Islam not only prohibits unjustified dispute and controversy but also forbids a truthful person to indulge in such an act.

Imam Ali, peace be on him, says: "A person cannot attain perfect faith except when he abandons dispute, even though he may happen to be a truthful person."[36]

The Holy Prophet, peace be on him and his progeny, says: "I enjoy authority over a House above Paradise, another House within Paradise and still another House in the Garden of Paradise. They are for one who abandons dispute and controversy even though he may be right."[37]

For this very reason Islam declares that some actions like A'tikāf (Retirement to a masjid for worship) and Hajj are invalidated by dispute Imam Jafar Sadiq (P) interprets it in this way: "You might be swearing "By Allah, yes" and "By Allah, no"[38] and this is the lowest stage of strife and controversy.

* * * * *

Social Responsibilities

In the capacity of being the first guardians of their children the parents should do their utmost to equip their children with outstanding and noble human qualities. The only way to decorate them with these qualities is "character building". After proper moral and spiritual training and education, the next phase for the man of Islam, is to prepare himself to reconstruct his social environment and to transform it into the light of Islam, filled with justice and virtue.

According to the logic of Islam, Islamic brotherhood is the most deep-rooted unity which creates mutual relationship and responsibility.

It is the duty of every Muslim to exhort others to do good and to combat corruption. These two duties, which are known, in Islamic Jurisprudence, as *'Amrbil Ma'ruf* and *Nahy 'anil Munkar*, enjoin upon all Muslims to keep a constant watch on the society. If they find anybody deviating from the path of justice and truth, they must invite him to the right path and if they find anybody committing a crime or sin, they should restrain him from doing so.

Islam asks every Muslim to keep his social spirit fully alive and hold dear the collective interests. It calls upon every individual to be responsible to all other members of the society and the society to be responsible to all the individuals. All the Muslims have a right to criticize and reform each other and play their role in the formation of a healthy society.

The subject of "exhortation to do good and restrain from doing evil" has been repeated in many verses of the Holy Qur'an. At times the Holy Book praises Muslims for having performed this duty[39] and at others it introduces it as a part of good actions.[40] And at times it also encourages Muslims to practise this good act by mentioning the exhortations of Luqman to his son.[41] And on some occasions Allah's Blessings are promised to those who discharge this important duty.[42]

Islam says that if you desire that cruelty and injustice should not prevail in your society and the society should not face destruction, do not forget to make a general scrutiny and constructive criticism.

Imam Ali Riza, peace be on him, says: "Invite others to good and check corruption, otherwise the tyrants will prevail upon you. At that time those among you who are good will invoke Allah's Mercy, but their invocations will not be accepted."[43]

Imam Ali, peace be on him, says: "The earlier nations perished because they committed sins and their religious heads did not prevent them from doing so."[44]

Again, the Holy Prophet, peace be on him and his progeny, says: "My followers will always be endowed with beneficence and prosperity, provided they invite others to goodness and restrain them from doing evil deeds and co-operate in good actions. However, if they fail to do so some of them will prevail upon others and they will find no helper either on earth or in the heavens."[45]

If some persons can prevent others from committing corruption but do not do so, Islam considers them to be accomplices of sinners.

Imam Baqir, peace be on him, says: "Allah addressed Prophet Shu'ayb, peace be on him, and said, "I shall torture 100,000 of your followers out of whom 40,000 persons will be evil-doers and 60,000 will be good ones". Shu'ayb, peace be on him, said, "O Allah! So far as the bad persons are concerned it is quite right but why should you torture the good ones?" The revelation came: "Because they did not admonish the wicked and did not get annoyed with them for My sake".[46]

The order to bid to do good and forbid the evil is subject to some special conditions. One of the conditions is the possibility of its being efficatious. The least that a person should do is that he should not look at the sinner with a cheerful face.

Imam Ali, peace be on him, says: "The Holy Prophet ordered us to meet the sinners with grim and dejected faces."[47]

Human beings are not equal to one another in the matter of taking into consideration the goodness or evil involved in various fields. On the other hand since the standard of knowledge, strong intellect, age, maturity and experience vary from individual to individual, it often happens that one's interest in something makes one deaf and blind and conceals its defects from one's eyes. In that event it becomes necessary that people should render intellectual help to one another and protect one another from falling into error.

Islam, therefore, ordains that Muslims should not fail to tender advice to one another and should communicate to others whatever they know about the goodness or badness of something and should not be negligent in doing their utmost in this behalf.

The Holy Prophet, peace be on him and his progeny, says: "On the Day of Judgement Allah will accord a higher status to one who has been more active in tendering advice to the people."[48] "Everyone should tender advice to his brother just as he is vigilant himself."[49]

Imam Ja'far Sadiq, peace be on him, says: "You should tender advice to Allah's creatures, for you will not find an act better than this".[50]

Islam has insisted on the performance of this social duty so much so that it considers stinginess in the matter of tendering advice to others to be 'dishonesty'.

Imam Ja'far Sadiq, peace be on him, says: "A person who observes his brother doing something improper and does not prevent him from doing it in spite of being in a position to do so, has betrayed him".[51]

Education and Training of Child

Islam attaches much importance to the training of children and has held the parents responsible in this regard.

The Holy Prophet (peace be on him and his progeny) says: "The parents are responsible with regard to their children in the same manner in which the children are responsible with regard to their parents."[52] "Allah blesses those, who assist their children in doing good things which they do themselves."[53]

At times the burden of this responsibility has been placed more on the shoulders of the father and it has been given a priority to the rights of a father.

Imam Ali, peace be on him, says: "The child has a right on his father and the father too has a right on his child."[54]

Islam considers training during childhood to be very important because the soul of a child is ready to accept every impression.

Imam Ali, peace be on him, says: "The heart of a newly-born child is like a virgin soil which accepts every seed that is sown on it."[55]

The Holy Prophet, peace be on him and his progeny, has considered the selection of a nice name for the child and giving him proper training as well as the selection of an appropriate profession for him to be the responsibilities of the parents.[56]

There is no doubt about the fact that from the psychological point of view the name of a person has a special effect on his mentality and mode of thinking and throughout his life he remains subconsciously under its influence. It is for this reason that Islam takes so much care in the matter of selection of a name and says: "The most appropriate name is one which makes man remember that he is the servant of Allah and similar is the case with the names of the prophets who were the embodiment of human virtues and an emblem of perfection."[57]

Islam abhors those names which make man egoistic, proud and negligent like Harith, Mālik, Khalid etc.[58]

Islam considers that people with good names shall be given good respect.

The Holy Prophet, peace be on him and his progeny, says: "When you name a child 'Muhammad' give him due respect, make room for him in the assemblies and do not be peevish towards him."[59]

Islam also attaches a greater importance to religious instruction.

Imam Ali, peace be on him, says: "One of the rights of a child is that his father should teach him the Holy Qur'an.[60] Islam also orders: "When the children complete their fifth year and can distinguish between their right and left hands, make them sit facing the *Qibla* and order them to perform *Sajda* (prostration). When they complete their sixth year, teach them prayers. And after they have attained the seventh year make tem learn the essentialities of *Wuzu* (ablution). And when they become nine years old, make them perform *Wuzu* and offer prayers in full and be strict with them on this account."[61]

Islam also considers archery and swimming important.

Imam Ali, peace on him, says: "Teach your children swimming and archery."[62]

Islam considers the first seven years to be a period of playful life for the children and orders that they should be given full liberty in this regard.

Imam Ja'far Sadiq, peace be on him, says: "Up to seven years of age, a child should play; for another seven years he should be taught how to read and write and for still another seven year he should learn about lawful and unlawful things."[63]

In fact even the initial seven years form a part of his training period. On the very day of the birth of child, *Azān* and *Iqāma*, which aim at the declaration of the Oneness of Allah and the invitation to Islam and the exhortation to perform good deeds, should be recited in his ears.[64]

In order to ensure that the children acquire full freedom in life during youth, Islam indicates two periods of their upbringing viz. the first seven years which is the playing period of a child; the next seven years is considered to be the period of his complete absorption in learning and acquisition of knowledge about various affairs of life; and still another seven years is considered to be a part of the half of the life span for the active participation in life's affairs.

It is as the Holy Prophet, peace be on him and his progeny, says: "A child is a master for seven years, a slave for another seven years and a minister for the next seven years."[65]

Islam lays much stress on being kind to the children. The Holy Prophet, peace be on him and his progeny, says: "A good act is written in the record of virtuous deeds for one who gives a kiss to his child."[66]

A person came before the Holy Prophet, peace be on him and his progeny, and said: "I have never kissed a child". When he turned and left, the Holy Prophet, peace be on him and his progeny, said to those present: "This stone-hearted person is one of the people of Fire".[67] (i.e. he will go to Hell).

Islam has forbidden beating a crying child. The Holy Prophet, peace be on him and his progeny, says: "Do not beat a child who is crying because for the first four months his crying is the testimony of the Oneness of Allah and for the following four months it is for blessings on the Holy Prophet and his progeny and for the next four months it is an invocation for the parents."[68]

Islam ordains that the male children should be circumcised as early as possible. The Holy Prophet, peace be on him and his progeny, says: "Purify (circumcise) your sons on the seventh day because the tissues then build up quickly and the wound heals up easily."[69]

Knowledge and experience has proved that milk has a great effect on the morals and mentality of a child, and therefore, Islam has prescribed special conditions for a nursing-maid. The Holy Prophet, peace on him and his progeny, says: "Keep your children away from the milk of women who are insane or adultresses, because through the milk baser traits are transmitted to the child."[70]

In order that the ears of the child should become acquainted with the remembrance of Allah and the realities of Islam from the moment of its birth, Imam Ja'far Sadiq, peace be on him, says: "When a child arrives in the world, recite *Azān* in its right ear and *Iqāma* in its left ear."[71]

Islam ordains that a child's *Aqiqa* should be performed i.e. an animal should be slaughtered for its sake by way of alms. Imam Ja'far Sadiq, peace be on him, says: "*Aqiqa* is necessary for a well-to-do man. As regards a poor person he should also do it, when his circumstances permit. And in case it is not possible for him to do it, he is under no obligation in this behalf. Every child that is born is under pledge in respect of his *Aqiqa*."[72]

In this manner the person of a newly-born child has been made a means of help to the poor.

In order to keep the spirit of children perpetually vigorous and fresh and to protect them from psychological problems, Islam has forbidden giving a preferential treatment to one over the other.

The Holy Prophet, peace be on him and his progeny, says: "Observe justice in dealing with your children in the same manner in which you expect them to observe justice in being kind and good to you."[73]

However, in contrast with the vicious practice of the Dark Age of Ignorance (before the advent of Islam), when the new-born daughters were buried alive, Islam permits that daughters may be given perference over sons.

The Holy Prophet, peace be on him and his progeny, says: "Whoever goes to the bazaar and purchases a present for the members of his family and brings it to them is like one who spends on the needy. However, (at the time of division) he should prefer daughters to sons because whoever pleases his daughter is like one who frees a slave from among the descendants of Prophet Iṣmā'il."[74]

* * * * *

Duties of the Children

Father and mother are two precious beings. Everyone knows their value, and looks upon them with respect. Islam, too, has stimulated this internal inclination of man which emanates from a sentimental and rational source and has indicated their value in a becoming manner through detailed and repeated statements, and has ordered the children that they should not neglect the respect for their parents even for one moment.

In the Holy Qur'an obedience to parents has been mentioned at many places along with the obedience to Allah and in some cases it has been mentioned as the first recommendation to the children of Adam.

At one place the Holy Qur'an says: *Your Lord has ordained that you must not worship anything other than Him and that you must be kind to your parents. If either or both of your parents should become advanced in age, do not express to them words which show your slightest disappointment. Never yell at them but always speak to them with kindness. Be humble and merciful towards them and say, "Lord, have mercy upon them as they cherished me during my childhood."*[75]

And on another occasion it says: *We enjoined man to show kindness to his parents, for with much pain his mother bears him and he is not weaned before he is two years of age We said: Give thanks to Me and to your parents. To me shall all things return."*[76]

The Holy Prophet says: "Goodness and benevolence towards father and mother is superior to prayers, fasting, Hajj, Umra and Jihad and carries a greater recompense."[7] "Two doors of Paradise are opened for a person whose day commences when his parents are pleased with him."[78]

The following tradition, quoted from Imam Ja'far Sadiq, peace be on him, confirms that the recompense for doing good to parents excels that for Jihad.

"A man came to of the Holy Prophet and said: "I like to perform Jihad in the cause of Allah, but my mother is not at all inclined towards my doing so." The Holy Prophet replied: "Go back and remain with your mother. I swear by the Lord who has sent me on a true mission that to remain with one's mother for one night (and serving her and doing good to her) is better than performing Jihad in the cause of Allah for a year."[79]

In another place he said: "Go back and remain with your mother because Paradise lies underneath the feet of one's mother."[80]

Islam considers kindness to parents to be the criterion of excellence and virtue. Imam Ja'far Sadiq, peace be on him, narrates as under: "One day when the Holy Prophet was in the company of some persons, his foster-sister came. The Holy Prophet accorded her due respect. He was extremely pleased to see her. He spread a sheet of cloth for her to sit on, and then began conversing with her. The girl departed and some time later her brother (who was the foster — brother of the Holy Prophet) came. The Holy Prophet did not, however, accord similar respect to him. One of those present asked: "O Prophet of Allah! What was the reason for this different treatment when this person happens to be a man?" The Holy Prophet replied: "The reason is that the girl is more respectful to her parents."[81]

Islam considers the right of parents to be the greatest of all rights and prefers it to everything else. Once a man came to Imam Ja'far Sadiq, peace be on him, and said: "My parents are Sunnis. The Holy Imam replied: Do good to them in the same manner in which you are under obligation to do good to those who believe in our *Walāyat:* that is who are our followers."[82]

And one who neglects to perform this duty or becomes the source of his parents' wrath is really very unfortunate. The Holy Prophet said: "Two doors of Hell are opened towards a person who causes the wrath of his parents."[83] "Be afraid of being disobedient to your parents or becoming the object of their wrath because the fragrance of Paradise covers a distance of five hundred years' time and reaches the nostrils of a man but it does not reach at all those with whom their parents are annoyed."[84]

And as we have learned from the verse of the Holy Qur'an (mantioned earlier) the lowest degree of such disobedience is that one should display weariness before them.

Imam Ja'far Sadiq, peace be on him, says: "If the Lord had considered anything to be lower than 'Uf' (word of disgust) he would have prohibited it. One of the stages of disobedience is that one should cast a fierce glance at one's parents."[85]

It should also be kept in view that the Prophet says: "The right of an elder brother over his younger brother is similar to the right of a father over his child."[86]

* * * * *

Service to Humanity

There are a number of problems which cannot be solved by one person alone, but, if he is assisted by some others, he can overcome the difficulties involved in them.

In principle, human life has no meaning without co-operation and, without it, it is transformed into animal life. It is for this reason that Islam insists that its followers should assist their brethren-in-faith in solving their problems and not leave them alone to face difficulties.

The Holy Prophet, peace be on him, says: "One who does not take interest in the affairs of Muslims is not a Muslim. And that person, too, is not a Muslim who hears a Muslim calling for help and does not respond to his call."[87]

Imam Ja'far Sadiq, peace be on him, says: "If a brother-in-faith comes to a person and seeks help from him and he does not help him in spite of being in a position to do so, Allah makes him help one of our enemies and then tortures him on this account."[88]

"If a person possesses a house and a brother-in-faith needs it for purposes of residence and he does not give it to him, Almighty Allah addresses the angels and says: 'O My angels! Here is a creature of mine who observes stinginess in lending his house to another creature of Mine. I swear by My Glory and Dignity that I will not provide him with a residence in Paradise."[89]

"If a brother-in-faith seeks help from a person and he, in spite of being in a position to help him, does not do so Allah will resurrect him on the Day of Judgement in such a condition that his hands will be tied to his neck and will keep him in the same condition till the accounts of all the people have been settled."[90]

On the other hand the spiritual reward fixed by Allah for such an act is so important and precious that similar reward has been promised for a very few other acts.

The Holy Prophet peace be on him and his progeny, says: "Allah has given Paradise to some persons who rule there (and enjoy a dignified position). They are the persons who have been meeting the needs of their brethren."[91] Imam Ali said that he heard the Holy Prophet saying "One who fulfills the needs of a brother Muslim is like one who has been worshipping Allah throughout his life."[92]

The Holy Prophet said: "Allah makes Paradise obligatory for one who helps a Muslim and diverts devastating water and fire from him (i.e. one who rushes to assist victims of flood and fire and save them)."[93]

And Imam Baqir, peace be on him, says: "whenever a person seeks my assistance I hasten to provide it to him lest he should become in a position to dispense with it and I may be deprived of the blessings attached to it'."[94]

Similarly Imam Ja'far Sadiq, peace be on him, says: "A Muslim who helps another Muslim to fulfil the latter's need is like one who has performed Jihad in the cause of Allah."[95]

"It neverhappened that a Muslim fulfilled a want of a fellow Muslim and Allah has not proclaimed that His blessings were with Him and that He would not give him anything short of Paradise.[96]

Imam Sadiq (P) says: On the Day of Judgement Allah will fulfil 100,000 wishes of a person who fulfills one of the wishes of a brother-in-faith of his. The first of them will be Paradise for himself and the other will be Paradise for his kinsmen and friends and brethrenin-faith of his. The first of them will be Paradise for himself and the other will be Paradise for his kinsmen and friends and brethren-in-faith provided they are not idol-worshippers.[97]

"Allah will make matters easy for a believer who solves the problems of a brother, and if he conceals his (i.e. brother Muslim's) error or secret, Allah will conceal seventy of his secrets. By Allah! So long as a person is the helper of his Muslim brother Allah remains his Helper."[98] — Usool-e-Kafi

Safwān Jammāl, one of the companions of Imam Ja'far Sadiq and Imam Musa Kazim, peace be on them, says: "I was present before Imam Ja'far Sadiq, peace be on him, Maymun, a resident of Makkah, arrived and complained about his indigence and lack of means to undertake about his indigence and lack of means to undertake journey to his home town. The Holy Imam ordered me to get up and assist him. I got up and with Allah's help succeeded in meeting his needs and then returned to the assembly. Imam enquired from me about the development and I told him that Allah had granted that man's needs.

The Holy Imam said: "Remember! In my view assisting a brother Muslim is better than going round the Ka'bah seven times."[99]

And in the end the Holy Imam says: "Almighty Allah has said thus: People get their sustenance from Me (and they are My creatures). Hence I like him more who is more kind to them and strives to meet their needs."[100] — Usool-e-Kafi

No doubt, making Muslims happy becomes the source of one's happiness on the Day of Judgement. Imam Musa Kazim, peace be on him, says: "There is a group of Allah's servants who strive to meet the needs of the people. They will enjoy peace of mind on the Day of Judgement. And Allah will make him happy on the Day of Judgement who makes one believer happy."[101]

In short helping one's fellow-beings is so much important that Allah gives spiritual reward even for an intention and resolution to perform it. Imam Muhammad Baqir, peace be on him, says: "At times it so happens that a Muslim seeks help from another Muslim and the latter, though inclined to help him, is not in a position to do so, Allah will send him to Paradise for this very resolution."[102]

The conclusion of this dicussion is contained in the following words of Imam Husayn son of Imam Ali, peace be on them: "The requests which people make to you are Blessings of Allah. So do not feel weary and uneasy."[103]

Imam Ali, peace be on him, says: "How surprising it is on the part of a person who is approached by a brother Muslim for help and he fails to help him and does not consider himself fit for performing a good act. Does this act not carry any spiritual reward which he should covet? Or can he not mitigate Allah's wrath by this means? Really, should one observe abstemiousness even in the matter of morals and virtues?"[104]

Hence, by taking together these explicit statements quoted from the pioneers of Islam and other traditions, which it is not possible to amplify here, it becomes quite clear that Islam considers extension of help to the needy Muslims and taking steps for public welfare to be at par with the most important and most sublime worship and has made every Muslim responsible for the performance of this great duty, and does not permit negligence or carelessness in this regard.

* * * * *

Good Deeds

Contrary to the thinking of some narrow-minded persons that religion does not care for things other than various forms of worship and obligatory and unlawful matters, Islam attaches great importance to public welfare like contruction of Masjids, orphanages, propagation centres, bridges and water reservoirs and improvement of roads. In short, Islam lays great stress upon every thing which contributes to the welfare and well-being of the people.

The Holy Prophet, peace be on him and his progeny, says: "One who passes his days and nights and does not care for the affairs of the Muslims (does not strive to solve any problem of the society) is not a Muslim."[105]

When the Holy Prophet, peace be on him and his progeny, was asked about the person whom Allah likes most, he replied: "He is the person who is more useful to the Muslim society than others".[106] And he said in other words: "The best among the people is the one from whom people benefit more."[107]

To such good deeds, Islam gives the name of alms recurring benefits.

Imam Ja'far Sadiq, peace be on him, says: "The record of the activities of everyone is closed after his death and thereafter he does not receive any reward or punishment except in three cases: The first one is the 'alms recurring benefits' (useful works) which he leaves behind himself; another is a good habit, which he leaves as his remembrance, and the third one is a dutiful child who prays for his deliverance (and if he has committed any sin his child makes amends for it".[108]

The Holy Qur'an says: *"Wealth and children are the bounties of this life. But deeds of lasting merit are better rewarded by your Lord."*[109]

Besides attaching so much importance to 'alms recurring benefits' viz. sacred buildings and endowments, Islam particularly stresses on the construction of Masjid which is the very basis for Islamic propagation and teachings, and it has made special recommendations in this behalf.

The Holy Prophet, peace be on him and his progeny, says: "One who constructs a Masjid, the Omnipotent Allah will grant him a house in Paradise".[110]

And the Holy Qur'an says: *And those persons who build Masjids and visit them, who believe in Allah and the Day of Judgement, attend to their prayers and pay Zakat (religious tan) and who fear none but Allah so these it may be that they are the rightly guided ones."*[111]

Islam's view with regard to social matters becomes clear from the fact that a comparatively small matter like levelling the streets of Muslims has been given so much importance. The Holy Prophet, peace be on him and his progeny, says: "Allah gives spiritual reward equal to that of reciting four hundred verses of the Holy Qur'an to a person who removes from the path of the Muslims that which inconveniences them."[112]

Whenever Imam Sajjad, peace be on him, passed through a road and saw a stumbling block lying on it he used to dismount from the animal on which he was riding so that he might remove it with his own hand.[113]

The Holy Prophet, peace be on him and his progeny, said: "It is incumbent upon every Muslim to give alms (and do favours to others) every day." Someone said: "How is it possible for anyone to do such a good deed every day?" The Holy Prophet replied: "When a person removes impediments from the path of the Muslims it is treated to be 'alms'.[114]

Helping the Oppressed

Islam appeared in a society in which cruelty and oppression were fully current along with other evils. Rich and powerful tyrants oppressed their subjects and other weak people as much as possible, and made them submit to their authority. There were also some who kept silent on account of fear or for some other reasons and thus practically endorsed the action of the tyrants by their silence. Hence the oppressors continued their oppressions as far as possible.

Islam besides threatening and condemning the oppressors and considering them distant from Allah's Blessings also, seriously took to task the second group of people who remain silent and do not strive to rescue the oppressed and has warned them of Divine Wrath.

Imam Ja'far Sadiq, peace be on him, says: "When a Muslim, in spite of being in a position to assist his brother, abstains from doing so, Allah also abstains from assisting him in this world as well as in the Hereafter."[115]

Islam strictly orders its followers to campaign against the tyrants and to assist the oppressed.

Imam Ali, peace be on him, says to his son: "Always campaign against the tyrant and help the oppressed".[116]

The Holy Prophet, peace be on him and his progency, says: "Allah appoints an angel to keep safe from the Fire of Hell on the Day of Judgement, that person who saves a believer from the oppression of a cruel person."[117]

Imam Ja'far Sadiq, peace be on him, also says: "It is better for a Muslim to help his oppressed brother than to fast and to sit in *A'tikāf* (seclusion) for one month in Masjidul Harām."[118]

Imam Muhammad Baqir, peace be on him, says: "Once a true believer lived in the country of a cruel king. The king was very keen to oppress the troe believers. The man was, therefore, compelled to leave his country and seek refuge in the country of non-believers and there he took up abode in the house of an infidel.

The infidel accorded him respect and gave him asylum. When the time of the infidel's death drew nearer Allah revealed to him thus: "I swear by My Dignity and Glory that if there had been a place in Paradise for the infidels I would have rewarded you but Paradise is forbidden to the infidels. However, O fire! Take hold of him but do not hurt him."[119]

In one of his remarks about assisting the oppressed, Imam Ja'far Sadiq, peace be on him, says clearly: "It is the duty of every Muslim to assist a Muslim (against the tyrants)."[120]

* * * * *

Mutual Co-operation amongst Muslims

At the time of the advent of Islam, the entire Arabia presented a scene of battlefield and was burning in the fire of corruption, contention, mischief and disturbance. People of that peninsula had always been at loggerheads with one another and their hearts were filled with acute rancour. However, Islam declared the mutual love amongst them to be the basis of its programme of inviting people to Allah. The Holy Prophet recited the following verse before them: *The believers are a band of brothers. Make peace among your brothers and fear Allah so that you may be shown mercy.* "[121]

Then the Holy Prophet, peace be on him and his progeny, embarked opon this task with high ambition and practically established brotherly relationship between two groops of Muslims. From that day onwards the phrase brethren-in-faith along with the phrase kinsmen became current and the former became more in vogue.

In order to root out rancour and animosity Islam ordains to establish peace and tranquillity among your brethren-in-faith.

At the time of his last moment Imam Ali, peace be on him, advised his children as under:

"My children! I advise you to adopt piety, keep your affairs organized and always make peace between yourselves because I have heard your grandfather, the Holy Prophet, peace be on him and his progeny, saying that Allah regards creating of peace between two persons to be superior to offering prayers and fasting for one years"[122]

For these very reasons the great leaders of Islam attached much importance to this subject, so much so that they kept some money with some of their companions so that if there was some financial dispute between two persons the same should be settled through that money.

Abu Hanifa, the Hajj goide says: "Once I was disputing with a person in connection with an inheritance. Mufazzal bin Umar passed by us. He observed us for a moment and then invited os to his residence. He settled the affair between us for four hundred dirhams and himself paid the amount to os. Then he said: "Remember! This money is not mine. Imam Ja'far Sadiq, peace be on him, gave it to me and ordered that as and when two faithful persons are disputing over some property, the matter should be settled by means of this money."[123]

Islam has imposed mutual responsibilities upon Muslims and called them the 'rights of brethren-in-faith'.

Imam Ali, peace be on him, quotes from the Holy Prophet, peace be on him and his progeny, as saying: "Every Muslim has thirty rights over another Muslim which he should either perform or the other should spare him from the performance thereof; a Muslim should overlook the errors of his brother-in-faith and should have pity on him when he is in trouble, should guard his secrets, should not talk about his shortcomings, should accept his apology, should defend him when others degrade him, give him good counselling and preserve mutual friendship with him, should pay his debts, should visit him when he is sick and should escort his foneral in the event of his death, should accept his invitation and his presents, should recompense him for his gifts, and thank him for his favours, should render him proper assistance, should protect his honour and meet his needs and make him achieve his purpose. If he sneezes he should invoke benediction for him. He should guide him to his lost things, answer his salutation, treat his statements to be correct, consider his gift to be good, confirm his oaths and be friendly with his friends. In case he is the oppressor, he should be stopped from doing evil and in case he is the oppressed one, the requisite assistance is to help him in receiving his dues. He should not leave him alone to face hardships and should consider good for him that thing which he considers be good for himself and should not desire for him that thing which he does not desire for himself."[124]

Imam Ja'far Sadiq also quotes the Holy Prophet, peace be on him and his progeny, as saying: "A believer has seven rights over another believer which the latter must discharge: He should respect him openly and be friendly with him in his heart. He should make him partake in his wealth, visit him when he is sick and escort his funeral on his death. And even after his death he should not say anything except good about him."[125]

Imam Muhammad Baqir, peace on him, said: "Some of the rights of a believer upon his brother are: He should satiate him when he is hungry, conceal his secrets, make his difficulties easy for him (assist him in his difficulties), pay his debts and protect his children after his death."[126]

Imam Ja'far Sadiq, peace be on him, also says: "A believer is the brother of the other believer and he is like an eye and a guide for him. He does not commit breach of trust with him, does not oppress him, does not deceive him and fulfils th promise made with him."[127]

* * * * *

Behaviour towards the Servants

Even today the behaviour of some persons towards their servants is just like that shown by the masters towards their slaves during the Dark Age of Ignorance.

Islam has seriously capaigned against this way of thinking and has considered the relationship between the master and the servant to be a relationship of mutual assistance on the basis of mutual respect and protection based on the concept of human rights and freedom.

The biographies of the leaders of Islam, besides their sayings, clearly indicate that they fully observed equality and respect in the matter of their servants and treated them like helpers and not like beasts of burden.

The Holy Prophet, peace be on him and his progeny, says: "They are your brothers whom Allah has made your subordinates. Hence if a person has a brother subordinate to himself, he should give him to eat what he eats himself and to wear what he wears himself and should assist him in doing difficult jobs".[128] He also said: "As and when you order your slaves (and servants) to do a difficult job, assist them yourselves."[129]

He also said: "The worst person is he who travels alone, and turns away his guest and beats his slave".[130]

Imam Ali Riza, peace be on him, instructed his two servants named Yāsir and Nādir. "If you see me standing by your side at the time when you are taking your meals, do not move from your place (do not pay me any respect until you have finished with your meals".[131]

Imam Ali, peace be on him, purchased two shirts, one of which cost three dirhams and the other two dirhams. He kept the cheaper one himself and gave the other to Qambar (his servant). Qambar said: "You are better suited to wear this shirt because you mount the pulpit and address the people". Imam Ali replied: "Qambar! You are young and still enjoy the prime of youth. I feel ashamed before Allah that I should seek precedence over you in the matter of dress because I have heard the Holy Prophet, peace be on him and his progeny, saying: "Give them (slaves and servants) to wear whatever you wear yourselves and give them to eat what you eat yourselves."[132]

Some people are of the view that so long as they are not harsh with their servants, the latter do not obey them. This way of thinking is, however, incorrect, because they are more obedient when they are treated well.

The Holy Prophet, peace be on him and his progeny, says: "Be kind to and cheerful with your servants, because by doing so your wishes are complied with more properly".[133]

In fact the methods of looking after household affairs should be learnt from Islam. Islam enjoins that we should observe a good system even in the case of servants and entrust a particular job to everyone of them. Imam Ali, peace be on him, says to his son: "Ask each one of your workers to perform a particular job, because in this way they do not pass on jobs to one another".[134]

On the other hand the servants too should not exceed their limits and they should pay due regard to the rights of their masters. It is said that Imam Ja'far Sadiq, peace be on him, once sent a slave of his for some work. He went and did not return in time. The Holy Imam went after him and found him asleep. He kept standing there till the man woke up. Then the Imam said to him: "O man! Why do you sleep during the night and during the day? Let the night be yours in which you may sleep but let the day be mine".[135]

Zakat
the Share of the Needy

In the modern world the indigence and poverty of a large number of people and the glaring class distinctions have attracted the attention of the intelligentsia who are striving hard to remedy this ailment and reduce this dangerous gap between different classes.

In order to prevent accumulation of wealth and eradicate th evils of poverty, Islam has prescribed the law of alms and Zakat. According to this law the rich persons are under obligation to pay every year a fixed percentage of their wealth to the needy and destitute.

The Holy Qur'an has mentioned it at numerous places (e.g. Surah al-Baqarah verses 40, 104 and 173; Surah al-A'raf verse 155; Surah al-Hajj verse 42 and Surah al-Mo'minun, verse 4) and it has given it so much importance that it has usually been mentioned along with the greatest of all religious duties namely the offering of prayers *(Salāt)*. For example it says: *"Offer prayers and pay Zakat, for you will be rewarded for whatever good work you do"*.[136]

The leaders of Islam have mentioned the philosophy underlying the law of Zakat and have thereby encouraged the people to pay it. Imam Ja'far Sadiq, peace be on him, says: "Zakat has been prescribed so that the rich people should be tested and the poor should be helped. If people had been paying Zakat for their wealth there would have been no indigent Muslim. It means that through this right fixed for the poor by Allah, the poor would become free from need. Hence, if poor and hungry persons are found, it is on account of the sin committed by the rich and it is only appropriate that Allah may withhold His Blessings from those people who have not attended to the rights of the needy".[137]

He also says: "Allah ha sfixed a share for the poor in the wealth of the rich and made the poor as partners in their assets. No rich person deserves praise unless he pays that right viz. Zakat. By means of Zakat the lives of the poor are guaranteed and with this act, a Muslim is called a Muslim".[138]

The following words of Imam Ja'far Sadiq, peace be on him, also deserve attention: "Allah has fixed 25 dirhams as Zakat out of 1000 dirhams because He has created the human beings and knows the extent of their needs. He knows that out of every 1000 persons 25 are poor (i.e. the number of weak persons and those who cannot do any work and those who are in need of immediate help is within these limits) and has fixed their share accordingly. And if the number of such persons had been more than this, He would have fixed a larger share for them, because Allah is their Creator and is aware of their condition".[139]

Islam has strictly warned the rich, and informed them of the dangers which spring out of class difference. The Holy Prophet, peace be on him and his progeny, says: "Ensure your wealth by paying Zakat".[140]

This is so because it is evident that most of the wicked deeds, corruption and thefts and above all the inauspicious melody of communism crop up from poverty and acute need.

Whatever has been said above was with regard to the payment of Zakat from the economic point of view. However, it should not be forgotton that its piritual aspect also enjoys at least as much importance.

Imam Ali, peace be on him, says: "Zakat, along with prayers, has been held for Muslims to be a means of proximity to Allah. It becomes an atonement for the sins of a person, who pays it willingly, and protects him from the fire of Hell. Hence none should pay it with a heavy heart and feel sad on account of its payment".[141]

On another occasion he says: "Do not forget to pay Zakat, for Zakat quenches the wrath of Allah."[142]

For the above mentioned persons Islam has strongly condemned non-payment of Zakat and has threatened the well-to-do people, who refrain from paying it.

Imam Muhammad Baqir (P) quotes from Imam Ali (P), who quoted from the Holy Prophet, peace be on him and his progeny: "If people refrain from paying Zakat, Allah's Blessings will also be withheld from the earth".[143]

Imam Ja'far Sadiq, peace be on him, also says: "One who refrains from paying the minimum amount of Zakat (one carat) is neither a believer nor a Muslim".[144]

Islam attaches so much importance to this social act that the Holy Prophet, peace be on him and his progency, formally turned out of the Masjid some persons who considered this th rights of the poor. He said: "Whoever of you does not pay vital act to be something quite ordinary and had failed to pay the rights of the poor. He said: "Whoever of you does not pay Zakat should leave 'our Masjid' and should not offer prayers in it".[145]

Though Islam accords due consideration to economic freedom and aquisition of personal property, yet it says: "Allah has made gold and silver coins (money and wealth) to be the means of the welfare of the people, so that they may meet their needs in different walks of life and achieve their ends. Hence the entire wealth of those, who accumulate a good deal of it but comply with Allah's orders and pay Zakat (i.e. the rights of the poor) shall become pure and lawful".[146]

But at the ame time Islam considers the non-payment of the rights of the poor to be an unpardonable sin and says: "A person who accumulates sufficient belongings and gold and silver and practises stinginess and does not pay Allah's right (and in its stead) converts it into gold and silver utensils (and leads a luxurious life) shall deserve Divine wrath". Almighty Allah says: *"A day will arrive when these coins will be made red hot with the fire of Hell and will be tattoed on their foreheads, backs and the lateral sides".* (Surah Tawbah, 9 : 35).

* * * * *

The Financial Rights

In order to reduce the grave distance between different classes, Islam has fixed, besides Zakat, other rights of the needy in the wealth of the well-to-do people and the rich and praises those people, "Who have themselves opened an account in their wealth and have determined a right in it for the indigent persons of the society - besides Zakat, which is their established right".[147]

Imam Ja'far Sadiq, peace be on him, says thus in connection with such rights: "Almighty Allah has fixed other rights, besides Zakat, in the property of the rich and He says: "Only those persons can withstand hardships who determine a right in their wealth for the poor. This right is besides Zakat and is a right which a person makes obligatory upon himself. He should fix it according to his means and pay it daily or once in a week or once in a month. And Allah says again: "Make a good loan to Allah". This is in addition to Zakat. He further says: "Those people who spend in the way of Allah openly and secretly".

"And again *mā'oun* (whose objectors are reproached by Allah) is also the same thing that money should be lent or something may be given on loan or a good deed may be done. And one of the things which are counted as assets besides Zakat in the sympathetic consideration about which Allah says: *And the people who hold it firmly and about which Allah has given orders. Hence anyone who acquits himself of the duties which Allah has made obligatory upon him has performed what was due from him*".[148]

Imam Ja'far Sadiq, peace be on him, says again: "Do you think that Allah has fixed only Zakat in your wealth? (If it is so, you are mistaken). That which Allah has fixed besides Zakat is more than Zakat and the same should be spent on your relatives and on those who ask you for it".[149] The Holy Imam was asked again as to whether Allah by saying: "Those who fix a right in their wealth for those who ask for it or are needy" meant something other than Zakat? He replied: Yes, by it those people are meant whom Allah has given wealth and who take out of it 1000 or 2000 or 3000 or something more or less than that and give it to their relatives or spend it on the helpless people of their community".[150]

However, Islam considers those rich persons to be virtuous who meet all financial obligations consisting of Zakat and rights of the relatives, the beggars and the needy.

Imam Ja'far Sadiq, peace be on him, said to Ammār Sābāti: "Have you much wealth? He replied: "Yes". The Imam asked: "Do you pay Zakat which Allah has made obligatory? He replied in the affirmative. Then the Holy Imam said: "Do you segregate a certain amount of your wealth for the poor?" He replied: relatives? "He said: "Yes". The Imam asked: "Do you help your brother-in-faith also? He replied: "Yes". Then the Holy Imam (encouraged) him and) said: "O Ammār! Wealth exhausts, human body decays but the action lasts. And the Reckoner is alive and He does not die. O Ammār! Whatever you send in advance belongs to you but whatever you leave behind will never reach you".[151]

* * * * *

Charity in the Cause of Allah

Charity in the cause of Allah sometimes called *Sadaqa* in the terminology of tradition (*Sadaqa* is charity in the cause of Allah). It is in itself such a wonderful thing that very few of the recommended precepts have perhaps been given an importance equal to it.

From the view-point of Islam charity exercises great influence upon everything including life, wealth and riches and above all the Blessings of Allah. The Holy Prophet, peace be on him and his progeny, says: "On the Day of Judgement everyone will rest under the shadow of his charity until the matters are settled between the people".[152]

"Secret charity in the cause of Allah quenches the Flame of Allah's Wrath".[153]

Imam Ja'far Sadiq, peace be on him, says: "Every Muslim who clothes a destitute Muslim remains under Allah's Protection, till the shreds of that cloth last".[154]

"Treat your sick kindly in the cause of Allah. Seek your sustenance by means of charity, for before it reaches the creature, it reaches the Hand of the Creator".[155]

Imam Muhammad Baqir, peace be on him, says: 'Goodness and kindness in the path of Allah eradicates poverty, increases a man's life-span and protects him from seventy different types of dangerous deaths.[156]

It is, however, much better that one should do this noble act while he possesses good health and stamina and not in the shape of a will at the time of his death.

The Holy Prophet, peace be on him and his progeny, was asked as to which charity is better. He replied: "That one which you give personally when you are alive and in control of your affairs; when you hope to live and are afraid of indigence, and not that you should postpone it till you are about to die and then you say to give that much to one and that much to another."[157]

* * * * *

Do not let them feel Inferior or Humiliated

There is no doubt about the fact that all these recommendations and insistence about charity have mostly been with a view to relieving the indigent from their pitiable condition and to remove their mental agony by meeting their financial needs. And the person who gives charity attains a higher moral and spiritual satisfaction by means of this pious act and thus he adorns himself with fresh virtue and excellence.

In case, however, charity is motivated by making the receipient feel obliged then on the one hand not only the real object is not achieved but a severe damage is also done to the spirit of the recipients and on the other hand it becomes known that this act in fact was not for Allah' sake and consequently one who thus spends money does not derive any moral or spiritual benefit. For this very reason the Holy Qur'an, while mentioning the subject of charity in the way of Allah, invites the attention of the people on many occasions to the fact that this act should be for Allah's sake only and should not be followed by letting the recipients feel obliged on account of the favour done to them.

At one place it says: "Those, who spend their property in the cause of Allah and do not make the recipient feel obliged or humiliated, shall receive their reward from Allah. They shall have no fear nor will they be grieved."[158]

And in two other verses following this it considers such an act to be the cause of loss of spiritual reward and benefit of charity and by comparing an act purely for the sake of Allah with the one other than this it says: *"Believers, do not make your charities fruitless by reproachfully reminding the recipient of your favour or making them insulted, like the one who spends his property to show off and who has no faith in Allah or belief in the Day of Judgement. The example of his deed is as though some soil has gathered on a rock and after a rainfall it turns hard and barren. Such people cannot benefit from what they have earned. Allah does not guide the unbelievers. The example of those who spend their property to please Allah out of their firm and sincere intention is like the garden on a fertile land which after a heavy rainfall or even a drizzle yields double produce".* [159]

And in many statements of the leaders of Islam also it has been mentioned clearly that the spiritual reward of a good action is lost by reminding the recipient of the favours done to him. The Holy Prophet, peace be on him and his progeny, says: "Allah nullifies the charity of a person who does good to a Muslim and then hurts him by reminding him of the favours done to him".[160] He also says: "And Allah does not pay any attention to a person and He does not purify his heart if that person reminds the recipient of the favour done to him".[161]

Hence, for the achievement of Allah's favour it has been ordered that if anything is given to a person he should not be considered to be low but should be respected. Imam Ali, peace be on him, says: "When you give something to a person who requests for it, take your hands upto your mouth and kiss them because charity is accepted by Allah".[162]

It is perhaps for this very reason that it has been ordered that charity should, as far as possible, be given secretly. The Holy Prophet, peace be on him and his progeny, says: "There are seven groups of people whom Allah will keep under the shadow of His Blessings on the Day of Judgement. One of them consists of the people who give charity and keep it a secret so much so that even their right hand does not know what they give with their left hand".[163]

57

Moderation

As the foundation of true social life has been laid on moderation and maintenance of equilibrium, the sacred religion of Islam has not ignored moderation and equilibrium in any circumstances and even in the matter of daily expenditure it praises those persons "who are neither extravagant nor niggardly but keep the golden mean".[164]

Extravagance and lavishness are condemned by Islam and are considered to be a great defect in a man.

Imam Ja'far Sadiq, peace be on him, says: "Perfection lies in three things and one of them is moderation in life".[165]

Imam Muhammad Baqir, peace be on him, says: "There is no goodness in the one who is not moderate in his life because this thing (i.e. not being moderate) is not beneficial for him either in this world or in the Hereafter".[166] And the Holy Qur'an says: *"Do not squander your wealth wastefully for the wasteful are Satan's brothers".*[167]

* * * * *

Granting a Loan

While the religion of Islam has considered different types of purchase and sale to be lawful, it has declared usury to be unlawful, in whatever shape it may be i.e. whether in connection with purchase and sale or in connection with lending and borrowing.[168]

However, as one is compelled to take loan at some time or another, Islam encourages the wealthy persons to grant loan to others.

Imam Ja'far Sadiq, peace be on him, says: "If a Muslim grants a loan to a brother Muslim for the sake of Allah (and not for interest) that loan is considered to be a 'Charity' till such time that it is repaid".[169]

The Holy Prophet, peace be on him and his progeny, says: "There is a writing on the gate of Paradise to the effect that the reward for charity is 10 times and the reward for loan is 70 times as high. I enquired from Jibril as to why it was so when the property of one who gives charity does not return to him, whereas a loan is repayable, Jibril replied that it was becuase one who takes charity may not be in need of it whereas one who takes a loan really needs it.

Hence charity is sometimes given to a man who deserves it and at other time to one who does not deserve it. it is for this reason that the reward for a loan is greater than that for charity and munificence".[170]

However, on the other hand Islam does not permit everyone to obtain loan and considers it to be justified for only those people who really need it, because being a debtor is the cause of humiliation for a person.

The Holy Prophet says: "Refrain from becoming a debtor because debt is a matter of shame for man. During the night it keeps him busy with itself and during day it makes him feel ashamed before the creditor".[171] And as anxiety, agitation and disturbance of mind get on one's nerves it is possible that debt may shorten the life of man. It is on this account that Imam Ja'far Sadiq, peace be on him, says: "Reduce your debts as far as possible because life increases by their reduction".[172]

For these very reasons the Holy Prophet, peace be on him and his progeny, says: "I seek refuge in Allah (from two things) — from blasphemy and from debt". The people asked: "Do you consider blasphemy and debt to be at par with each other?" The Holy Prophet, peace be on him and his progeny, replied: "Yes!"[173]

It is perhaps for this reason that at times a debt becomes the cause of blasphemy.

However, none of these things prevents a needy person from taking a loan. Imam Musa Kazim, peace be on him, says: "Whoever makes efforts to earn the requirements of life equal to his personal needs as well as the needs of his family is like one who performs Jihad in the way of Allah. However, when his expenses exceed his income he may take loan from others. It is for Allah and His Messenger to provide him the needs of his family and if he dies without having cleared his debt it is necessary for the Imam to repay the same from the public treasury of the Muslims".[174]

The Holy Prophet, peace be on him and his progeny, says: "Allah is with the debtor provided he has not committed a sin against Allah with that loan".[175]

Furthermore, when Imam Ja'far Sadiq, peace be on him, was asked about the correctness of the following incident: "A man from amongst the Ansar died when he owed a debt of two dinars and the Holy Prophet, peace be on him and his progeny, did not perform his funeral prayers but asked others to perform the prayers although another person had undertaken to repay his debt. They were under the impression that borrowing is an unlawful act and it was on this account that the Holy Prophet, peace be on him and his progeny, had declined to perform his funeral prayers", the Holy Imam said: "Yes. The incident is correct. The Holy Prophet did so because others should take responsibility in the very first instance for the repayment of his debt (and thus comfort him) and besides people should also have taken a lesson and should not have considered 'debt' to be something unimportant but in spite of this, borrowing is not a sin."[176]

Just as Islam declares borrowing to be lawful and encourages the rich to advance loans, it also makes the debtors responsible for the repayment of the loan as early as possible.

Imam Ja'far Sadiq, peace be on him, says: "Amends can be made for every sin by means of Jihad in the cause of Allah and martyrdom except for a loan for which there is no expiation or atonement other than its repayment or its being forgiven by the creditor".[177]

Hence the Holy Prophet says: "After the mortal sins there is nothing more serious than that a person should die in debt and should not leave anything for its repayment."[178]

One of the case in which Islam attaches importance to intention also, besides action, is with regard to the repayment of a debt, because it says that, in case a person is not in a position to make immediate repayment of a loan, it is necessary for him to be keen to repay it.

Imam Ja'far Sadiq, peace be on him, says: "My son! You should know that if a person takes a loan and has it in view that he has to repay it he is in Allah's Protection till he puts his intention into practice. However, if he does not care for its repayment he is a thief."[180]

Islam says that when a person is in a position to repay his

debt he should not be negligent in this behalf. The Holy Prophet, peace be on him and his progeny, says: "If a person, not withstanding his being in a position to repay another's right, shows negligence and carelessness in its repayment, his daily recompense is like punitive tax imposed on a person who forcibly usurps the property of others."[181]

Imam Muhammad Baqir, peace be on him, says: "If a person withholds the right of a Muslim, in spite of being in a position to pay it, fearing that if he pays it he would become poor, he should know that Allah is more competent to make him poor as compared with his wish to become independent of need by withholding the rights of others".[182]

However, Islam also orders the creditors that they should not demand repayment of loan at an inappropriate time and should not press a debtor for repayment when he is not in a position to make it.

Imam Ali Riza, peace be on him, says: "Just as it is not lawful for a debtor not to repay the loan in spite of his being in a position to do so, it is also not lawful for a creditor to put the debtor under pressure".[183]

In this connection the Holy Qur'an says clearly: *"If your debtor be in (financial) straits, grant him a time until he can discharge his debt? but if you waive the sum as charity it will be better for you, though you know it".*[184]

Islam considers it becessary for the debtors to make repayment of loans at the appointed time by whatever means possible even though they may be obliged to sell their belongings. However, the necessities of life like residential house etc. are exempted from this rule.

Imam Ja'far Sadiq, peace be on him, says: "A house cannot be sold for repayment of loan because it is necessary for everyone to have a shelter to rest in."[185]

It is reported that Muhammad bin Abi Umayr, a distinguished companion of Imam Ja'far Sadiq, peace be on him, was a draper and he became bankrupt. His entire property was lost and he became extremely poor. However, he had a claim of ten thousand dirhams against a man. When that man came to know about his need he sold his residential house for 10,000 dirhams and brought the money to him. Muhammad bin Abi Umayr asked: "What is it?" He replied: "It is the debt which I owe you". Muhammad said: "Have you inherited this amount?" The man replied: 'No'. Muhammad then said: 'Has any one given it to you as a gift?'. The man said: 'No!' Muhammad again asked: "Have you sold a garden or an orchard?" The man said: 'No'. Muhammad asked: "Then how have you been able to possess this money?" The man replied: "I had a house which I have sold out to repay your debt". Muhammad bin Abi Umayr said: "It has been reported to me from Imam Ja'far Sadiq, peace be on him: "No one should sell his house for the sake of repaying the debt". Pick up your money. I do not need it. Although I need every penny but I will not take this amount".[186]

To ensure that the rights of creditors are not lost, Islam orders that after the death of a debtor his debt should be paid first and thereafter his property should be divided among his debt, out of his property.

The Holy Prophet, peace be on him and his progeny, says: "The first thing which should be provided for out of the property of a dead person is his shroud. Then comes the turn of his debt and thereafter the property is divided between his heirs".[187]

Even if the time fixed for the repayment of debt has not yet arrived, it becomes payable with immediate effect, in the event of the death of the debtor.

Imam Muhammad Baqir, peace be on him, says: "If a debt is payable by a person at an appointed time but he dies before that time, the debt becomes payable with immediate effect".[188]

However, if another person stands surety for the repayment of a debt, the responsibility of the debtor to the creditor comes to an end.

Imam Ali Riza, peace be on him, says: "If a person who owes a debt dies and another person guarantees its repayment the responsibility for the repayment of the debt is transferred to the surety".[189]

Forgiveness and Toleration

In order to suppress and crush their adversaries some persons resort to pay them in the same coin and meet wickedness with wickedness. However, Imam Ali, peace be on him, says: "Punish your opponents with kindness and ward off the harm done by them by means of a good reward".[190]

It means that to forgive a mistake is the best method of stopping its repetition. Hence, the Qur'an says in connection with the qualities of the pious people: "People who control their anger and forgive the shortcomings of the people".[191] And then orders that the Muslims: "Should forgive and overlook. Don't you wish Allah to forgive you? He is Forgiving and Merciful".[192] And again it says: "He that forgives and seeks reconciliation shall be rewarded by Allah".[193]

Forgiveness and toleration are qualities which ensure success and prosperity in this world as well as in the Hereafter. The Holy Prophet, peace be on him and his progeny, says: "Should I lead you to goodness in this world as well as in the Hereafter? Visit him, who has abandoned relations with you. Do good to him, who has deprived you. And fogive him, who has oppressed you".[194] He further say: "It is necessary for you to be forgiving, because forgiveness and toleration increase the honour of man. Forgive, so that Allah may make you respectable".[195]

However, it should be remembered that forgiveness carries value when one is in a position to take revenge and it behoves only that person (to forgive) who possesses the necessary power.

Imam Ali, peace be on him, says: "Forgive your enemy when you have the upper hand over him and consider it to be thanksgiving for the power which you possess".[196] "The person most suited to forgive is he, who possesses more power to punish".[197]

We can understand the importance of forgiveness when we see that while emphasizing the infallibility of *Ahlul Bayt* (the chosen descendants of the Holy Prophet) Imam Ja'far Sadiq, peace be on him, says: "We come of the family whose second nature is to forgive those who have oppressed us".[198] He also says: "To forgive, while possessing power to punish is the way of the propehets and the pious people".[199]

* * * * *

Hypocrisy
and Double-dealing

Islam has campaigned seriously against hypocrisy or double-dealing and has warned its followers sternly against it. There are numerous verses of the Holy Qur'an and the traditions of the leaders of Islam which condemn hypocrisy and double-facednes.

The Holy Qur'an in connection with some hypocrites and their end says: *"There are some who declare: We believe in Allah and the Day of Judgement", but they are not true believers. They deceive Allah and the believers. However, they have deceived none but themselves, a fact of which they are not aware. A sickness exists in their hearts to which Allah adds more sickness. Besides this they will suffer a painful punishment as a result of the lie which they tell. When they are asked not to commit corruption in the land, they reply, "We are only reformers". They are corrupt but do not realize it. When they are asked to believe as everyone else does, they say, "Should we believe as fools do?" In fact, they are fools but they do not know it. To the believers they profess belief but in secret they say to their own devils "We were only mocking". In fact Allah mocks them and gives them time to continue blindly in their transgressions. They have traded guidance for error but their bargain has had no profit and they have missed the right guidance. Their case is like that of one who kindles a fire and when it grows bright Allah takes away their light leaving him in darkness. They cannot see. They are blind, deaf and dumb and cannot regain their senses. Or it is like that of a rainstorm with darkness, thunder and lightning approaching. They cover their ears for fear of thunder and death. (Allah encompasses those who deny His Words). The lightning almost takes away their vision. When the lighting brighteons their surroundings, they walk, and when it is dark, they stand still. Had Allah wanted, He could have taken away their hearing and their vision. Allah has power over all things".* [200]

Allah will not forgive, or guide those to the right path, who first believe, then disbelieve, again believe and disbelieve, and then increase their disbelief.

The Holy Qur'an further says: *"Tell the hypocrites that for them there will be a painful torment. Do those who establish friendship with the disbelievers instead of the believers seek honour? Let them know that all honour belongs to Allah".* [201]

For the hypocrites and the disbelievers, Allah has prepared Hell wherein they will live forever. Hell is their proper punishment. Allah has condemned them and they will suffer a permanent torment like those who lived before you, whose power, wealth and children were much greater than yours. [202]

The Holy Prophet, peace be on him and his progeny, says: "A hypocrite is like the branch of a date-palm tree which has been cut off from the tree and its owner intends to utilize it for a building but it is not suitable for it and then he wishes to use it for some other purpose but is disappointed again and in the end he has no alternative left but to burn it and destroy it".[203] (In short the hypocrites are not only useless persons but dangerous and poisonous elements in whichever society they may be).

The Holy Prophet, peace be on him and his progeny, says: "Hypocrisy is to show oneself to be more pious outwardly than what actually one is internally".[204]

He also mentions the sign of a hypocrite as under: "A hypocrite is one who tells lies when he speaks, does not keep his promises and commits breach of trust".[205]

Imam Ja'far Sadiq, peace be on him, quotes from Luqman as under: "A hypocrite is one whose words and deeds do not accord with his internal thoughts and his appearance is different from his actual personality".[206]

People who practise hypocrisy are called 'double-faced' and 'double-tongued' in the terminology of tradition. Imam Muhammad Baqir, peace be on him, says thus about the hypocrites: "One who possesses two faces and two tongues is a bad person. He is one who praises his brother-in-faith in his presence and slanders him in his absence. If his brother attains a status he envies him and if he is involved in some difficulty he leaves him alone and does not help him".[207]

The Holy Prophet, peace be on him and his progeny, says: "One who is a hypocrite in this world will be having two tongues of fire on the Dooms Day".[208]

* * * * *

Mutual Trust

It is evident that before everything else society needs 'mutal trust and confidence' of its members because unless the people trust one another and look upon one another with confidence and respect, they cannot smoothly continue their social life, solve their problems by mutual help and maintain proper relations. The dangers of lack of mutual trust are so obvious that they need not be discussed in detail.

In order to expand and strengthen mutual trust among its followers Islam prohibits them from suspecting one another and considers it to be a sin. The Holy Qur'an says: *"Believers, avoid immoderate suspicion, for in some cases suspicion is a crime"*.[209]

Imam Ali, peace be on him, says: "Bad opinion about a good person is one of the greatest crimes and worst kind of injustice".[210] "It is unjust that one should decide about a reliable person according to one's own supposition".[211]

Islam orders that the words of a brother-in-faith should be taken in good faith. Imam Ali, peace be on him, says: "Till such time a word carries a good sense do not attach a bad meaning to it".[212]

Islam has declared mutual trust and good opinion to be the right of Muslims over one another. Imam Ja'far Sadiq, peace be on him, says: "One of the rights of a believer over his brother is that he should corroborate what he says and should not contradict it".[213]

However, Islam considers bad supposition to be peculiar to those who are themselves ill-bred and wicked. Imam Ali, peace be on him, says: "A wicked person does not hold a good opinion about his brother and is always suspicious about him because man by virtue of his instinct considers everyone according to his own nature".[214]

It should, however, be kept in mind that it is the duty of Muslims not to place themselves in a situation which may invite calumny viz. they should not do anything which may make others suspect them. And if such a situation does arise they should clarify the real position. It was on this account that while the Holy Prophet, peace be on him and his progeny, was once sitting with one of his wives named Safia and a man from amongst the Ansar happened to pass by and the Holy Prophet made it known to him that the woman was his wife. The man said, "O Prophet of Allah! Is it possible that I should entertain any suspicion about you?" The Holy Prophet then said, "O man! Satan penetrates into human body like blood. I, therefore, feared lest it should misguide you to hold a bad opinion".[215]

Islam has strictly prohibited all such things as may possibly cause mutual suspicion among the Muslims e.g. back-biting, hearing a person slandering others, peeping at the secrets of others etc. etc.

* * * * *

Truthfulness

Truthfulness is one of the most basic fundamentals for the establishment of mutual social relations. Islam has, therefore, attached much importance to truthfulness as a moral value and the Holy Qur'an has mentioned it on various occasions.

To show the importance which truthfulness enjoys in the eyes of Islam it is sufficient to say that whenever the Holy Qur'an wants to praise a prophet it makes a selection out of his virtues and introduces him to be a truthful person.

The Holy Qur'an has mentioned Prophet Ibrahim, peace be on him, along with this attribute.[216] It has also glorified Prophet Yusuf, peace be on him, with this virtue.[217] It also praises Prophet Ismā'il, peace be on him, for truthfulness[218] and also extols Prophet Idress, peace be on him, on this account.[219] It also narrates about other distinguished personalities and true servants of Allah that they 'possessed truthful tongues".[221]

Islam considers truthfulness to be the excellent sign of man's merits. Imam Ja'far Sadiq, peace be on him, says: "Do not be misled by one's praying or fasting too much, because many persons develop a habit in this behalf and cannot forsake it. On the other hand judge people in the light of their truthfulness and honesty and test them keeping in view these two merits.[222]

Islam considers goodness of an action to be dependent upon truthfulness. Imam Ja'far Sadiq, peace be on him, says: "If a man has a truthful tongue, his action is also correct and pious".[223]

The Holy Prophet, peace be on him and his progeny, promises intercession to those people who are truthful[224] and the first advice which he tendered to Imam Ali, peace be on him, was to be truthful and never to utter a lie".[225]

Islam considers salvation to be accompanied by truthfulness. Imam Ali, peace be on him, says: "Make truthfulness your second nature because salvation depends on truthfulness".[226]

All these are recommendations made by Islam about truthfulness. However, the reproaches and threats which it attaches to falsehood are more serious. The Holy Qur'an declares liars to be the persons who do not believe in Allah[227] and considers them to be devoid of Divine guidance[228] and thus it says about their fate: "On the Day of Judgement you will see the liars with black faces and those who imputed false things to Allah".[229]

Imam Ja'far Sadiq, peace be on him, says: "Excessive falsehood causes light from one's heart and brightness from one's face to disappear".[230]

Hence, in order that the badness of this act may become patently clear, Imam Muhammad Baqir, peace be on him, says: "Allah has closed the door of every evil deed with a lock, the key of which is drinking wine, because when a person gets intoxicated he becomes liable to commit any crime, as he loses his sense of proportion, which normally stops him from because its consequences are more evil and inauspicious".[231]

On another occasion Imam Hasan Askari, peace be on him, has directly declared falsehood to be the key to curses and evils[232] and it is for this very reason that Imam Baqir, peace be on him, calls it the destroyer of faith.[233]

Imam Ali, peace be on him, says: "One does not enjoy the taste of faith unless he forsakes falsehood whether this falsehood be in seriousness or in jest".[234]

The Holy Prophet, peace be on him and his progeny, says: "It is possible that a believer may be timid or miser but it is not possible that he may be a liar".[235]

Besides all this, falsehood is not beneficial even in the worldly life. The Holy Prophet, peace be on him and his progeny, says: "Falsehood decreases the means of man's sustenance".[236]

Imam Ali, peace be on him, says: "Being habituated to falsehood results in indigence and adversity".[237]

The Holy Prophet says: "Refrain from falsehood even if you consider it to be advantageous for you, because it contains perdition and adversity of which you are not aware".[238]

Islam orders that one should refrain from associating with the liars. Imam Ali, peace be on him, says: "It is appropriate that a Muslim should not associate with a liar".[239]

Imam Sajjad, peace be on him, advises his son Imam Muhammad Baqir, peace be on him, in the following words: "Refrain from associating with people of five categories and do not coverse nor travel with them. Out of them the first one is that of the liars, because they are like a mirage which shows far off things nearer and the things which are near are shown to be far off".[240]

* * * * *

Trustworthiness

In the foregoing discussion the stress laid on truthfulnes by Islam has become clear in a brief manner and presumably you noticed at that stage that in most of the traditions the subject of trustworthiness has also been mentioned along with truthfulness. The importance of trustworthiness in the eyes of Islam can well be understood by this because it is one of most important bases for the prosperity of human society.

On one occasion the Holy Qur'an orders the Muslims explicitly to return to the owners the things left by them in their custody.[241] And at another place it has mentioned trustworthiness to be one of the primary qualities of the believers.[242] It has also introduced the Prophets like Noah, Hud, Sāleh, Lot, Sho'ayb and Musa, peace be on them, as trustworthy messengers.[243]

The Holy Prophet, peace be on him and his progeny, says: "A person who is not trustworthy is devoid of a strong and complete faith".[244]

Islam considers trustworthiness to be the first trait of a companion. When Imam Ja'far Sadiq, peace be on him, was asked about the rules of companionship during journeys he replied: "Protect the thing entrusted by him (i.e. by your companion) to you and return it to him".[245]

Imam Ja'far Sadiq, peace be on him, says: "Whenever a person entrusts anything to you do not commit a breach of trust even if that person may happen to be the murderer of Imam Husayn".[246]

"If the murderer of Imam Ali entrusts his sword to me and I accept the trust I shall not misappropriate it and shall return it to him as and when he asks for it".[247]

Islam declares that trustworthiness also creates a good impression on one's life. Imam Ja'far Sadiq, peace be on him, tells his son: "My son! Trustworthiness guards the faith and the worldly affairs of man. Be trustworthy so that you may always be free from want".[248] And on another occasion he says to one of his companions: "I recommend two things to you: one of them is truthfulness and the other is trustworthiness, for these two are the key to the means of sustenance".[249]

The Holy Prophet, peace be on him and his progeny, also says: "Trustworthiness increases one's means of sustenance and breach of trust is the cause of poverty and indigence".[250]

* * * * *

Visiting the Sick

The sick are usually broken-hearted and dejected persons, who are soundly in need of affability, kindness and spiritual contentment, because they consider themselves hepless and disabled and at times lose hope completely. It is evident that in such circumstances visiting friends and brothers-in-faith is a source of great consolation for them and it provides them comfort and mental satisfaction. In view of this Islam recommends very strongly that the sick should be visited and the act of enquiring about their health should not be neglected.

The Holy Prophet, peace be on him and his progeny, says: "Every Muslim who visits a sick person is absorbed in Allah's Blessings and during the time he is seated by the sick he is benefited by the Divine Mercy. If he visits the sick man in the morning 70,000 angels pray for him till evening and if he visits him in the evening 70,000 angels pray for him till morning".[251]

Islam orders that when you visit the sick you should enquire about their health and pray for them, because it is possible that by this means their hearts may be consoled.

The Holy Prophet, peace be on him and his progeny, says: "Visit the sick and escort the funerals of the dead so that you may be reminded of the next world. Pray for the sick person and say: "O Allah! Cure him and treat him with Your medicine and keep him safe from calamity".

When you visit a sick persons, take with you a present for him, even if it may be very small. The Holy Prophet, peace be on him and his progeny, says: "Whoever is willing to feed a sick person shall be provided by Allah with the fruits of Paradise".[252]

Once when some companions of Imam Ja'far Sadiq, peace be on him, were going to visit a sick person he met them on the way and asked them to stop. When they stopped he asked them: "Are you carrying with you an apple or quince or citron or some perfume or a piece of aloeswood?" They replied in the negative. Thereupon, the Holy Imam said: "Don't you know that such things ensure peace of mind of a sick person?"[253]

One who visits a sick person should not expect reception or victuals from him. So much so that the Holy Prophet, peace be on him and his progeny, has said that one should not eat anything while sitting with a sick person or else he would lose the spiritual reward accompanying the visit.[254]

Islam tells that one should not disturb a sick person for three days (during which period the nature of his ailment is not usually clear). Imam Ali, peace be on him, says: "A sick person should be visited after three days............"[255]

It is also necessary that the visit should not be a source of inconvenience and uneasiness to the patient. It is, therefore, proper that one should not sit with him for a long time.

Imam Ali, peace be on him, says: "Among those who visit the sick that person is rewarded more who stays with the patient for a short time unless he knows that he desires him to stay further".[256]

Imam Ja'far Sadiq, peace be on him, says: "It is better that while you visit a sick person you should place your hand on his hand and should get up soon from his side. The fact is that the visit of a foolish person is more troublesome to a patient than his own ailment" (because it causes him more inconvenience)".[257]

Islam orders the Muslims to assist the sick persons in discharging their daily requirements. The Holy Prophet, peace be on him and his progeny, says: "One who assists a sick person in meeting his needs is absolved from his sins whether he succeeds in this task or not".[258]

Sympathy with the Bereaved

Whatever consoles an afflicted and bereaved person to some extent and reduces his grief and gloom amounts to condolence with him. Islam has, therefore, stressed upon this subject and a great reward has been promised for it in a number of traditions. Imam Ja'far Sadiq, peace be on him, says: "One who consoles a bereaved person earns a reward equal to his without losing anything as the bereaved person is entitled to a great reward)".[259]

It is evident that members of a bereaved family are too much disturbed for some days to think of themselves or of their food. Hence, Islam has ordered that (contrary to what has become customary these days!) their neighbours should arrange for their food for three days. Imam Ja'far Sadiq, peace be on him, says: "It is appropriate that the neighbours of a bereaved person should feed him for three days".[260] He also says: "To prepare meals in the presence of the bereaved people is one of the customs of the Dark Age of Ignorance and the course prescribed by Islam is that food should be taken for them in the manner recommended by the Holy Prophet, peace be on him and his progeny, with regard to the family of Ja'far son of Abu Talib, peace be on him".[261]

Islam has not only made sympathy with the afflicted people necessary but, as a matter of principle, its entire programme is based on sympathetic care and service to humanity. While praising the companions of the Holy Prophet the Holy Qur'an says: *Muhammad is the Messenger of Allah and those with him are stern to the disbelievers yet kind among themselves".*[262] And while praising some of them it says: *"Those who enjoin fortitude, mercy and kindness".*[263]

Imam Ja'far Sadiq, peace be on him, says: "There are three types of people whose prayer is certainly accepted. Out of them one is a Muslim, who prays for such Muslim who has been sympathetic towards him, and similarly a Muslim who curses that one who could help him and could meet his need but shirked it".[264]

* * * * *

Friendship

Islam has attached great importance to the subject of friendship and always instructed its followers to mingle with good and pious men.

The Holy Prophet, peace be on him and his progeny, said: "Whenever you see one of the gardens of Paradise open before you, benefit from it". The people asked: "O Prophet of Allah! Where is the garden of Paradise?" The Holy Prophet, peace be on him and his progeny, replied: "I mean association with the believers and those who have faith in their Lord".[265]

The Almighty Allah in the Holy Qur'an instructs His Prophet thus: *"Be patient with those who worship their Lord in the morning and evening seeking His pleasure. Do not overlook them to seek the worldly pleasure, nor obey those whose hearts We have made heedless of Our rememberance and who follow their own desires beyond all limits".*[266]

The Holy Prophet, peace be on him and his progeny, says: "A good friend is better than solitude, but solitude is better than mingling with bad people".[267]

"The most lucky person is he ho associates with noble-minded people".[268]

"One always absorbs the ways of his friend".[269]

The Holy Prophet, peace be on him and his progeny, defines a good friend in these words: "He is the one whose very sight makes you remember Allah, whose conversation increases your knowledge, and whose deeds remind you of the world in the Hereafter".[270]

Islam says that two friends should act as preachers for each other and each one of them should point out the shortcomings of the other. The better friend is he who performs this duty in a better way. Imam Ja'far Sadiq, peace beon him, says: "My most beloved friend is he who points out my faults to me".[271] "When a person finds his friend in error and can prevent him from it, but does not do so, he commits a breach of trust with him".[272]

Islam has encouraged the Muslims so much to associate with pious people that Imam Ja'far Sadiq, peace be on him, says: "The enemy (Satan) overpowers a person whose heart does not give him good counsel and whose soul does not prevent him from committing sins and above all who also does not possess a pious friend".[273]

Islam similarly prohibits association with mean and ignorant persons. The Holy Prophet, peace be on him and his progeny, says: "The wisest person is he, who shuns the company of ignorant people".[274] Imam Ali, peace be on him, says: "The company of bad people becomes the cause of low esteem of the good people".[275] "A bad companion is one who justifies the sins committed against Allah before the eyes of the people".[276]

The leaders of Islam have prohibited mingling with the persons who are devoid of decent human qualities and moral virtues.

Imam Muhammad Baqir, peace be on him, says: "Do not associate with a fool, a miser, a liar and a timid person, because a foolish friend, while thinking that he is doing you good, will cause you harm, and a miserly friend will take from you but will not give you anything. In time of need, the timid friend will run away from you as well as from his own parents, and a liar, who tells too many lies, says that which cannot be believed, and it is not, therefore, possible to benefit from his ideas and thoughts".[277]

The Holy Prophet, peace be on him and his progeny, has called a bad friend 'a dead body' and he says: "Association with the dead makes the human heart die and 'the dead' are the persons, who have lost their faith and are ignorant of the Laws of religion".[278]

Imam Ja'far Sadiq, peace be on him, says: "Test your friends in respect of two qualities and in case they possess these two, associatie with them otherwise shun their company: Offering obligatory prayers at their proper time and doing good to their brother-in-faith in weal as well as in woe".[279]

* * * * *

The Decencies

Many people think that happiness and adversity are the direct result of factors like riches, status and authority. However, according to Islam, happiness springs from matters which increase man's spiritual and moral values. Their fundamentals have been explained in the sayings of the leaders of Islam — one of them being cheerfulness and decent behaviour. Imam Ja'far Sadiq, peace be on him, says: "Good behaviour is one of the factors of human prosperity".[280]

And that being so it is not surprising that the Almighty Allah commends His Prophet for his noble character as He says: *"Yours is a sublime nature"*.[281] And Allah also bases the rapid advancement of Islam on this factor and says: *"Had you been harsh and cold-blooded, they would have surely deserted you"*.[282]

Islam accords a special consideration to sublime nature and decent behaviour. Imam Ali, peace be on him, says: "The faith of one who possesses decent morals is more complete".[283]

Imam Ja'far Sadiq, peace be on him, says: "Whoever is more well-behaved is wiser than others".[284]

"The Lord has granted you Islam. You, too should guard it well by being forgiving and tolerant".[285]

At times Islam invites people to think about the good spiritual effects of proper behaviour and good morals. For example the Holy Prophet, peace be on him and his progeny, says: "The spiritual reward of one who possesses good morals is like that of one who fasts and worships continuously".[286] "Piety and good morals are the things which will lead most of my followers to Paradise".[287]

Imam Ja'far Sadiq, peace be on him and his progeny, says: "The spiritual reward given by Allah for decent behaviour and good morals is equal to that of struggling in His path".[288]

"Good morals melt the sins (and make them disappear) just as the sun melts snow on the face of the earth".[289] "And (on theother side) misconduct spoils the good deeds of man just as vinegar spoils honey".[290]

The Holy Prophet, peace be on him and his progeny, says: "An immoral person can never repent of his sins, for whenever he forsakes one sin he will become involved in still a graver sin".[291]

At times Islam mentions the social and individual losses which man has to face on account of bad morals and also describes the advantages which accrue from good morals. Imam Ja'far Sadiq, peace be on him, says: "Doing good to the people and behaving properly towards them makes the cities populous and increases the span of life".[292]

"An immoral person remains involved in torture and anguish".[293]

The Holy Prophet, peace be on him and his progeny, tells his kinsmen: "O sons of Abdul Muttalib! You cannot please all the people with money but you can meet them with cheerful faces and good behaviour so that you may be liked by them, for wealth is limited in any case, but the decent morals and cheerfulness are inexhaustible".[294]

Imam Ja'far Sadiq, peace beon him, when asked about good behaviour, replied: "Good behaviour is that you should be kind to the people, speak with them in a nice manner and meet them with a cheerful face".[295]

* * * * *

Redeeming the Promise

Fidelity is a sacred word which is received with respect everywhere and enjoys extraordinary importance.

Islam considers fidelity to one's promise to be one of the most excellent human traits and considers that man to be 'righteous' who keeps his promise.[296] The Holy Qur'an explicity orders: *"Keep your promises, because you will be called to account for your promises".*[297] Almighty Allah commends Prophet Ismā'il, peace be on him, a great Prophet of Allah in these words: "He was as good as his word, a Messenger and a Prophet".[298]

Islam considers 'keeping promise' to be one of the essentials of the faith. Imam Ali, peace be on him, says: "Redemption of a promise is one of the signs of the believers".[299] The Holy Prophet, peace be on him and his progeny, says: "One who does not keep his promise, has no faith".[300] "One who believes in Allah and the Day of Judgement, keeps his promise when he makes it".[301] And again Imam Ali, peace be on him, says: "To fulfil one's promise is a sign of faith".[302]

Islam considers going back on one's promise to be a sign of hypocrisy. The Holy Prophet, peace be on him and his progeny says: "There are four signs of a hypocrite. One of them is going back on one's promise".[303]

As already mentioned above the Holy Qur'an praises Prophet Ismā'il, peace be on him, for being 'as good as his word'. Imam Ja'far Sadiq, peace be on him, says: "Prophet Ismā'il,

85

peace be on him, promised to meet a man at Safah, a place situated outside Makkah. The Prophet stayed there for a long time but that man did not turn up. People of Makkah were trying to find out his where-abouts but they could not know where he was. At last a man chanced to pass by him and said: 'O Prophet of Allah! We have become weak and have been ruined in your absence' Prophet Ismā'il, peace be on him, said: 'I have made a promise to such and such person that I would stay here and shall not move away till he comes'. The people went to that man and said: 'O enemy of Allah! You have made a promise wih Allah's Prophet and failed to fulfil it!' The man then recollected and came to Prophet Ismā'il, peace be on him, and said: 'O Prophet of Allah! Forgive me for I had forgotten my promise'. It was on this account that the Almighty Allah revealed the verse about him".[304]

Imam Ja'far Sadiq (P), also says: "The Holy Prophet, peace be on him and his progeny, promised a man that he would sit on a stone till he came back. That man went away and the sun rose and the weather became hot. The companions of the Holy Prophet said "O Prophet of Allah! What difference would it make if you come and stay under a shade? The Holy Prophet replied: "I have promised to meet him here and if he does not replied: "I have promised to meet him here and if he does not turn up I will stay here till the Day of Judgement".[305]

In fact this is a lesson which makes the importance of keeping a promise abundantly clear. It is the principle the observance of which in our social life can solve most of our problems.

* * * * *

Consultation

Everyone reflects as to how he should solve the problems of his life and what policy he should adopt to acquit himself well of his responsibilities. One of the best methods of surmounting the difficulties is to make consultations and to benefit from the advice of others.

Imam Ali, peace be on him, says: "There is no support like consultation".[306] "Consultation is next to guidance".[307]

Imam Ja'far Sadiq, peace be on him, says: "No one can be misled by consultation".[308]

The Holy Prophet, peace be on him and his progeny, says: "The prudent way of doing things is that you should consult others to follow their advice".[309] And the Holy Qur'an itself directs the Holy Prophet, to consult his companions[310] and praises those persons who accept the Divine invitation and consult others in their affairs.[311]

Islam forbids obstinacy and stubbornness. Imam Ali, peace be on him, says: "He who is adamant does not achieve his purpose. However, if he consults others, he shares their wisdom."[312]

Imam Ja'far Sadiq, peace beon him, says: "He who persists in his views is sitting on a precipice".[313]

Imam Ali, peace be on him, tells his son Muhammad: "He who insists on his words involves himself in difficulties and he who seeks assistance from the views of others becomes aware of his mistakes and errors".[314]

Islam does not permit us to consult everyone. On the other

87

hand it describes the persons who are pious, experts and competent to be consulted. Imam Ja'far Sadiq, peace be on him, says: "Consult about your affairs the man, who fears his Lord".[315] "Always consult those people who are wise and pious, because such persons do not utter anything except good, and do not oppose them, because this will be harmful to your faith as well as to your worldly affairs".[316] On another occasion he says: "Consultation has some limitations which must be observed failing which more loss will accrue from it than gain. The person whom you consult should be wise, free, friendly and intelligent, so that he may realize your purpose. For, if he is wise, you will gain; if he is free and pious, he will try to advise and guide you; if he is your genuine friend, he will guard your secrets; and if he understands your purpose properly, it will be possible for him to tender you his best advice".[317]

Islam does not give any consideration to one's status as we have seen that Almighty Allah orders even His Prophet to consult his companions. Imam Ja'far Sadiq, peace be on him says: "Do not imagine that a man becomes inferior by consulting others. On the other hand Allah exalts him and makes him successful in his affairs and he comes in close proximity to Allah".[318]

Imam Ali Riza (P) says in praise of his father, Imam Musa Kazim (P) son of Imam Ja'far Sadiq, peace be on them: "Though he excelled all others in wisdom, yet he used to consult a black slave of his and said: "Often it so happens that Allah solves many problems through his tongue".[319]

Islam forbids consultation with those who are devoid of good qualities and possess undesirable habits. The Holy Prophet said to Imam Ali, peace be on them: "Do not consult a timid person because he will make matters difficult for you, and do not consult a covetous person, because he will encourage you to do something and to make your inclination intense and will not care for expediency in the matter".[320]

Just as Islam recommends that people should consult one

another it also gives strict orders to Muslims not to deceive anyone while tendering advice but to think of his betterment and suggest their honest views. Imam Ali, peace be on him, says: "I hate one who deceives a Muslim while tendering advice".[321] "One who tenders advice is supposed to be honest".[322]

* * * * *

During Journey

As most of the gifts of life and successes and experiences can be acquired by travelling in different parts of the world the leaders of Islam have encouraged the people to undertake journeys and to have a change for a while in the schedule of their daily lives. The Holy Prophet, peace be on him and his progeny, says: "Travel so that you may remain hale and hearty. Travel so that you may derive benefit and get a windfall".[323]

However, numerous rules have been prescribed for a person for the period he is away from his home and every one of them is important from the spiritual and social view-point. One of these rules is that as and when a person gets ready to undertake a journey he should, as soon as possible, find out a companion for himself. The Holy Prophet, peace be on him and his progeny, says: "Should I tell you who the worst man is? He is the one who travels alone and turns away his guest and beats his slave"[324]

Islam has directed the people to remember Allah in all circumstances and orders that while undertaking a journey one should not forget invocation.

The Holy Prophet, peace be on him and his progeny, says: "The best protection of a traveller for his family is that while proceeding on his journey he should perform two rak'ats of prayers and say: 'O Lord! I entrust to You my ownself, my family, my property, my children, my life in this world as well as the next; my trusts and my prospects of life in the Hereafter are under Your trust and custody'. Without doubt Allah grants the wishes of the one who performs this act".[325] (and protects him as well as what belongs to him).

As opposed to the belief of the Arabs who considered certain hours to be good for journeying and others to be inauspicious, Islam says travel whenever you like and entrust yourselves to Allah and spend in His way. Imam Ja'far Sadiq, peace be on him, says: "Give alms and leave your house as and when you like".[326] The Holy Imam was again asked: "Is it abominable to undertake a journey on certain days, for example on Wednesday?" He replied: "Whenever you wish to go on a journey commence it by giving alms and recite 'Ayatul Kursi" (Surah al-Baqarah, 2 : 257)[327]

Again Imam Muhammad Baqir or Imam Ja'far Sadiq, peace be on them, says: "Whenever my father under-took a journey on the last Wednesday of a month or on any other day which the people consider inauspicious for journeying he used to give alms and then left the house".[328]

Fellow-travellers should observe love and affection for one another and should end their journey with cheerfulness. The Holy Prophet, peace be on him and his progeny, says: "Magnanimity of a traveller lies in that he should make others share with his provisions and should behave well towards them and should not commit sin".[329]

Imam Ja'far Sadiq, peace be on him, says: "Magnanimity during the course of journey lies in that you should carry abundant provisions (for the journey) and distribute it among your fellow travellers. When you part with your fellow travellers you should guard their secrets and while travelling you should cut jokes with them but not in such a way that it displeases Allah".[330]

The Holy Prophet, peace be on him and his Progeny, also says: "One of the good deeds is that when some persons undertake a journey they should share the provisions collectively because doing so is more pleasant for them and is also praiseworthy from the view-point of good morals".[331]

"It is magnanimous on the part of a man that he should carry good provisions for his journey".[332]

Fellow-travellers should consider themselves equal to one another and should not seek preference over others and everyone of them should pride himself upon having served the other. The Holy Prophet, peace be on him and his progeny, says: "The chief of a group is one who serves others while performing a journey".[333]

Once the Holy Prophet, peace be on him and his progeny, was travelling along with others. On the way it was decided to slaughter a sheep and prepare food. One of his co-travellers said: "I shall slaughter the sheep". Another took the responsibility of stripping the sheep of its skin. Still another undertook to cut the meat into pieces. It was also decided that a fourth person should cook the meat. The Holy Prophet then said: "I, too, shall collect firewood". His companions, however, said: "O Prophet of Allah! We shall do this job as well". The Holy Prophet replied: "I am aware that you can do this job but Allah is not pleased with a servant of His who is with his companions and claims a special position among them". Then he stood up and began collecting firewood.[334]

Furthermore, Imam Sajjad, peace be on him, always travelled with those people who did not know him and settled with them that he would serve them during the course of the journey. Once, while he was travelling with some persons, a man saw him on the way and identified him. He went up to the fellow travellers of the Holy Imam and said to them: "Do you know who this man is?" They replied in the negative. Thereupon, he told them that he was Imam Sajjad, son of Imam Husayn, peace be on them. When they came to know about the Holy Imam they fell on their knees and kissed his feet and then said: "O son of the Prophet of Allah! Did you wish us to fall a prey to the Fire of Hell? Just imagine, had we misbehaved towards you with our hands or tongues was it not certain that we would have been annihilated? What was the reason for your behaving in this manner?" The Holy Imam replied: "Once I was travelling with some people who knew me and paid me great respect on account of (my relationship with) the Prophet of Allah so I was afraid that you too might act in the same way and for this reason I considered it appropriate not to introduce myself to you".[335]

Islam also orders its followers to respect the rights of their fellow-travellers and to discharge the same in an appropriate manner. It is for this reason that the Holy Prophet, peace be on him and his progeny, says: "If a traveller falls sick on the way he has a right over his fellow-travellers to wait for him for three days".[336]

Islam orders that when a person wishes to part with his fellow-traveller, he should escort him a few steps and then bid him farewell. Imam Ja'far Sadiq, peace be on him, says: "Once Imam Ali, peace be on him, happened to travel with a *Zimmi* (a non-Muslim who lives under the protection of Islam). The *Zimmi* asked him about his destination. Imam Ali told him that he was going to Kufa. When they reached the cross-roads the Holy Imam proceeded on the way on which his fellow-traveller was going. The *Zimmi* was surprised and asked: "Did you not intend to go to Kufa?" Imam Ali replied: "Yes! The *Zimmi* said: "Then the way to Kufa is the other one and you have passed beyond it". Imam Ali replied: "I know it". Then the man said: "Then why are you coming along with me?" Imam Ali replied: "No doubt, good companionship lies in that one should escort one's companion at the time of separation and our Holy Prophet Muhammad, peace be on him and his progeny, has ordered us accordingly". The *Zimmi* wondered and said: "Has your Prophet given such orders?" Imam Ali, replied: "Yes" Then the man said: "People do not follow him without just cause. People have been inclined towards him for his supreme morality and that is why they obey him. Hence I too hereby declare that I have adopted your religion". Then he accompanied Imam Ali to Kufa and when he came to know as to who he was he embraced Islam on his hand".[337]

Islam prefers that when a person returns from a journey he should not forget to bring a present, however small it may be, because such an act promotes love and affection between the traveller and the members of his family. Imam Ja'far Sadiq, peace be on him, says: "If one of you goes on a journey and then intends to return, he should bring a present for his family according to his means, even though it may be a piece of stone".[338]

According to Islam the pilgrims and other persons who undertake journeys for religious purposes are entitled to special respect. Imam Sajjad, peace be on him, says: "If a person looks after the household affairs of one who has gone to perform pilgrimage of the House of Allah, his spiritual reward is like that of the one, who has gone to Makkah and has kissed the Black Stone".[339] He also says: "O People! Those of you, who have not gone to perform the Hajj, please the pilgrims, shake hands with them and pay them due respect because this behaviour will make you share the spiritual reward with them".[340]

Islam also orders that a traveller should end his journey with invocation in the same manner in which he commenced it with invocation.

Imam Ja'far Sadiq, peace be on him, says: "When a traveller returns from his journey and reaches home, he should not commence any work unless he has washed his body and made himself clean. Thereafter, he should offer two rak'ats of prayers and prostrate himself before Allah and thank him 100 times".[341]

* * * * *

Jihad

It should not be imagined that a revolutionary movement and a public-spirited campaign based on truth and righteousness, can make its headway without being confronted with opposition and obstruction. It is but natural that profiteers and self-seekers who find their interests in jeopardy or persons who cannot realize the true facts in their true perspective, and possibly consider them against their interests, try as far as possible to overthrow the new regime and create obstructions in its way.

The Divine religion of Islam, too, which was not content only with making certain things obligatory or unlawful but considered the enforcement of a correct and useful social system to be one of its basic targets, could not be exempted from confrontations.

It is evident that the advancement and success which springs from Islam necessitates self-sacrifice and devotion in the path of Allah which is called 'Jihad', and which has been made obligatory for the Muslims who possess competence and who fulfil certain special conditions. It is for this reason that Islam, which in itself is a supreme and sacred code of life and which governs the individual as well as the social system of life, has acquired its grandeur and glory. Imam Ali, peace be on him, says: "Allah has made Jihad obligatory in order to ensure the glory and grandeur of Islam".[342]

The Holy Prophet, peace be on him and his progeny, says: "Perform Jihad so that you may leave honour and supremacy as a remembrance for your children".[343]

"Good qualities are under the shadow of the sword and it is only the sword which keeps the people upright (and makes them follow the right path). The sword is the key to Paradise and Hell".[344]

Imam Ali, peace be on him, considers the glory of this world and of the Hereafter to be lying under the shadow of Jihad and says: "Allah has made Jihad obligatory and given it grandeur and treated it to be the support of the faith. By Allah! Without Jihad neither the life in this world nor in the Hereafter can be prosperous".[345]

It is evident that if negligence is observed in the performance of this sacred duty and the Muslims fall into a state of terror this sacred religion will become weak owing to the transgresssions and encroachments of the unbelievers, and its followers, too, will be humiliated and will become subjects of foreign despotic rule. Gradually they will also be subdued in the matter of belief and laws.

The Holy Prophet, peace be on him and his progeny, says: "If a person forsakes Jihad, Allah makes him degraded and helpless in his life and he also falls a prey to perdition and deviation in the matter of his faith".[346]

Imam Ali, peace be on him, Says: "Jihad (struggling in the cause of Allah) is one of the gates of Paradise which the Almighty has opened for His distinguished servants. Jihad is the dress of piety and a strong Divine armour and shield. If one abstains from Jihad intentionally Allah disgraces and involves him in various difficulties. And on account of his having considered this great obligation to be ordinary he deviates from the rightpath and falls in adversity and will not get any share according to justice and equity".[347]

Almighty Allah has attached so much importance to this great duty that He mentioned it in more than 140 verses of the Holy Qur'an and also considers the Mujahids and fighters to be entitled to glory and supreme position and says: "You must not think that those who were slain in the cause of Allah are dead. They are alive, and well provided for by their Lord; pleased with His gifts and rejoicing more than those whom they left behind and who have not yet joined them and have nothing to fear or to regret? rejoicing in Allah's Grace and Bounty. Allah will reward the faithful".[348]

Once, when Imam Ali, peace be on him, was encouraging his companions and friends to perform jihad, a young man stood up and enquired from him about the spiritual reward for the Muslim Mujahids. The Holy Imam said: "I was riding a camel in the row of the Holy Prophet, peace be on him and his progeny, and we were returning from the Battle of 'Zātus Salāsil'. I then put the same question (regarding the spiritual reward for those who fight in the path of Allah) to him and he replied: "When Mujahids decide to perform Jihad, Allah decides to free them from the Fire of Hell, and when they prepare to proceed for Jihad, He is proud of them before the angels, and when they take leave of their families, the doors, the walls and the house weep for them and they become free from sins like a snake which sloughs off its skin".[349]

Islam does not make Jihad obligatory for everyone and it has exempted the women, the old men, the blind, the disabled persons and those involved in financial difficulties, from the obligation of Jihad.[350]

Islam grants high status to the soldiers, Imam Ja'far Sadiq(P) says: "There are three groups of people whose prayers are granted and one of them is the group of soldiers. You should, therefore, be careful as to how you remember them in their absence".[351]

The Holy Prophet, peace be on him and his progeny, says: "A person who conveys the message of a soldier is like the one who frees a slave and has a share in his spiritual reward".[352] "And Allah's angels will welcome and greet the person, on the Day of Judgement, who encourages a soldier and applauds him".[353]

In the Battlefield

In the battles and campaigns in which the non-Muslims took part before as well as after the advent of Islam there was no obstacle or impediment in the way of the soldiers indulging in murder, assault and theft of property, because the battles were based on force and subjugation and not on faith, principles and humanity. However, with the dawn of Islam a new chapter was opened in the matter of Jihad, because Islam forbade all sorts of campaigns and battles except those which were fought for the prevention of oppression or eradication of corruptions and tribulations.

The Holy Qur'an says: *"Fight for the sake of Allah those who fight against you but do not attack them first. Allah does not love the aggressors".* [354]

Hence it is evident that the basis for the battles fought by Islam was only prevention of cruelty and oppression and there was no other underlying motive either political or economic. Hence the Holy Qur'an says: *"Fight against them until trouble terminates and Allah's religion reigns supreme. But if they mend their ways, fight none except the oppressors".* [355]

These and other similar verses clearly indicate the real purpose of Islamic battles and put an end to the idle and spiteful gossips of the enemies of Islam in this regard.

Hence, it is to achieve this very end that the Muslim warriors are under obligation, as and when they encounter a group or a community, to invite them, in the first instance, to accept Islam, and to make known to them their readiness for reconciliation, in case they embrace Islam, or agree to pay *Jizya* (i.e. tax paid by non-Muslims residing in areas controlled by Muslims in return for the protection accorded to them).

The Holy Prophet said to Imam Ali, peace be on them "Never fight against a man without first inviting him to Islam. By Allah if He makes you to guide one person only it would be better than ruling the whole world".[356]

Islam orders that Muslim warriors should always keep their real target in view and should know that the object of Jihad is to quench the fire of mischief, to prevent cruelty and oppression, and to invite people to the right path. Furthermore, they should always commence their war slogans with the Name of Allah Imam Ali, peace on him, says: "The Holy Prophet, peace be on him and his progeny, ordered us that before participating in a battle we should specify a slogan and should recite the Name of Allah".[357]

Again, Islam says that Muslims should fight with those people only, who obstruct the advancement of this sacred object and act as an impediment. Therefore, the Holy Prophet, peace be on him and his progeny, says: "Do not hurt their old people and children" (i.e. of the unbelievers).[358]

In short, Islam has forbidden every act which may be contrary to this sacred object. Imam Ja'far Sadiq, peace be on him, says: "As and when the Holy Prophet, peace be on him and his progeny, decided to send an army to fight a battle, he used to call the soldiers and exhort them thus: "Proceed with the Name of Allah and in the path of Allah and as the Prophet of Allah. Do not commit breach of trust with your enemies or mutilate their bodies or deceive them. Do not kill their old men, women and children. Do not plunder the trees unless it becomes absolutely necessary to do so. Everyone among the Muslims, whether big or small, should take care of one unbeliever and provide him asylum. He should be under protection so as to attend the Word of Allah. If he follows you he will become one your brothers-in-faith and if he abstains from doing so send him to his place and seek help from Allah".[359]

Here remains one point which is considered to be the distinction of Islam — that every Muslim is entitled to provide asylum to one or more unbelievers (the number has been quoted to be up to ten).

The Holy Prophet, peace be on him and his progeny, says: "The responsibility and pledge of all Muslims is one and the same and even the smallest among them can take advantage of it".[360] Imam Ja'far Sadiq, peace be on him, explains this tradition as under: "If a Muslim army besieges a group of unbelievers and then one of the unbelievers comes and says: 'Provide me a shelter so that I may meet your chief and converse with him.' And if any Muslim gives him an asylum it is incumbent upon all distinguished Muslims to honour that pledge".[361]

Imam Ja far Sadiq, peace be on him, again says: "Imam Ali, peace be on him, approved the action of a slave who was under protection and who had given protection to the unbelievers, and said: "He too is one of the believers".[362]

It appears from this that besides according respect to the Muslim warriors generally, and treating all Muslims to be equal to one another, Islam uses every opportunity to end warfare and seeks to find out some justification for ending strife through reconciliation. Imam Ja'far Sadiq, peace be on him, says: "If a group of Muslims besieges a city and its residents become helpless and ask for refuge, and the Muslims, for some reason or the other reject their request and despite this the besieged people get the impression of having been granted asylum and they surrendered themselves, in that case they will be treated as having been given protection".[363]

* * * * *

On the Seat of Justice

Islam does not approve of differences and confrontations. Imam Ali, peace be on him, in this connection says: "Refrain from differences and disputes becuase these things poison the minds of the brothers-in-faith against one another and sow the seeds of discord in them".[364]

It cannot, however, be denied that owing to clash of interests, people are sometimes compelled to have to resort to trial and judgement. Islam orders that in that event they should refer to persons who are competent to give dicisions. And, in order to encourage competent persons to adjudicate, Imam Ali, peace be on him, says: "The best people are those who decide justly".[365]

Imam Ali, peace be on him, gave the following orders to Mālik Ashtar to find out such persons: "Select the wisest person in the land for administration of justice among the people. He should be a person for whom this task is not hard and the litigating parties should not be able to prevail upon his views. He should not persist in his mistake and should not be incapable of returning to truth when he recognizes it. He should ot be covetous. He should not consider a matter superficially in arriving at a decision and should give very deep thought to it in case of doubt. Above all he should depend on reason and should not be annoyed by the lengthy explanations proposed by the litigating parties. He should be more patient than everyone else in bringing truth to light and when the real position becomes crystal clear his judgement should be explicit and decisive. He should be a person who is not elated by the praise of the people and who is not influenced by the words of deceitful persons. And such persons are very rare".[366]

Islam has forbidden women from acting as judges and Imam Baqir, peace be on him, says in this regard: "A woman should not adjudicate and should not be a ruler".[367]

Islam has strongly repressed unjust adjudication and has severely reprimanded oppressive judges so much so that the Holy Qur'an has declared them to be transgressors,[368] and at another place it calls them tyrants[369] and at still another place it calls them unbelievers.[370] Furthermore, Imam Ja'far Sadiq, peace be on him, says: "Whoever gives a wrong decision which is opposed to Divine orders, even with regard to two dirhams, is an unbeliever".[371]

Besides all this Islam considers such a state of affairs as a root cause of the cessation of Divine blessings. Imam Ja'far Sadiq, peace be on him, says: "When the rulers become oppressive in their decisions the sky withholds rains".[372]

And in order to present the status of a judge in its true perspective the Holy Prophet, peace be on him and his progeny, says: "The tongue of a judge is between two flames of fire, and when he arrives at a decision regarding a case his destiny is decided. If he takes a just decision he goes towards Paradise and if he does not do so, he is drawn towards Hell".[373]

Islam has prescribed some code of conduct for a judge which fully indicates the great efforts made by this Divine religion for the establishment of justice.

Imam Ali, peace be on him, says to Muhammad son of Abi Bakr, who was appointed by him as the Governor of Egypt: "Spread your plumage for the people of Egypt and keep your flanks level for them and remain cheerful in their presence. Observe equality even in the matter of looking at them so that the strong may not expect injustice on your part for the protection of their interests and the weak may not lose hope of receiving justice from you".[374] And the Holy Prophet, peace be on him and his progeny, orders: "Whoever wishes to arbitrate between the people should oberve equality between them in all respects so, that he may not differentiate between them in the matter of casting a glance or making a sign or allotting a place. He should also not raise his voice against anyone of them unless he does so with the other also".[375]

Once Imam Ali, peace be on him, deputed Abul Aswad Duwayli to act as his agent in a case, but suspended him before the end of the proceedings of the case. When he asked the reason for that the Holy Imam replied: "Because I found that your voice was louder than the voice of your colleagues".[376]

Islam has forbidden the judges to help anyone of the litigating parties in any manner whtatsoever. Hence, the Holy Prophet, peace be on him and his progeny, has forbidden a judge to prompt a witness.[377]

To ensure that a judge is always accessible to the people, Islam has prohibited him from keeping a mediator.

The Holy Prophet, peace be on him and is progeny, says: "If a person enjoys authority over the people in some manner and appoints a mediator for himself Allah will not be kind to him on the Day of Judgement although on that day he will be helpless and needy".[378] And Imam Ali, peace beon him, also directed Shurayh to hold court in Masjid (and any other place where people had access to him and the proceedings assumed the shape of an open court) and desist from adjudicating at his house.[379]

It is evident that when a person is hungry or angry or is feeling sleepy, it is very difficult for him to give a correct decision. Hence the Holy Prophet, peace be on him and his progeny, has prohibited a judge from deciding a case while he is angry or hungry or is feeling sleepy.[380]

It is interesting to note that, with a view to ensuring that the judges and persons, who rule over the people, do not make any distinction between them, Islam has prohbited them from making transaction in purchase, sale and trade, except with those persons, who do not know them, because it is possible that by means of such transactions mutual acquaintance or friendship may influence them and it may hinder the administration of justice. Hence Imam Ali, peace be on him, says: "If a governor engages himself in trade, he cannot administer justice"[381]

It has also been related that once Imam Ali, peace be on him, went to the bazaar to purchase a shirt. There he met two sellers but as they knew him he refrained from purchasing the shirt from them. Eventually he came across a third person who did not know him and bought the required shirt from him for three dirhams.[382]

Islam has also prohibited a judge from making one of the litigating parties his guest. It so happened that once a person was the guest of Imam Ali (P) and later he came before him along with his adversary in a certain case. When Imam Ali, peace be on him, realized that the man had been his guest for this purpose, he was very much annoyed and said to him: "Don't stay with me, for the Holy Prophet, peace be on him and his progeny, has forbidden the judge to accord hospitability to one of the two litigating parties".[383]

It must be mentioned here that Islam has made strenuous efforts to uproot the giving and taking of bribes in a Muslim society, so much so that in many traditions a man who accepts a bribe has been called an unbeliever.[384] The Holy Prophet, peace be on him and his progeny, says: "May Allah curse the one who gives a bribe and the one who takes it and still the other one who acts as a mediator between the two".[385] He has also said: "Refrain from taking bribe because it is a blasphemous act and one who takes bribe is deprived of Paradise".[386] And with this object in view Imam Ali, peace be on him, instructs Mālik Ashtar: "Give him (the judge) ample means and make his life so comfortable that there should be no excuse left for him and he should not need anything from the people".[387]

* * * * *

Work and Effort

The real object of Islam is to guide and to ensure the intellectual and spiritual magnificence and moral excellence of the people, yet it also attaches much importance to a sound and respectable economy which is one of the prerequisites for the achievement of this end. Hence it considers these two things to be associated with each other and believes that with the betterment of economic condition, efforts can be made for spiritual evolution as on the other hand indigent persons soon become involved in various deviations. The Holy Prophet, peace be on him and his progeny, therefore says: "Affluence is a good help to achieve piety".[388] And Imam Ja'far Sadiq, peace be on him, says: "The world is a good means to acquire the benefits of the Hereafter".[389]

Islam exhorts the Muslims not to depend on others, because besides other things, it is possible that by depending on others one may become involved in different kinds of sins. Imam Ja'far Sadiq, peace be on him, says: "One who depends on others and is a burden on the society is devoid of the Blessings of Allah".[390]

For this reason Islam has always encouraged the people to work hard and to refrain from indolence. Imam Musa Kazim, peace be on him, says: "Allah hates a lazy person".[391]

Imam Ja'far Sadiq, peace be on him, says: "There are three types of persons whose invocations are not granted. Out of them one is a man who sits at home and does not go in search of his daily bread and says: "O Lord! Provide me sustenance". Allah replies: "Have I not opened for you the way for the sustenance?"[392]

"Do not get weary of earning the expenses of your life. Our forefathers also made efforts for their sustenance and searched for it".[393] Imam Ali, peace be on him, says: "Allah likes an honest worker"[394] Imam Musa Kazim, peace be on him, says: "Whoever seeks his sustenance by lawful means to meet his own expenses as well as those of his family is like one who performs Jihad in the way of Allah".[395]

It was for this reason that the leaders of Islam also remained busy in work, and, when some superficial observers, who thought that Islam consisted of a set of prosaic prayers only, raised objections to their hard work, they received harsh replies. One of such persons named Muhammad bin Munkadar says: "One hot day I went out of Madina. Imam Baqir, peace be on him, saw me. He was an obese person and was leaning on two of his slaves. I said to myself: "Allah be praised. It is strange that an old man from among the elders of Quraysh is busy in his worldly affairs!" I decided to give him an advice. So I went up to him and greeted him. He replied in a loud voice when his face was sweating. I said: "May Allah bless you! You are an old man from among the elders of Quraysh! Why are you after worldly affairs in this heat with all this inconvenience? How, would you like it that you may die in this condition?" The Holy Imam replied: "If I die in this condition, I will be dying while obeying the Commands of Allah. It is this merit for which the members of my family and I are not dependent on your help nor that of other people.[396]

* * * * *

Framing, Animal Husbandry and Trade

We have discussed in the foregoing pages that on the whole Islam has asked man to work and to shun lethargy. However, while mentioning the type of vocations it encourages three of them most viz. farming, animal husbandry and trade and gives them greater importance.

(i) **Farming:** On many occasions farming has been declared to be the best profession.

Imam Ja'far Sadiq, peace be on him, says: "In the eyes of Allah no profession is better than farming".[397] A man said to him: "I have heard some people saying that farming is a disapproved and abominable profession". The Holy Imam replied: "They are mistaken. Engage yourselves in farming and in planting trees. By Allah! There is no profession more preferable than farming".[398]

Furthermore, the Holy Prophet, peace be on him and his progeny, was asked once as to which commodity is good. He replied: "It is the agricultural produce which one has raised himself and has paid its requisite dues".[399]

Islam says that farming is the source which generates wealth. Hence Imam Ali, peace be on him, says: "If a person possesses water and earth and is still poor, Allah deprives him of His Blessings".[400]

(ii) **Animal Husbandry:** From Islamic point of view 'animal husbandry' is one of the sources of blessings. Hence, the Holy Prophet, peace be on him and his progeny, once asked one of his relatives: "Why don't you have (the source of) blessing in your house? He asked: "In what does blessing lie?" The Holy Prophet, peace be on him and his progeny, replied: "A milch sheep! Whoever has a milch sheep or a she-camel or a cow possesses the source of blessings, for these are the stock of prosperity".[401] He also said: "Possess sheep. Sheep are good assets".[402] "You should rear sheep and engage yourself in farming".[403]

Islam wishes that Muslims should always remain self-respected, honourable and powerful. Hence it encourages them to procure various means of achieving respectability and it has attached great importance in this behalf to the possession of an easy-paced animal for riding. Imam Ja'far Sadiq, peace be on him, says: "Keep an animal for riding, because such animals are auspicious, and you meet your needs through them and their sustenance is with Allah".[404] And he also says: "It is a good luck for a man to possess an animal which he rides at times of need, and thus pays the rights of his brethren".[405]

The Holy Prophet, peace be on him and his progeny, has also considered possession of an easy-paced animal for riding to be something auspicious for man.[406]

It should be remembered that in those days animals were the only means of transport and the motor vehicles had not yet been invented. However, in any case, the Holy Qur'an considers all means of transport to be a divine blessing for man and recommends that one should remember Allah while boarding them.

It says: "It is He Who has created everything in pairs and the ships and the cattle for you to ride so that perhaps when you ride them you will recall the bounties of your Lord and when you establish your control over them you would say "Glory belongs to Him who has made them subservient to us when we would not have been able to do so oursevles. To our Lord we shall all return".[407]

(iii) **Trade:** The Holy Prophet, peace be on him and his progeny, says: "If blessing is divided into ten parts, nine parts of it would be found in trade".[408]

On the Day of Judgement the honest traders will be associted with righteous people".[409] And Imam Ja'far Sadiq, peace be on him, says: "There are three types of persons who will enter Paradise without being called to account. They are the just leader, the truthful trader and the old man, who ends his life while having remained obedient to Allah".[410]

Imam Ali, peace be on him, says: "Engage yourself in trade for by this means you will become independent of the wealth of the people".[411] And Imam Ja'far Sadiq, peace be on him, also says: "Trade sharpens one's wisdom".[412] "And abandoning of it reduces wisdom".[413] "Do not forsake trade lest you should be humiliated. Engage yourself in trade and Allah will bless you".[414]

* * * * *

What the Businessmen should know

In the foregoing discussions the importance of work and effort (including trade and business) in the eyes of Islam has been clarified to some extent. However, it should be remembered that trade is respectable when it is associated with the remembrance of Allah and the observance of the principles of justice. Hence, the Holy Qur'an praises those persons whose trade and transactions do not make them forget the Almighty Allah.[415]

Imam Ali Riza, peace be on him, says: "When you are busy in purchase and sale and the time for prayers arrives you should leave your transaction and rush to offer the prayers and the trade should not entangle you all by yourself. The Almighty Allah has commended a group of persons and says: 'Men whom neither trade nor profit can divert from remembering Him'. These were the persons who traded but when it was time to offer prayers they left their work and came to the masjid. The spiritual reward and recompense of such persons is more than those (the monks) who leave work and business and engage themselves in worship and prayers only".[416]

However, it is much better that one should run one's trade and business in one's own town and one should, by this means, serve one's own people. Imam Ja'far Sadiq, peace be on him, says: "It is auspicious for a man that his place of business should be in his own town and he should be having good friends and obedient children".[417]

In Islam only those transactions which are useful for the

individals and the society are treated to be lawful. However, transactions, which involve interest and which are certainly harmful for a proper economy, have been prohibited as they are are unlawful. Hence, Islam orders that before being engaged in trade it is necessary for the people to learn its rules and regulations, so that they may not be guilty of unlawful acts.

Imam Ali, peace be on him, said thrice: "Jurisprudence (knowledge of legal matters) comes first and then comes trade".[418] "And when a person engages himself in trade without knowledge (of laws relating to it), he gets himself involved in 'interest'.[419]

In Islam that trade, which is accompanied by good manners and excellent qualities, is good. The Holy Prophet, peace be on him and his progeny, says: "Whoever buys or sells things should possess five qualities or else he should neither buy nor sell. He should refrain from taking interest; should not swear; should not hide the defect of a thing; should not praise a thing while selling it, and should not find fault with it after purchasing it".[420]

And Imam Ali, peace be on him, says: "O people of the bazzar! Fear Allah and do not swear, for, although swearing creates market for a commodity, it takes away blessings from it".[421]

Islam offers every opportunity to remind one about Allah. It, therefore, recommends that while visiting the bazaar one should remember Allah.

Imam Ja'far Sadiq, peace be on him, says: "When you enter the bazaar say: "O Lord! I seek from You the goodness of the bazaar and its people and seek Your protection from its mischief and corruption. O Lord! I seek Your refuge from oppressing anyone or being oppressed by others. O Lord! I seek Your refuge from Satan and his hordes and from persecution by the licentious sinners. Allah is sufficient for me and there is no god but He, I rely on Him and he is the Lord of the Great Throne".[422]

Islam orders that Muslims should be fully conversant with the code of business and condemns ignorance about commercial matters. Hence, when a person enquired from Imam Muhammad

Baqir (P) about the method of purchase and sale he replied: "If you settle with your brother that you will sell something to him at the cost price you may do so, otherwise you should be cautious in business transactions".[423] He also says: "It is good for you to talk frankly with the buyer otherwise in business a buyer is likely to be deceived. From Religion's view-point this deal is a total loss".[424] However, this situation is till such time that an agreement is not reached and after that it is not proper for either the seller or the buyer to discuss about the cost price of the commodity anymore. Imam Ja'far Sadiq, peace be on him, says: "The Holy Prophet, peace be on him and his progeny, has forbidden reduction in price after an agreement has been concluded".[425] However, a Muslim trader should not be impatient and if on a certain day he does not make any profit he should not get discouraged. The Holy Prophet, peace be on him and his progeny, says: "People come across a time when they complain against their Lord. For example they say: "By Allah! I have not made any profit since such and such day and have throughout been feeding on my capital". What happens to them? Has not Allah given them the capital?"[426]

Islam orders that if a buyer regrets having purchased a commodity the seller should cancel the transaction and take back the commodity from him. Imam Ja'far Sadiq, peace be on him, says: "On the Day of Judgement Almighty Allah will forgive the shortcomings of a believer who agrees to return the commodity purchased by him from a Muslim or take back the commodity sold to a Muslim".[427]

Islam orders that one should not interfere in the transactions of others and one should not disengage them from each other. The Holy Prophet, peace be on him and his progeny, has prohibited the people from doing so.[428]

Islam insists upon the sellers that they should procure good stuff. Imam Ja'far Sadiq, peace be on him, said to a dealer of wheat: "Purchase and sell good material because when you sell something good, people will say: "May Allah bless you and the one who supplied this material to you".[429]

Islam strongly prohibits hoarding and withholding of commodities till their prices may go up, and it declares such activities to be unlawful. The Holy Prophet, peace be on him and his progeny, says: "If a person purchases wheat and keeps it for forty days so that its price may go up and then sells it, this sin of his cannot be covered even if he gives away the entire sale proceeds in charity".[430]

As a matter of principle Islam lays down that there should be no black-marketing of commodities in any case.

Imam Ja'far Sadiq, peace be on him, once gave 1000 dinars to one of his slaves so that he might invest it in trade on his behalf. He bought some commodity and proceeded to Egypt along with a caravan of traders. When they reached the gate of th city they were informed by some persons coming out of it that the commodity which they had brought was in great demand and was scarce there. When they understood the delicacy of the situation they swore collectively that they would not accept less than one hundred per cent profit. In this way the slave of the Holy Imam also earned 1000 dinars as profit on an equal amount of capital. He put each of these sums in separate bags and, on his return to Madina placed the two bags before the Imam. Imam Ja'far Sadiq, peace be on him, was surprised and enquired about the matter. When he came to know the facts of the case he picked up his own capital and returned the profit to the slave and said: "I do not need this interest on my capital". He then added: "It is easier to fight with a sword than to earn lawful means of living".[431]

The leaders of Islam attached great importance to the conditions of the bazaar and the observance of the principles of justice. Hence, we read in the biography of the Commander of the Faithful, Imam Ali, peace be on him, that during the period of his rule he inspected the bazaars of Kufa every day. At that time he used to carry a particular bifurcated lash on his shoulder and stood at the end of every bazaar and uttered these words with a loud voice: "O traders! Fear Allah!" As soon as th voice of the Holy Imam was heard, all people stopped work and listened to him attentively: "Do not consider the blessings of labour to be rigorous. Seek proximity with the customers. Adorn yourselves with patience. Refrain from falsehood and swearing. Avoid cruelty and oppression and procure the rights of the oppressed and the afflicted. Shun usury. Do not sell lesser. Do not buy commodities from people at under-cut prices and do not spread corruption on earth". Then he walked throughout the bazaars and thereafter returned to his headquarters to look after the public affairs".[432]

Islam permits the religious rulers to supervise the work of the traders and craftsmen especially in the matter of fixing reasonably fair prices for various commodities and merchandise. Imam Ali, peace be on him, says to Mālik Ashtar: "Accept my recommendation with regard to the traders and craftsmen and advise them to do good, whether they may be those residing in the town and are doing business, or those who move about peddling their goods, or those who serve the people with their physical labour, because they are the source of profit and the backbone of the country's economy, and they procure their stock through difficult ways amidst wilderness and distant seas and dangerous hills and deserts and amidst places where no one lives and where no one dare go. They are peace-loving and mild persons who never create any disturbance. Supervise their activities in your own presence and in different parts of the town.

"In spite of all this, however, you should know that some of them are exacting and stingy, who hoard goods for their gain and fix the prices of things in various transactions according to their own discretion. People usually talk about this complaint and it is indeed bad for the ruler of the town. Hence you should prevent hoarding, because the Holy Prophet, peace be on him and his progeny, has prohibited it. You should ensure that their transactions should take place in a fair and just manner and with correct scales and fair prices so that injustice may not be done either to the buyer or to the seller. And when anyone of them is guilty of hoarding after having been prohibited by you, award him proper punishment which should not be too harsh or severe".[433]

* * * * *

Formation of a Family

Like other inherent instincts the sexual power of man is something natural which has been endowed by Almighty Allah since the very first day. It is evident that, if this instinct is not satisfied by marriage, which is the only legal method, the people will either be compelled to satisfy it by unlawful means or this power will be completely wasted, and in either case there will follow a chain of moral, social and hygienic evils.

For this reason Islam has attached great importance to this vital matter and the Holy Prophet, peace be on him and his progeny, therefore, says: "The worst among your dead are those who remained unmarried".[434]

Imam Ja'far Sadiq, peace be on him, says: "Two rak'ats of prayers offered by a married person are better than 70 rak'ats offered by a bachelor".[435]

And the Holy Prophet, peace be on him and his progeny, says: "Whoever marries, ensures half of his faith".[436] "Allah has not sent me with a law prescribing monastic or secluded life. On the contrary He has appointed me as a Prophet with a moderate and simple religion. I fast and offer prayers. I have my spouse too. Whoever loves me should follow my tradition. Matrimony is my tradition".[437]

The thing which deserves attention is the intense friendship and kindness 'which is generated by conjugal alliance and makes life sweet, happy and peaceful.

The Holy Qur'an says: "And one of His signs is that He

created mates for you from yourselves that you may find peace in them and He creates between you love and compassion".[438]

It should, however, be remembered that conjugal life should not be established for sexual satisfaction only. On the contrary its primary object should be to procreate useful and pious progeny, so that the number of the followers of truth should keep on increasing. The Holy Prophet, peace be on him and his progeny, says: "Marry and produce offsprings so that you may multiply, because on the Day of Judgement I shall pride myself on the number of my followers as also of miscarried children".[439]

"What is it that restrains faithful persons from entering into matrimony? It is possible that Allah may give them a child who may honour the earth by saying, 'There is no god, but Allah".[440]

There are many who avoid performing this vital act of entering into conjugal life on account of some superstitions and do not marry especially on account of fear that it may later involve them in financial difficulties. Such persons should be told that adverse financial conditions should not prevent them from entering into matrimonial alliance. The Holy Prophet, peace be on him and his progeny, says: "One who does not marry on account of poverty and indigence has entertained a bad opinion about the Almighty because He says: 'If those who marry have been needy and poor, Allah will make them independent by His Blessings".[441]

The Holy Prophet, peace be on him and his progeny, also says: "Marry to acquire your sustenance, because blessing has been placed among women".[442]

Islam also considers it a great service to make efforts for the conjugal life of two persons and to arrange for the preliminaries thereof.

The Holy Prophet, peace be on him and his progeny, says: "Allah provides houris to the person who makes efforts to arrange the matrimony of two believers, so that they may be united".[443]

Islam considers marriage to be a sacred and religious matter and, therefore, considers purity of faith to be a prerequisite for a spouse. The Holy Prophet, peace be on him and his progeny, says: "One who chooses a woman for her beauty only does not find in her what he desires and Allah ignores a person who marries a woman for her wealth. It is, therefore necessary that you should select a faithful and pious spouse".[444]

And Imam Ja'far Sadiq, peace be on him, says: "When a man marries a woman for her wealth or beauty, Allah leaves him to himself, and, if he selects a faithful and pious woman, Allah gives him wealth as well as beauty".[445]

Islam forbids taking ignorant and foolish women in marriage. Imam Ali, peace be on him, says: "Avoid matrimonial alliance with foolish and ignorant women, because association with them is a calamity and the child born of such a woman would be good-for-nothing and worthless".[446]

Notwithstanding what has been mentioned above, Islam has left the selection of a spouse at the sweet will of a husband and considers the interference and imposition by the parents to be inappropriate. Hence when a person said to Imam Ja'far Sadiq, peace be on him: 'I wish to marry and have also selected a woman, but my parents have another woman in view', the Holy Imam replied: 'Marry the woman whom you like and leave the other".[447]

It is evident that this recommendation applies only when a person is not influenced by infatuation and sudden outburst of emotions.

It should be admitted that a great difficulty which has cropped up these days for the young men and makes them desist from marrying, is the heavy amount fixed for a dower and the cumbersome ceremonies and undue demands of many women.

No doubt Islam considers the dower of a woman to be her admitted legal right and it is payable by man however enormous it may be. It is for this reason that the Holy Qur'an says: "If you wish to divorce a woman in order to wed another, do not take back from her the dower you have given her even if it happened to be a gilded hide of a cow".[448]

However, morally, Islam considers heavy dower and excessive expectation to be a misfortune on the part of a woman and extols those women, whose dower is light and whose expenses are moderate and who are more fit for multiplication of the offsprings.

The Holy Prophet, peace be on him and his progeny, says: "Inauspiciousness lies in three things viz. a woman, an animal for riding and a house. The inauspiciousness of a woman lies in that her dower is heavy and she may with severe difficulty give birth to offsprings".[449]

"The best women from among my followers are those who are more beautiful and whose dower is lesser".[450] And Imam Ja'far Sadiq, peace be on him, also says: "The auspiciousness of a woman lies in the lightness of her dower and in her fertility, and her inauspiciousness lies in her excessive expenses and infertility".[451]

* * * * *

What Married Couples should know

The number of divorce cases is increasing year after year and the demon of domestic strife is showing itself with a still more dreadful appearance. All are anxious to find out the reason for this unfortunate state of affairs and have not yet realized that as a matter of fact the main reason for this is that married couples do not perform their duties properly.

Islam has determined certain responsibilities for husband and wife, the proper discharge of which would not only reduce mutual differences and the number of divorce cases, but would also create a sort of mutual love and affection in the family which would make their life sweet, pleasant and peaceful.

The Holy Prophet peace be on him and his progeny, describes a good woman in these words: "The best of your women is she, who gives birth to many children; is loving and chaste; lives honourably in the family, and is humble before her husband; adorns herself only for her husband, and protects herself from others; pays heed to what her husband says and obeys his orders; accedes to his wishes in privacy, safeguards his property and never spends or bestows gifts from her husband's property".[452] He further says: "After being a Muslim the greatest gain for a man is a faithful woman, who, when she sees him, becomes happy and obeys his orders, protects his property and her own honour in his absence".[453]

Islam has strongly recommended that a woman should show humility and respect to her husband. The Holy Prophet, peace be on him and his progeny, says: "If I wished to direct that a person should prostrate himself before another (i.e. if it had been permissible to prostrate oneself before anyone except Allah) I would have ordered the women to prostrate themselves before their husbands".[454]

Islam also makes it clear that, if a a woman obeys her husband, it means that she has performed one of the best acts of her life. Imam Musa Kazim, peace be on him, says: "Jihad of a woman is to lead a good conjugal life".[455]

And the Holy Prophet, peace be on him and his progeny, also says: "If a woman does not perform her duty towards her husband, she has failed to obey Allah".[456]

It should not be forgotten that as against the duties of women Islam has also placed heavy responsibilities on men towards their wives. Islam orders that husbands should behave kindly towards their wives. Imam Sajjad, peace be on him, says: "Allah more likes that man, who provides better means of comfort for the inmates of his family".[457]

The Holy Prophet, peace be on him and his progeny, says: "The best among you is he who cooperates with his family".[458] "The duty of man towards his wife is that he should treat her as his equal partner in the matter of food and dress, should not slap her and should not quarrel with her".[459]

Imam Ali Riza, peace be on him, says: "It is proper for a man that he should not be harsh to his wife and children, so that they may not pray to Allah for his death".[460]

Islam has given so much importance to the rights of women that according to some traditions it permits the religious ruler that when a man does not discharge his responsibilities, the religious ruler may in special and specified conditions bring about separation between them. Imam Muhammad Baqir, peace be on him, says: "If a person has a wife whom he does not give her dress to cover herself with or food to satisfy her hunger, the Imam (or religious ruler) is authorized to bring about their separation".[461]

Islam has strongly recommended that a wife should be provided assistance and her needs should be met by her husband. Imam Sajjad, peace be on him, says: "If I enter the bazaar and purchase some meat for my family with the money that I am carrying, this act is better for me than setting a slave free".[462]

Furthermore, when the Holy Prophet, peace be on him and his progeny, saw Imam Ali assisting Fatima Zahra peace be on them, in some household affairs he encouraged him to do so and said that that behaviour carried Divine reward. He further says in this connection: "If a person helps his spouse in household affairs, Allah records for him spiritual reward equal to the number of hair on his body and as if he had fasted during days and offered prayers during nights for one year". And after uttering a few words he says: "A person, who does not disdain serving and assisting his wife and children, will be admitted by Allah into Paradise without taking any account of his deeds". In the end he says: "No one serves his spouse except the one, who is one of the very truthful persons, or martyrs, or a man for whom Allah has desired the goodness of this world as well as of the Hereafter".[463]

Islam prefers that married couples should co-operate as far as possible by adjusting themselves with each other's habits, and should overlook the inconvenience which they experience from each other. The Holy Prophet, peace beon him and his progeny, says: "If a man tolerates the behaviour of his wife, Allah grants him spiritual reward equal to that earned by Prophet Ayub, peace beon him, for his contentment and patience, and if a woman tolerates the behaviour of her husband the Almighty grants her the position of Asiya, daughter of Muzāhim and wife of Pharaoh".[464]

Islam prohibits hurting a woman. The Holy Prophet, peace be on him and his progeny, says: "The best man among the Muslims is he, who is gentle to his wife and treats her kindly".[465] He also says: "Is it proper that one should beat one's wife and thereafter share her bed?"[466]

Islam also recommends that women, should be shown extraordinary kindness. The Holy Prophet, peace be on him and his progeny, says: "Jibril recommended to me so much about a wife that I thought that she should not at all be divorced except when she is guilty of unchastity".[467] He further says: "If a man places a morsel of food in the mouth of his wife, he earns spiritual reward for his behaviour".[468]

Besides all this, Islam also orders women to behave towards their husbands properly and in a loving manner. The woman who does not behave towards her husband modestly, and compels him to do things which are beyond his means, none of her prayers and good acts will be acceptable and the Lord is displeased with her".[469] "If a woman troubles her husband with her tongue Allah will, on no account, spare her from punishment and will not accept her good deeds until and unless she pleases her husband. This is so even though she fasts during days and prays during night and frees slaves for the sake of Allah and mounts easy-paced animals in the path of the Lord and yet she will be the first person who will be thrown into the Fire (of Hell). And similar is the case with a man who maltreats his wife".[470]

One of the matters to which Islam has attached importance is the adornment and ornamentation of the woman, Islam says that the woman should adorn herself before her husband in a pleasant and decent manner, so that his eyes and thoughts do not turn towards other women.

Imam Muhammad Baqir or Imam Ja'far Sadiq, peace be on them, says: "It is better for a woman to adorn herself with gold and she should not refrain from ornamentation. Let it be with only a necklace. It is also not appropriate for her to give up the use of henna (which was in vogue in those days as a means of adornment) even if she is past her prime".[471]

Islam similarly orders men to adorn themselves for their wives, so that they (i.e. women) may not get attracted to someone else.

Imam Ali Riza, peace be on him, says: "Adornment of

123

man for the sake of his wife adds to her chastity".[472] And then a person asked him perhaps by way of criticism: "Have you dyed your hair?" He replied: "Yes, with henna and 'Kitam' (name of a special grass). Do't you know that this act carries spiritual reward, because the woman expects from you the same thing, which you expect from her. And there are many women who deviate from the path of chastity owing to the carelessness and faults of their husbands".[473]

* * * * *

Cleanliness and Purity

Some non-Muslim writers have expressed the view that Islam has not given any detailed orders about the health and hygiene of the people. This view is not, however, correct because this Divine religion has made particular recommendations about cleanliness which is essential for health and hygiene.

Islam has given important hygienic orders regarding the cleanliness of everything ranging from drinking water to residence, dress and even the deep well of water. The Holy Qur'an, while enumerating Allah's Blessings on mankind says: *"Have We not placed high mountains upon it (earth) and given you fresh water for you to drink?"*[474]

Islam recommends the use of clean utensils. It was on this account that the Holy Prophet, peace be on him and his progeny, preferred to drink water in Syrian cups (which were considered to be clean and fine utensils in those days) and used to say that those were the best containers for that purpose".[475]

The matter which modern medical science wishes to control and calls it 'microbes' was checked in earlier ages and given different names. The Holy Prophet, peace be on him and his progeny, forbade the blowing of breath into water.[476] And Imam Ali, peace be on him, says: "Do not drink water from the broken side of a vessel and similarly from the side of its handle (which is naturally contaminated) because Satan sits there".[477] And the Holy Prophet peace be on him and his progeny, says: "Do not drink from the side of the handle of a vessel, becasue dirt gets collected there".[478] And Imam Ja'far Sadiq, peace be on him, says: "Do not drink water from the nozzle of a vessel or from its broken portion because demons drink water from there".[479]

Furthermore, the Holy Prophet, peace be on him and his progeny, has prohibited the contamination of drinking water with water contained in one's mouth. He has also prohibited drinking from flowing water like animals.[480]

After drinking water, the next important topic is that of eating food. In order that one's hands should be clean Islam orders that one should perform ablution before taking one's meals.

The Holy Prophet, peace be on him and his progeny, says: "The life of a person, who performs ablution before taking his meals, is prolonged and his body becomes secure against diseases".[481]

Performing of ablution before taking meals prevents a person from poverty and indigence, and performing it after having taken meals prevents him from insanity and keeps his eyesight good".[482]

Islam has given detailed instructions regarding the cleanliness of one's body and commends everything which helps the achievement of this sacred object.

Imam Ali, peace be on him and his progeny, says: "Hammam (bath-house) is a good place, because (on the one hand) it reminds one of Hell and (on the other hand) removes dirt and impurities from the body".[483]

Imam Ja'far Sadiq, peace be on him, says about the purity of the water of the bath-house: "If it be possible for you to sip the bath-house water, sip it".[484]

It means that the bath-house water should be so clean and pure that it may be fit for drinking.

The Holy Imam recommends the washing of head with marsh-mallow. Imam Ja'far Sadiq, peace be on him, says: "Washing the head with marsh-mallow (blue in colour) keeps one safe from headache and keeps one secure from poverty and indigence and prevents one from dandruff".[485]

Islam orders shortening of the hair of the moustaches and shaving the armpit to ensure satefy from dirt. The Holy Prophet, peace be on him and his progeny, says: "No one should let the hair of his moustaches grow long because Satan takes his abode there and conceals itself in it".[486] "And one should also not let the hair of one's armpit grow long because Satan takes its abode there also".[487] Imam Ali, peace be on him, says: "Removing the hair of the armpit makes its bad odour disappear".

It is evident that there is much more possibility of dirt being accumulated under the nails. Hence the Holy Prophet, peace be on him and his progeny, orders the people that they should cut their nails.[489] However, he has prohibited them from cutting them with their teeth[490] because in that event the dirt collected under the nails reaches one's mouth.

To ensure that people get inclined towards one another Islam recommends the use of perfumes and similarly other oils which are the means of adornment. Imam Musa Kazim peace be on him, says: "It is not appropriate for a man to forsake the use of perfume on any day".[491]

It was one of the attributes of the Holy Prophet, peace be on him and his progeny, that he liked to oil his hair and felt uneasy on account of dishevelled hair. He used to say "Oiling one's head wards off grief and worry".[492]

And more important than all these things is the brushing of the teeth and keeping them clean. The Holy Prophet, peace be on him and his progeny, says: "Angel Jibril laid so much stress on the brushing of the teeth that I thought that the Almighty Allah was going to make it obligatory".[493] "If it had not been difficult for my followers I would have ordered them to brush their teeth before every prayer". (i.e. I would have made it obligatory for them five times a day).[494]

Imam Ja'far Sadiq, peace be on him, says: "Brushing of the teeth is one of the routines of the prophets".[495]

Furthermore, Islam recommends the rinsing of the mouth with water *(Mazmaza)* and sniffing up water through the nostrils and then expelling it out *(Istinshāq)* to ensure purification of mouth and nose. Imam Ali, peace be on him says: "*Mazmaza* and *Istinshāq* have been recommended to keep the mouth and the nose clean".[496]

Although Islam does not attach any importance to the quality of dress, it attaches much importance to its cleanliness. The Holy Prophet, peace be on him and his progeny, says: "Whoever procures a dress should cleanse it".[497]

Imam Ja'far Sadiq, peace be on him, sbys: "Clean dress humiliates one's enemy".[498]

Islam abhors houses which are filthy and filled with dirt and considers it to be a trait of dirty Jews. The Holy Prophet, peace be on him and his progeny, says: "Keep your houses clean and do not be like dirty Jews".[499] And Imam Muhammad Baqir, peace be on him, says: "Keeping one's house clean keeps poverty and miseries away".[500] Imam Ali, peace be on him, says: "Keep your house clean of cobweb because it is the cause of poverty".[501]

It is interesting to note that in all cases Islam considers uncleanliness to be a source of poverty.

Besides the fact that Islam cosniders the desecrating of Masjid to be unlawful and declares its consecration to be compulsory, it has lso laid great stress on its purification from dirt and filth. As such the Holy Prophet, peace be on him and his progeny, says: "Allah forgives the one who sweeps a Masjid on Thursday and removes dust from it, even if it may be equal to the collyrium of an eye".[502] "And if a person keeps a Masjid neat and clean, the Lord grants him spiritual reward equal to that of setting free a slave".[503]

The Holy Prophet has forbidden the habit of spitting in a Masjid and says: "A man who refrains from spitting in a Masjid will meet Allah on the Day of Judgement in a happy mood and his record of actions will be placed in his right hand".[505]

It is an undeniable fact that contamination of ground under fruit-bearing trees and the banks of wells and canals from which drinking water is drawn is the cause of various ailments. Hence the Holy Prophet has forbidden to defecate at such places and similarly Imam Ali, peace be on him, has prohibited urinating in flowing water.[507]

* * * * *

The Dress We should Wear

Notwithstanding the fact that Islam has restrained its followers from indulging in luxuries and ornamentation and leads them towards virtues, spiritualism and blessings of the next world, it has also prohibited monastic life and abstinence from the bounties of this world. The Holy Qur'an explicitly objects to the mode of thinking of the monks and says: *"Say: 'Who has forbidden you to benefit from the bounties of Allah, to wear decent clothes, or to eat good things) which He has bestowed upon his servants?"*[508]

Hence this Divine religion orders its followers to wear decent and respectable dress. Imam Ja'far Sadiq, peace be on him, says: "Wear good dress, for Allah is the source of goodness and likes goodness, but be careful that you should procure your dress by lawful means".[509] And on another occasion he says: "There are three things regarding which Allah does not take any account from his faithful servant and one of them is the dress which he wears".[510]

It should, however, be remembered that Islam allows the use of adornments when they are utilized for Allah and in the path of Allah, and orders that while wearing a new dress one must remember the Almighty. Imam Ali, peace be on him, says: "The Holy Prophet, peace be on him and his progeny, advised me that whenever I wore a new dress I should says: I praise the Lord who has given me this new dress so that I may be respectable among the people. O Lord! make this dress auspicious for me so that by using it I should endeavour to seek Your pleasure and should make Your Masjids populous".[511]

Imam Ja'far Sadiq, peace be on him, says: "When you wear a dress say: O Lord! Cover me with the dress of faith and adorn me with piety. O Lord! Grant me strength to wear away this dress with constant use while remaining obedient to You and Your Prophet".[512]

Islam exhorts its followers to keep the dress and its accessories neat and clean. Imam Ja'far Sadiq, peace be on him, says: "Allah is the source of beauty, and likes beauty and dislikes depression, because, when He endows a blessing on a servant of His, He likes to see its effect". People asked the Holy Imam as to how man displays the effect of Divine blessings, he replied: "One should keep his dress tidy and use perfume, white-wash his house and keep it clean from dirt. Allah likes lighting of a lamp before sunset as doing so wards off poverty and enhances the source of man's livelihood".[513]

Imam Ali, peace be on him, says: "Neat dress clears off worry and grief from the heart of man".[514]

At the same time Islam condemns the wearing of a delicate, thin and soft dress which habitautes one to self-indulgence. Imam Ali, peace be on him, says: "Wear coarsely woven dresses and refrain from wearing declicate ones".[515]

Imam Sajjad, peace be on him, also says: "If human body wears a declicate dress it rebels and commits sins against the Lord".[516]

The Holy Prophet, peace be on him and his progeny, says to Abu Zar: "Wear rough and coarsely woven dress so that pride may not overpower you".[517]

However, Islam also prohibits wearing of an unusual dress with the object of presenting oneslef in the eyes of the people as a religious and pious person.

Imam Sajjad, peace be on him, says: "If a person wears a dress by means of which he intends to become famous and renowned, Allah will make him wear a dress of fire on the Day of Judgement".[518]

And it is surprising that at times some people who were ignorant of the realities of Islam also objected to the leaders of the faith wearing decent dress instead of coarse dress, just as a man appeared before Imam Ja'far Sadiq, peace be on him, and said: "I have heard that your grand father Imam Ali, peace be on him wore coarse dress and his shirt used to cost about four dirhams only but now I see that you are wearing a decent dress". The Holy Imam replied: "Yes. Imam Ali, peace be on him, used to wear such a dress when it was not something unusual. However, such dress is out of fashion these days and if anyone uses such dress how he will make himself conspicuous among the people. The best dress is that which is in vogue at a particular time".[519]

Islam prohbits wearing of a dress by which one may pride himself over others and the Holy Prophet thus spoke to Abu Zar: "Before the advent of Imam Mahdi there will be some people who will wear woolen dresses during winter as well as during summer so that they may pride themselves over others. The inmates of the heavens and of earth curse such people".[520] He also said: "If a person wears a dress and prides himself over others a Flame of Hell overtakes him and he will be rocking in it till the Day of Judgement".[521]

Islam has prohibited the wearing of a long flowing dress which was considered to be a source of pride by the Arabs in those days and which was likely to get soiled. It was for this reason that when Imam Muhammad Baqir once saw his son Imam Ja'far Sadiq, peace be on them, in an assembly, said to him: "My son! Make your dress tidy". Imam Ja'far Sadiq, peace be on him, got up and left the place and then returned. Those present thought that the dress of Imam Ja'far Sadiq had been dirty or impure but Imam Muhammad Baqir, peace be on him, told them that it was long and he had, therefore, asked him to shorten it".[522]

Islam has prohibited men from wearing the dress of women and vice versa. Imam Ja'far Saidq, peace be on him, says: "If the Holy Prophet saw a man wearing a dress resembling that of a woman or a woman having made herself resemble a man he used to admonish them".⁵²³

*****

Relation of Kinsmanship

Among the different relations in the society the relation of kinsmanship carries special respect by Islam and we have already learnt that assistance to one's relations has been treated to be a part of financial rights of the people over their prosperous kinsmen. It is for this reason that, wherever the Holy Qur'an mentions, assistance to one's relatives, it gives it a preference over spending on other needy persons. In this connection a mention may be made of the 26th verse of Surah Bani Israel[524] and the 38th verse of Surah al-Rum.[525]

In the narrations of the leaders of Islam great stress has been laid on the fact that giving importance to the relation of kinsmanship and considering it to be an honourable act ensures long life, prosperity and acceptance of good deeds and prayers.

Imam Ali Riza, peace be on him, says: "At times it so happens that if a man, who does not have more han three years life left, treats his kinsmen well and speaks affably with them, Allah extends his age by thirty years (i.e. ten times). And Allah does what He likes".[526]

Imam Ja'far Sadiq, peace be on him, says: "Treat your relations with compassion even if it be with a sip of water. The best thing with which you can maintain relationship is that you should protect your relatives from the curelty and oppression of others. Observance of relationship postpones death and makes a man praiseworthy".[527]

Imam Muhammad Baqir, peace be on him, says: "Observance of relationship makes one's actions sacred, averts calamities, increases wealth, prolongs one's age, enhances the means of sustenance and is a source of one's becoming popular. So fear Allah and be kind to your relations".[528]

Preservation of ties of relationship is important not only from the religious point of view but from the social point of view also. Hence Imam Ali, peace be on him, says: "Hold your relatives dear, because they are your wings with which you can fly and they are your roots to which you can return and they are your hands with which you can attack your enemies".[529]

It is on this account that the Holy Prophet, peace be on him and his progeny, says about persons, who do not observe relationship with their kinsmen: "One who does not observe relationship will not enter Paradise".[530]

The ties of kinsmanship are respectable in the eyes of Islam in all events so much so that even Muslims and unbelievers are at par with each other in this behalf. Hence, when a person said to Imam Ja'far Sadiq (P). "I have relatives who are not like me (i.e. they are not Muslims). Do they enjoy any rights over me?" The Holy Imam replied: "Yes. The right of kinsmanship cannot be cut off by anything. If they had been Muslims they would have enjoyed two rights over you, one of kinsmanship and the other of being Muslims".[531]

The tie of kinsmanship is so strong that even if it is cut off from one side it is incumbent upon the other side to maintain it. As such, when a person said to the Holy Prophet: "My kinsmen did nothing to me except that they oppressed me, separated from me and abused me. I have also forsaken them". The Holy Prophet, peace be on him, replied "Allah, too, will forsake you on this account". He said: "You should unite with one who has broken away from you and should give him, who has deprived you, and should forgive him who has oppressed you. If you do so Allah will help you".[532]

* * * * *

Hospitality

Entertainment of guests is one of the outstanding moral qualities. The nations who possess a larger share of this moral quality take pride in it and it is justified that they should feel proud. The importance of this matter in the eyes of Islam can be realized from the following words of Imam Ja'far Sadiq, peace be on him: "If two believers arrive at the house of another believer and he makes them eat their fill, it is like his having freed a slave".[533]

We can also understand the importance of this matter to a still greater extent from the following tradition quoted from Imam Ja'far Sadiq, peace be on him: "To feed four Muslims to the point of satiety is equal to freeing a slave from among the descendants of Prophet Ismā'il, peace be on him".[534]

Islam safeguards the personality of a new visitor or a guest and explicitly says that he is not a burden on the family (i.e. the host), but he has come along with his own sustenance and he is a blessing which is brought to the family. The Holy Prophet, peace be on him and his progeny, says: "A guest is a guide who leads to the path of Paradise".[535] And again he says: "When Allah wishes to do good to a family he sends a gift to it. That gift is a guest who comes with his sustenance and carries away the sins of the family with him."[536] He also says: "A guest never comes to a family except that he brings his sustenance with him."[537]

Islam encourages those persons, who are hospitalable, and

praises them for this good quality. Imam Ali, peace be on him, says: "On the Day of Judgement a hospitable believer will arise from his grave in such a condition that his face will be shining like the dise of the moon. The people will wonder and think to themselves as to whether he is a prophet. However, the angel accompanying him will introduce him and say: "He is the man who was hospitable and entertained his guests and thus he has no way other than that of entering Paradise".[538]

Islam glorifies and respects hospitable persons, whatever their belief or creed may be. Imam Ja'far Sadiq, peace be on him, says: "Once some captives were brought before the Holy Prophet, peace be on him and his progeny, for being executed (on account of the offence committed by them) A man was brought for being executed. Angel Jibril descended and requested the Holy Prophet, peace be on him and his progeny, for the postponement of that man's execution. The Holy Prophet, peace be on him and his progeny, sent back that man and called him again after the execution of his other companions. Jibril again appeared and said: "Your Lord says that this man used to feed others and was hospitable and remained patient in difficult circumstances". The Holy Prophet, peace be on him and his progeny, released him on account of this quality. When that man came to know the matter, he wondered and embraced Islam, and then said: "I swear by Allah Who has chosen you as His Messenger that I never returned any person without giving him my wealth".[539]

Islam has prescribed some special rules and manners regarding the entertainment of guests. As such Imam Ja'far Sadiq, peace be on him, says: "If a brother-in-faith of yours arrives at your place, serve him whatever is available with you. However, if you invite him to meals entertain him property".[540]

The Holy Prophet, peace be on him and his progeny, says: "The host should begin eating first and should finish it last of all so that the guests may eat with complete freedom and get satiated".[541]

137

Islam also says that one should escort his guest up to the door of the house. The Holy Prophet, peace be on him and his progeny, says: "One of the rights of the guest on the host is that the latter should escort him from the room to the gate of the house".[542]

Islam has forbidden rendering assistance to a guest for making his departure. It has been reported that once some Arabs were the guests of Imam Ja'far Sadiq, peace be on him. At the time of their departure the Holy Imam give them presents etc. but forbade his slaves to assist them in making preparation for their leaving. When asked about the reason for this action, he replied: "We are a family who do not assist their guests in their departure".[543] The Holy Imam by his behaviour wanted to make people understand that he was not worried because of the guests and was not at all happy on account of their departure.

On the other hand Islam also makes the guests realize that they should not stay at one place for more than three days lest the host should be disturbed.

The Holy Prophet, peace be on him and his progeny, says: "Whoever believes in Allah and the Day of Judgement honours the guests. Entertainment is for three days only and thereafter it amounts to alms".[544]

No doubt Islam orders the host to do his best to honour and entertain his guest so much so that the Holy Prophet, peace be on him and his progeny, says: "The rights of a guest consist in that you should provide him (even) a tooth-pick".[545]

However, notwithstanding this, Islam orders the guest to behave in such a manner that the host is not disturbed. It directs inter alia that he should sit at the place appointed by the host. As Imam Muhammad Baqir, peace be on him, says: "When one of you arrives at the house of a brother-in-faith he should sit at the place appointed by the owner of the house as he knows better the situation of the house and the parts of it which should not be made public".[546]

It has also been mentioned in the biography of our great

leader, Imam Ali, peace be on him, that one day a person invited him to meals and he replied to him thus: "I accept your invitation on three conditions". The man inquired: "What are those conditions?" The Holy Imam said: "You will not procure anything from outside the house, will not hesitate to offer whatever is available in the house, and will not disturb your family".[547]

* * * * *

Showing Love to Orphans

One of the unfortunate sections of the society is the children, who lose their parents when they are quite young and are deprived of love and affection. It is evident that if such children are left to themselves they would grow up to be careless and mischievous. Islam, therefore, orders its followers to do their best to look after such children and to bring them up under their supervision.

The Holy Qur'an says: *"They ask you about the orphans. Tell them: 'The best thing to do is what is for their good. They are your brethren if you would associate with them. Allah knows who is corrupt or a reformer. Had Allah wanted He would have brought upon you hardship. Allah is Majestic and All-Wise".* [548]

There is no doubt about the fact that such children are grieved and broken-hearted on account of the deficiency which they observe in themselves and suffer from an inferiority complex. What a good thing it would be if amends are made for their loss and proper care is provided to them as it would serve as a source of consolation to them.

The Holy Prophet, peace be on him and his progeny, says: "Allah makes Paradise essential for one who acts as guardian of an orphan and trains him properly so that he may become self-reliant.[549]

Imam Ja'far Sadiq, peace be on him, says: "Whoever puts an affectionate hand on the head of an orphan will be awarded by Allah a glow of light on the Day of Judgement, equal to the number of his hair, which will pass from below his hand".[550]

Imam Ali, peace be on him, in his bequest says to his children: "Fear Allah in the matter of orphans. Do not leave them satiated at one time and hungry at another and do not pamper them while they are with you".[551]

The practical aspect of kindness shown to orphans may be seen in the following tradition. The Holy Prophet, peace be on him and his progeny, says: "One day Prophet 'Isa, peace be on him, passed through a graveyard and saw with his special insight that one of the dead was being tortured. He again passed from there after a year and saw no signs of torture in that particular grave. He enquired from the Almighty about the matter. It was then revealed to him that the man was a sinner but he had a son who was pious and who had provided food and shelter to an orphan and repaired a road during the year in question and Allah forgave the sins of his father on this account".[552]

The Holy Prophet, peace be on him and his progeny, says again: "If a person looks after an orphan and meets his expenses, he and I will be close to each other in Paradise as fingers of a man's hand are close to one another".[553]

* * * * *

Respect for the Dead

The respect and honour which Islam considers important for Muslims are of two kinds: one, during the lifetime of a Muslim, and theother, after his death.

Just as Islam does not tolerate that a Muslim should be insulted during his lifetime so it prescribes respect and special ceremonies in the event of his death. Hence, it does not allow any disrespect shown to the dead bodies of Muslims. Imam Ali, peace be on him, says: "The same respect is given to a Muslim after his death as he enjoyed during his lifetime".[554]

Islam orders that the dead bodies should be cleansed and washed and it has made this act obligatory for others. The Holy Prophet, peace be on him and his progeny, says: "It is obligatory for my followers to wash their dead and offer prayers for them".[555]

Imam Ja'far Sadiq, peace be on him, says: "It is obligatory that the dead should be washed".[556]

It is also necessary that due attention should be paid to matters relating to modesty with regard to the dead bodies of the Muslims just as it is cared for during lifetime. The dead body of a man should be washed by a man and that of a woman by a woman, or by those who are their *Mahram* i.e. those who are so closely related that marriage between them is prohibited.

Hence, when Imam Ja'far Sadiq, peace be on him, was asked about the washing of the dead body of a woman who dies while journeying and is not accompanied by a woman or a

Mahram he replied: "She should be buried in her own clothes and similarly if a man dies and is not accompanied by anyone except a woman who is not his *Mahram*, he too should be buried in his own clothes".[557]

The dead body of a Muslim should be washed and shrouded and thereafter prayers should be offered for him.

The Holy Prophet, peace be on him and his progeny, says to Abu Zar: "O Abu Zar! Offer prayers for the dead. It is possible that this thing may make you grieve but still grief for the sake of Allah carries a good reward".[558]

The dead bodies of Muslims should be buried as early as possible. Te Holy Prophet, peace be on him and his progeny, says: "Honour and respect for a dead person lies in that he should be carried to his grave expeditiously".[559]

Islam orders that funeral of Muslims should be well attended, because by doing so one pays homage to them and one is also reminded of one's own death. The Holy Prophet, peace be on him and his progeny, says: "Visit the sick and attend the funeral precession of the dead so that you may be reminded of the Hereafter".[560]

Imam Ali Riza, peace be on him, says: "Whowever attends the funeral procession of one of our followers is absolved from his sins and becomes as innocent and void of sins as a newly born child".[561]

It should, however, be kept in view that while attending the funeral one should remember Allah and the Hereafter. The Holy Prophet, peace be on him and his progeny, said to Abuzar "While attending the funeral procession remind yourself of your own death and fear it, and remember that you too will meet it one day".[562]

Islam orders that one should cherish the good memories of the dead and pray for them, so that the Lord may forgive them.

It has been reported that one day the Holy Prophet, peace be on him and his progeny, was attending the funeral procession of a dead person. He heard some persons praising the departed soul and saying that he was a good man. The Holy Prophet, peace be on him and his progeny, said: "I swear by the Lord of the Ka'bah that the path to Paradise has become secure for this man because the believers have witnessed his goodnnss and Allah does not reject their testimony".[563]

In order to protect the honour of the dead bodies of the Muslims, Islam orders that he who washes a dead body, should not tell anyone about the defects which he observed in the dead body. The Holy Prophet, peace be on him and his progeny, says: "A Muslim, who washes (the dead body of) a brother Muslim and does not leave him dirty; does not look at his private parts; does not divulge his defects, and thereafter attends his funeral and offers prayer for him and then stays there till he is buried, is absolved from his sins".[564]

Islam also prohibits everything which is a cause of disrespect to the dead. The Holy Prophet, peace be on him and his progeny, says: "If I have to walk over a burning desert or fire, or to place my foot on the edge of a sharp sword, I would prefer it to trampling down the grave of a Muslim".[565] He also says: "The Almighty Allah has considered a few things to be undesirable for my followers. One of them is laughing in the graveyard or between the graves".[566]

However, Islam recommends that people should visit the graves occasionally and remember the departed souls and seek Allah's forgiveness for them. Imam Ja'far Sadiq, peace be on him, says: "It is one of the rights of a Muslim over another Muslim that he should visit his grave".[567]

* * * * *

Protection of Animals

As opposed to what some people think the problem of 'protection of animals' is not something which has been brought into existence by the present-day world. On the contrary it can be seen in the Islamic instructions in a more extensive and complete form.

Islam has placed the relations between man and animals under a fixed law and given the animals extensive rights. The gist of it may be observed in the following tradition. The Holy Prophet peace be on him and his progeny, says: "Every animal for riding has six rights over its master:
(i) Whenever he halts at a halting place, he should first provide it with fodder. (ii) Whenever he passes by water he should let it drink water. (iii) He should not beat it on its face because it praises Allah. (iv) He should not ride on its back except in the cause of Allah (i.e. he should keep riding on it only while performing the journey and should dismount it when, for example, he halts to converse with some other person for a long time). (v) He should not overburden it beyond its capacity. (vi) He should not compel it to go on a path which it is not possible for it to cover".[568]

Besides the above-quoted traditions many other responsibilities of man vis-a-vis animals have been mentioned in the sayings of the religious leaders, a summary of which is given below:
(i) Be careful about providing them fodder. Ima Musa Kazim,

peace be on him, says: "It is an honour for a man that his animals reserved for riding should be fat and fleshy" (viz. there should be no carelessness on the part of their master about providing them the necessities of life).[569]

When Imam Ali, peace be on him, distributed the war booty and fixed and shares of the warriors, he allocated to the rider, who had broguht two horses — one for riding and the other as a spare horse, three shares: two for his horses and one for him, and each of the foot-soldiers got only one share".[570]

(ii) Don't keep them thirsty. Imam Muhammad Baqir, peace be on him, says: "Allah likes cooling down the heat of sore livers. If a person quenches the thirst of animals, Allah will accommodate him under His own shadow on the Day, on which there will be no shadow available except His".[571]

(iii) Don't hit them on their faces. Imam Ja'far Sadiq, peace be on him, says: "There is a dignity and respect for everything and the dignity of the quardrupeds lies in their faces".[572]

(iv) The Holy Prophet, peace be on him and his progeny, says: "Don't mount the quadruped with legs flexed and don't make their backs as your seats".[573]

(v) The Holy Prophet, peace be on him and his progeny, says: "Three of you should not ride a quardruped at a time because the third person is accursed and is far from the Blessings of Allah".[574]

(vi) Lighten the burden of feeble animals at the halting place.

(vii) Don't overstay in dry deserts and do not make them your halting-place.

(viii) Drive slowly through jungles where water and grass are available, so that the animals may make use of them. The Holy Prophet, peace be on him and his progeny, says: "Almighty Allah likes gentleness and leniency. Hence if you travel with weak quadrupeds, bring down their load at each halting place and, if the desert is dry, pass through it and halt at the green land".[575] Imam Muhammad Baqir, peace be on him, says: "Drive slowly through green lands and try to cross the dry lands quickly".[576]

(ix) Don't drive the animals too fast. Imam Muhammad Baqir, peace be on him, says: "Do not accept the evidence of a pilgrim to Ka'bah, who reaches his destination earlier than all others, because by doing so he must have tortured his animal".[577]

(x) Don't beat the animals unnecessarily. The Holy Prophet, peace be on him and his progeny, says : "Beat the animals if they are refractory or vicious or run away, but refrain from beating them for slipping or falling down on the ground".[578]

(xi) Don't kill the animals (or birds) unnecessarily. The Holy Prophet, peace be on him and his progeny, says: "If a person kills a sparrow it will complain on the Day of Judgement and will say: "O Lord! Ask this person as to why he killed me without any reason".[579]

Imam Ja'far Sadiq, peace be on him, says: "A woman was subjected to Divine torture because she had fastened a cat which died of thirst".[580]

(xii) Don't slaughter an animal in the presence of another animal. Imam Ali, peace be on him, says: "Don't slaughter a lamb when it is looking at another".[581]

(xiii) It is better that you should not slaughter an animal which has been reared up by you. A man said to Imam Ali Riza, peace be on him: "I reared up a sheep in my house for one year and then I decided to sacrifice it. When I caught it and made it lie on the ground it looked at me. I felt pity for it and, therefore, waited for sometime and then slaughtered it". The Holy Imam replied: "I dislike this behaviour. Don't kill an animal which you have reared up yourself".[582]

* * * * *

ISLAM a code of social life

part 2

In the Name of Allah the Beneficent, the Merciful

A Few Words

In the first part of this book, we have studied some Qur'anic verses and traditions, that constitute the code of social life, and now in the second part, we are presetning without any elaboration some more traditions, which talk of moral, ethical and spiritual uplift of an individual; and ultimately of a society.

All the traditions collected in this part have been quoted from *Tuhaful 'Uqūl 'an Āle Rasūl* compiled by Abu Muhammad al-Hasan bin Sho'ba al-Harrāni, the prominent *muhaddith* (traditionalist) of the fourth century Hegira.

As the name of the book suggests, all the traditions in it are narrated on the authority of Ahlul Bayt, the Chosen Decendants of the Holy Prophet, peace be on them.

Hishām bin Sālim and Hammād bin 'Isa narrate that Imam Ja'far Sadiq, peace be on him, said: "My narration is the narration of my father, his is that of my grandfather, his is that of Husayn, his is that of Hasan, his is that of Ali, the Commander of the Faithful, his is that of the Holy Prophet and the narration of the Holy Prophet is the Command of Allah".[*]

"When we reply to a question in any matter, it is from the Holy Prophet. We do not speak of our own will".[‡]

That is why our Holy Prophet, peace be on him and his progeny, urged upon us to adhere to his Ahlul Bayt, who are

---
[*] Usūlul Kāfi, vol. I, p. 53.
[‡] Basāirud Darajāt, pp. 300 — 301.

purified and honoured personages as ordained by Allah in the Holy Qur'an. (Vide, Surah al-Ahzāb, 33 : 33)

The Holy Prophet, peace be on him and his progeny, has said: "I leave among you two inseparable precious entities i.e. the Book of Allah and my Ahlul Bayt. Whosoever adheres to these two shall be saved from going astray".*

We pray to Almight Allah to grant us strength to follow in the footsteps of Ahlul Bayt, so that we may be blessed in this world and the Hereafter.

* * * * *

---

*Sahih Tirmizi, vol. V, p. 328 printed by Darul Fikr, Beirut; Sahih Muslim, vol. V, p. 362 printed by 'Isa al-Halabi.

Sayings of Ahlul Bayt

DESIRE

Imam Ali, peace be on him, says: "(O Lord,) Your slave does not prolong his desire except that at last he forgets You".[1]

Imam Ja'far Sadiq, peace be on him, says: "Allah bestows numerous blessings on His slave which he does not desire and there are many desrious persons whose desires are fulfilled by others and there are many persons who meet their death and are deprived of their share".[2]

GIFT

The Holy Prophet, peace be on him and his progeny, says: "Accept gifts. The best gift is that of perfume which is comparatively light and sweet-smelling".[3]

GOODNESS

The Holy Prophet, peace be on him and his progeny, says: "Wearing dress reveals one's riches and doing good to one's servant crushes one's enemy".[4]

"Compensate one, who does good to you. And if you do not compensate him, praise him, for praise is his reward".[5]

"It is necessary for a man, to whom good is done, to praise the person, who has done good to him. If he does not do so, he is guilty of ingratitude".[6]

SINCERITY

The Holy Prophet, peace be on him and his progeny, says: "There are four signs of a sincere person: (i) His heart is sound (ii) His limbs are harmless (iii) He does good to others (iv) He refrains from doing evil".[7]

GOOD MORALS

The Holy Prophet, peace be on him and his progeny, says: "Good behaviour makes its owner attain the level of one who fasts during day-time and prays at night". He was asked: "What is the best gift which one can bestow upon one's slave?" He replied: "Good behaviour".[8]

"Amongst the believers one, whose morals are best possesses the most perfect faith".[9]

Imam Musa Kazim, peace be on hsm, says: "A generous person who possesses noble disposition is under the protection of Allah and He never ignores him and He takes him to Paradise. Allah never sent a prophet who was not geneorus. And my father always recommended to me to be generous and good-natured till he passed away".[10]

MANAGEMENT OF THE HOUSEHOLD

Imam Riza, peace be on him, says: "The reward for one who seeks sustenance to support his family is greater than one who fights for the cause of Allah".[11]

PERSEVERANCE

Imam Ali, peace be on him, says: "Safety lies in perseverance, and prayer is the key to achieve blessing".[12]

PRODIGALITY

The Holy Prophet, peace be on him and his progeny, says: "There are four signs of a prodigal:
(i) He prides himself on false things. (ii) He eats that which is not suitable for him. (iii) He is not inclined to do good. (iv) He

opposes everyone from whom he cannot derive benefit".[13]

Imam Ali, peace be on him, says: "Prudence with thrift is better than affluence with extravagance".[14]

MODERATION

The Holy Prophet, peace be on him and his progeny, says: "My Lord has recommended nine things to me:
(i) To be sincere secretly as well as openly.
(ii) To maintain justice, whether it is pleasant or not.
(iii) To be moderate in spending, whether I am poor or rich.
(iv) To forgive one who has been unjust to me.
(v) To give to one who has refused to give me something.
(vi) To befriend one who has severed connections with me.
(vii) That I should reflect while I am quiet.
(viii) That my speech should be *Zikr* (supplication).
(ix) The aim of my seeing is to take a lesson".[15]

FRIENDSHIP

Imam Ali, peace be on him, says: "Blessed is he, who, while being obedient to Allah, befriends the people and they befriend him".[16]

"The best way to win the hearts of one's friends and remove grudge from the hearts of one's enemies is to meet them cheerfully and enquiring about their welfare during their absence and being happy in their presence".[17]

HONESTY

The Holy Prophet, peace be on him and his progeny, says: "Honesty brings sustenance and dishonesty entails poverty and indigence".[18]

Imam Ali, peace be on him, says: "O Kumayl! You should understand and know that none is permitted to withhold the thing entrusted to him. Whoever narrates that we have accorded such a permission says something absurd and commits a sin and will be punished by being thrown into Hell, for he tells a lie. I swear that before breathing his last the Holy Prophet, said to me thrice: "O Abul Hasan return the thing entrusted to you by a good man or a sinner, whether it is big or as small as a needle and a thread".[19]

"Return to its owner the thing entrusted to you although he may have killed the children of the prophets".[20]

EQUITY

Imam Ja'far Sadiq, peace be on him, says: "Brothers among themsevles need three things to do. If they do them they remain firm, otherwise they part with one another and also become enemies. Those three things are: (i) Dealing equitably with one another, (ii) Being kind to one another. (iii) Not envying one another".[21]

CHARITY IN THE PATH OF ALLAH

Imam Zaynul 'Ābidin, peace be on him, says: "It is one of the morals of a believer that howsoever meagre his income may be he spends something in the path of Allah".[22]

Imam Musa Kazim, peace be on him, says: "Beware of refusing to spend for the cause of Allah and then spending twice as much in disobedeying Allah".[23]

The Holy Prophet, peace be on him and his progeny, says: "The hands are of three kinds: The one that requests, the one that gives and the one which is parsimonious. And the best of the hands is the one that gives".[24]

"Do not wear a ring on your forefinger and middle finger .... Do not keep your little finger bare".[25]

Imam Ja'far Sadiq, peace be on him, says: "Wearing a ring on one's hand is the Sunnah of the Holy Prophet".[26]

FAITH

The Holy Prophet, peace be on him and his progeny, says: "A believer is like an ear of corn which suddenly falls on the ground and then suddenly stands erect. And an unbeliever is like a hard tree which always stands erect possessing no sense (to bow his head before truth)".[27]

Imam Ali, peace be on him, says: "O Kumayl! Faith is either firm or a borrowed one. Take care that you may not be one of those whose faith is a borrowed one. Indeed it is proper that your faith should be firm, for then you proceed on a lighted path and are not misled".[28]

"The title of the book of a believer is cheerful disposition"[29]

PARSIMONY

The Holy Prophet, peace be on him and his progeny, says: "From amongst you the person most distant from me is one who is parsimonious and scurrilous".[30]

Imam Husayn, peace be on him, says: "A miser is one who shirks greeting others".[31]

Imam Ja'far Sadiq, peace be on him, says: "One who hates three things acquires three other things viz:
(i) One who hates doing evil deeds acquires respect.
(ii) One who hates pride acquires greatness.
(iii) One who hates stinginess acquires honour".[32]

MISTRUST

The Holy Prophet, peace be on him and his progeny, says: "Refrain from being suspicious about the people".[33]

BROTHERHOOD

Imam Ali, peace be on him, says: "How bad is holding apart after uniting; oppression after friendships and brotherhood, and enmity after kindness".[34]

"The believers are brothers of one another and nothing is more dear to a brother than his brother".[35]

"If you do not love your brother you are not his brother, because a believer is one who has faith in what we believe in, and whoever goes against it is guilty in regard to us and whoever is guilty regarding us is not amongst us and whoever is not amongst us shall go to Hell".[36]

FORBEARANCE

Imam Ali, peace be on him, says: "Learn forbearance, for forbearance is the friend and helper of a believer, and knowledge is his guide and modesty is his brother, and wisdom is his companion and patience is the commander of his army".[37]

Imam Muhammad Baqir, peace be on him, says: "There are no other two things which associate better with each other than forbearance does with knowledge".[38]

Imam Ja'far Sadiq, peace be on him, says: "There are three persons who are not recognized except on three occasions: (i) A forbearing person is not recognized except at the time of anger. (ii) A brave man is not recognized except in the battlefield. (iii) A brother and friend is not recognized till the time when you need his help".[39]

GOODNESS

The Holy Prophet, peace be on him and his progeny, says: "There are ten signs of a righteous person: (i) His friendship is for the sake of Allah. (ii) His enmity is for the sake of Allah. (iii) He becomes a companion for the sake of Allah. (iv) He parts company for the sake of Allah. (v) He is angry for the sake of Allah. (vi) He is pleased for the sake of Allah. (vii) He works for the sake of Allah. (viii) He seeks Allah. (ix) He fears Allah at the time of danger and fear. He is pure and sincere. He is modest and vigilant. (x) He does good to others for the sake of Allah".[40]

"The sign of an ignorant person is that he acts sluggishly while doing something good".[41]

Imam Ja'far Sadiq, peace be on him, says: "Four things are the attributes of the Prophets: (i) Righteousness (ii) Generosity (iii) Bearing unpleasant things with fortitude (iv) Standing up to defend the right of a believer".[42]

REBELLION

The Holy Prophet, peace be on him and his progeny, says: "The quickest evil is the punishment for rebellion".[43]

Imam Ja'far Sadiq, peace be on him, says: "The following three things, in whomsoever they are, are harmful for him: (i) Deceit (ii) Breach of promise (iii) Aggression. This is what the word of the Almighty Allah means when He says: *Does not the evil plot recoil only on those who make it?* (Surah Fatir, 35:41) *Now see what the result of their plot was. We destroyed them and their people all together.* (Surah an-Naml, 27:51) And the Almighty Allah says: *Men, it is your own souls against which you revolt. You enjoy this worldly life only for a while.* (10:24)".[44]

Imam Ja'far Sadiq, peace be on him, says: "A believer does not possess the following six attributes: (i) Severity (ii) Ignorance (iii) Jealousy (iv) Obstinacy (v) Falsehood (vi) Aggression".[45]

THE HELPLESS

Imam Ja'far Sadiq, peace be on him says: "How bad it is to take revenge upon the helpless".[46]

Imam Ali, peace be on him, says: "Remember Allah in respect of the helpless. Let them participate in your life".[47]

INDEPENDENCE AND POVERTY

The Holy Prophet, peace be on him and his progeny, says: "Seeking less assistance from the people is independence and seeking much help from them is abjectness and poverty".[48]

A man said in the presence of Imam Zaynul Abidin, peace be on him: "O Lord! Make me independent of others". The Holy Imam said: "No, it is not so, because people live in society. You should say: "O Lord! Make me independnnt of wicked people".[49]

Imam Musa Kazim, peace be on him, says: "If you are satisfied to the extent you need, the smallest thing of the world will be sufficient for you. And if you are not satisfied to the extent you need, there is nothing in the world which can satisfy you".[50]

REGRET

The Holy Prophet, peace be on him and his progeny, says: "Regret itself is repentance".[51]

Imam Ja'far Sadiq, peace be on him, says: "Salvation lies in three things viz: (i) You should control your tongue (ii) You should stay in your house, and (iii) You should regret your fault".[52]

Imam Ja'far Sadiq, peace be on him, says: "Three things entail regret: (i) Taking pride in something (ii) Boasting, and (iii) Using violence to acquire honour".[53]

RESIGNATION AND FORTITUDE

The following is an extract from the letter of condolence sent by the Holy Prophet to Ma'āz in connection with the death of his son.

"I learn that you are impateint on account of your son. Allah granted him to you till the time of his death and took away his soul at the appointed time. We are from Allah and we have to return to Him. Beware, lest impatience should destroy your spiritual reward. If you attain the spiritual reward attached to your calamity you will come to know that for those who are patient and resign themselves to the Divine Will, the calamity is very meagre and brief as compared with the great spiritual reward of Allah. You should know that impatience does not bring back a dead person and cannot restrain the Divine decree. Be cheerful and accept the destiny. It should not be that you may grieve on account of something, which is attached to you as well as to all other human beings and shall come at the time fixed for it. peace be upon you".[54]

PIETY

The Holy Prophet, peace be on him and his progeny, says: "Death is sufficient to take a lesson from and piety is sufficient for being rich".[55]

Imam Ali, peace be on him, says: "Speak the truth in all

circumstances; associate with the pious; shun the libertines; keep aloof from the hypocrites. and do not associate with the treacherous".[56]

"Truly speaking everyone is proceeding towards the Hereafter and the thing, which we are enamoured of, is the pleasure of Allah and the high ranks in Paradise, which every pious person inherits".[57]

PRIDE

Imam Ali, peace be on him says: "Whoever is self-conceited goes astray; whoever dispenses with his intellect stumbles; and whoever treats the people arrogantly is humiliated".[58]

Imam Muhammad Baqir, peace be on him, says: "By Allah, an arrogant person quarrels with the Almighty about the Authority of His Greatness".[59]

LAZINESS

The Holy Prophet peace be on him and his progeny, says: "There are four signs of a lazy person: Sluggishness to the extent of negligence; negligence to the extent of giving up one's duty; giving up one's duty to the extent of committing sin, and finally feeling annoyed to perform one's duty".[60]

The Holy Prophnt, peace be on him and his progeny, says: "There are three signs of a lazy person. He is sluggish till he becomes negligent. He is negligent till he loses; and he loses till he commits sin".[61]

Imam Muhammad Baqir, peace be on him, says: "Abstain from laziness and despondency, because these two are the key of all evils. One, who is lazy, does not pay the right of another and one, who is despondent, is not content with his own right".[62]

HUMILITY

Imam Ali, peace be on him, says: "The best ornament of a believer is humility; his beauty is his modesty; his dignity lies in understanding religion; and his honour is in abandoning absurd talk".[63]

Imam Muhammad Baqir, peace be on him, says: "Humility is that you should agree to sit at a place which is below your dignity and salute everyone you meet and do not contend even though you may be right".[64]

Imam Hasan Askari, peace be on him, says: "Humility is such a blessing that on account of it, the people are not jealous".[65]

WEALTH

The Holy Prophet, peace be on him and his progeny, says: "Wealth does not consist in owning a large quantity of goods. On the other hand it means having a heart which is free from want".[66]

REPENTANCE

The Holy Prophet, peace be on him and his progeny, says: "There are four signs of a repentant: (i) He acts only to please Allah (ii) He abandons falsehood (iii) He considers truth to be necessary (iv) He is fond of doing good deeds".[67]

Imam Ali, peace be on him, was requested to explain what sincere repentance is. He said in reply: "Heartfelt regret and asking forgiveness with the tongue and determining not to repeat the sin".[68]

Kumayl bin Ziyad said to Imam Ali (P): "O Commander of the Faithful! A person may commit a sin and then ask forgiveness. What is the limit of asking forgiveness?
Imam Ali replied: O son of Ziyad! It is repentance.
Kumayl asked: Is that all?
The Imam replied: No.
Kumayl asked: Then how is it?
The Imam replied: Whenever a person commits a sin he should say "I seek Allah's forgiveness" and should move.
Kumayl asked: What is meant by moving?
The Imam replied: He should move his two lips and tongue with the intention that he should be followed by reality.

Kumayl asked: What is reality?
The Imam replied: He should repent sincerely and determine not to repeat the sin for which he asks forgiveness.
Kumayl asked: Suppose I do so, will I be forgiven?
The Imam replied: No.
Kumayl asked: Why is it so?
The Imam said: Because you have not yet reached its root.
Kumayl asked: Then what is the root of asking forgiveness? The Imam replied: It is return to repentance from the sin for which you have asked forgiveness (and that is the first degree of the devout) and the abandonment of sin. 'Asking forgiveness' is a term which carries six meanings. (i) Regretting the past deeds (ii) Determination of not repeating that sin (iii) Paying the right of every creature to whom you are indebted (iv) Paying all the binding rights of Allah (v) Reducing the flesh which has grown on your body by unlawful means till your skin sticks to your bones and then fresh flesh grows between them. (vi) You should make your body taste the pain of submission as you made it taste the deliciousness of sin".[69]

TRUST IN ALLAH

Imam Riza (P) was requested to explain what 'trust in Allah' means. He replied: "It means that you should not fear anyone except Allah".[70]

The Holy Prophet, peace be on him and his progeny, says: "Whoever wishes to become the most powerful person should rely on Allah".[71]

Imam Ali, peace be on him, says: "Recite the name of Allah everyday and say: *La Hawla wa la Quwwata illa billah* (No one possesses power and strength except Allah) and rely on Allah".[72]

CALUMNY

The Holy Prophet, peace be on him and his progeny, says about calumny: "A person who suffers at the hands of a thief and continuously accuses the innocent people till his sin becomns greater than that of the thief".[73]

Imam Ali, peace be on him, says: "Whoever makes himself the object of calumny should not reproach one who holds an adverse view about him, and whoever keeps his secret hidden exercises control over himself".[74]

PEEPING AT THE SINS OF OTHERS

Imam Ja'far Sadiq, peace be on him, says: "Whenever you see that a person peeps at the sins of others and has forgotten his own sins, you should conclude that he has been captured by Divine plot".[75]

JIHĀD (HOLY WAR)

Imam Ali, peace be on him, says: "It is not possible to do *jihād* except in the company of a just Imam (leader) and there is no question of booty except in the company of a learnnd Imam".[76]

Imam Ali, peace be on him, says: "I remind you of Allah in the matter of *jihād* with your wealth, life and tongue. Indeed, only two persons perform *jihād:* A true Imam and one who obeys and follows him".[77]

FLATTERY

Imam Muhammad Baqir, peace be on him, says: "Flattery and envy do not form part of the morals of a believer except for acquiring knowledge".[78]

LOVE FOR WORLDLY PASSIONS

Imam Musa Kazim, peace be on him, says: "Allah sent revelation to Dawud, peace be on him: O Dawud! warn your friends against worldly passions, for the hearts of those, who hanker after them, are far from Me (My Mercy)".[79]

JEALOUSY

The Holy Prophet, peace be on him and his progeny, says:

163

"A jealous person has three signs: (i) Backbiting (ii) Flattery (iii) Taunting at the time of one's misfortune".[80]

Imam Ali, peace be on him, says: "The jealous persons are not happy — the kings have no friends and the liars lack courage".[81]

The Holy Prophet, peace be on him and his progeny, says: "Go ahead when there is a bad omen; do not take a decision when you are suspicious; and do not be aggressive when you are jealous."[82]

Imam Ali, peace be on him, says: "A believer is neither a flatterer nor jealous except for acquiring knowledge".[83]

"I have not seen any oppressor who resembles an oppressed person more than does one who is jealous".[84]

TRUTH

Imam Ali, peace be on him, says: "Indeed, the benefit which you derive from your world is that it should be good for your life in the Hereafter. Spend in the cause of truth and do not be a treasurer for others".[85]

"Recognize the right of a person who has recognized your right, whether he is exalted or unimportant".[86]

"You must fear Allah openly and secretly and should speak the truth at the time of happiness and anger".[87]

WISDOM

Imam Musa Kazim, peace be on him, says: "Do not teach wisdom to the ignorant, for by doing so you will do injustice to it; and do not withhold it from those who deserve it, for in that event you will do injustice to them".[88]

"Just as the people have left wisdom for you, you too should leave the world for them".[89]

The Holy Prophet, peace be on him and his progeny, said: "When you see that a believer is quiet, seek his proximity so that he may teach you wisdom. A believer talks less and works much. A hypocrite is talkative and works less".[90]

MODESTY

The Holy Prophet, peace be on him and his progeny, says: "Modesty emanates from faith".[91]

Imam Zaynul 'Ābidin, peace be on him, says: "Seeking help from the people brings about abjection, destroys modesty, reduces dignity and brings poverty; and seeking less from the people is independence".[92]

Imam Muhammad Baqir, peace be on him, says: "Modesty and faith are tied with one string. If one of them goes the other follows it".[93]

DECEIT

Imam Ali, peace be on him, says: "Do not neglect the deceit of Satan and say: "Every time I see something unlawful I withdraw my hand".[94]

"Do not practise deceit, for it is a part of the morals of mean people".[95]

INTELLECT

The Holy Prophet, peace be on him and his progeny, says: "The Almighty has divided intellect into three parts. The intellect of one who possesses all these parts is complete. And he, who does not possess even one of these parts, does not possess intellect. These three parts are: (i) Recognizing Allah well (ii) Obeying Allah fully (iii) Accepting Divine fate with complete patience".[96]

"Indeed everything good is recognized by means of intellect and whoever does not possess intellect does not possess faith".[97]

Imam Ali, peace be on him, says: "There is no wealth like intellect and no poverty is worse than ignorance".[98]

HUMILITY

The Holy Prophet, peace be on him and his progeny, says: "Let it not be that you should practise humility hypocritically, which means that the body is humble but the heart is not humble".[99]

Imam Ali, meace be on him, says: "Be extremely humble before your Lord when you achieve your object and are guided towards your aim".[100]

"O Kumayl, dignity does not lie in offering prayers, fasting, and giving alms; but dignity lies in offering prayers with a pure heart; your deeds should please Allah and your humility should be sincere. You should also see in what and on what you are offering your prayers because if they are not performed in a lawful manner they are not acceptable".[101]

SINCERITY

Imam Ali, peace be on him, says: "The first step of religion is to accept, understand and realize Him as the Lord; thorough understanding lies in conviction and confirmation, and the right conviction is to sincerely believe that there is no god but He. The true belief in His Oneness is to realize that He is so absolutely Pure and above nature, that nothing can be added to or subtracted from Him; because one should realize that there is no difference between His Being and His Attributes".[102]

"Seek sincerely from your Lord whatever you need, because to give or to withhold is in His Hand".[103]

CHEERFULNESS

The Holy Prophet, peace be on him and his progeny, says: "Cheerfulness destroys grudge".[104]

DISHONESTY

The Holy Prophet, peace be on him and his progeny, says: "A believer may be habituated to anything except falsehood and dishonesty".[105]

Imam Ja'far Sadiq, peace be on him, says: "If one entrusts something to a dishonest person, Allah does not guarantee its return".[106]

"A believer has not been created to tell lies or to commit treachery and there are two things which cannot combine in a hypocrite; a good mien and comprehension of Islamic faith".[107]

GOODNESS

Imam Hasan, peace be on him, says: "The goodness which has no evil about it, is thanking Allah for a blessing and enduring adversities with patience".[108]

Imam Zaynul 'Ābidin, peace be on him, says: "The best thing is that one should guard oneself (from sins)".[109]

"Help one, who seeks good from you. If he deserves it you have done your duty. And even if he does not deserve it you yourself deserve it. And if a person abuses you from your right side and then turns to your left side and apologizes to you, you should accept his apology".[110]

USING ABSUSIVE LANGUAGE

Imam Muhammad Baqir, peace be on him, says: "Allah hates an impudent person who uses abusive language".[111]

REMEMBERING ALLAH

The Holy Prophet, peace be on him and his progeny, says: "The best deeds are three in number: (i) You should pay the rights of the people. (ii) You should become equal to your brother for the sake of Allah (iii) You should remember Allah in all circumstances".[112]

"Allah's *Zikr* (Devotion to Allah) is better than only giving alms".[113]

"Allah rewards the person who always remembers Him".[114]

FRIENDSHIP

Imam Muhammad Baqir, peace be on him, says: "Twenty years' friendship is as good as relationship".[115]

Imam Ja'far Sadiq, peace be on him, says: "A friend can be tested by means of three things. If he possesses them he is a true friend, otherwise he is a friend in weal but not in woe: (i) That you may ask him to give you something. (ii) That you

167

may entrust something to him. (iii) That you may be associated with him in adverse circumstances".[116]

"If you wish to find out whether your friend is sincere you should annoy him. If he remains friendly with you in spite of this he is your brother, otherwise not".[117]

LENIENCY

Imam Musa Kazim, peace be on him, says: "Be lenient, for leniency is auspicious and ill-disposition is inauspicious. Indeed, leniency, goodness and cheerfulness make the houses prosper and increase sustenance".[118]

HYPOCRISY

The Holy Prophet, peace be on him and his progeny, says: "There are four signs of a hypocrite: (i) He is very keen to pray to Allah in the presence of others. (ii) He is lazy while alone. (iii) He seeks praise in every matter. (iv) He endeavours to pretend".[119]

"Do not do anything good to make a show of it and do not feel ashamnd to do it".[120]

PIETY

Imam Ali, pace be on him, says: "A pious person in the world is he, whose patience is not out of control in the face of unlawful things, an who is not prevented from thanksgiving by lawful things".[121]

The Holy Prophet, peace be on him and his progeny, says: "Piety consists in cutting short one's desires, thanking Allah for every blessing, and restraining oneself from things declared by Allah to be unlawful".[122]

A man asked Imam Zayun 'Ābidin, peace be on him: "What is piety? The Imam replied: There are ten stages of piety. The highest stages of piety are the lowest stages of continnence and the highest stages of contincene are the lowest stages of conviction and the highest stages of conviction are the lowest stages of submission. Indeed piety has been defined very finely in the sacred verse which says: *"You would not grieve for what you have missed, nor rejoice over what Allah has given you"*. (Surah al-Hadid, 57:23)".[123]

GENEROSITY

The Holy Prophet, peace be on him and his progeny, says: "Indeed, Allah likes him, who is generous in the discharge of his obligations".[124]

"When your leaders are good and your rich are generous and every work is done in consultation with all of you, the face of the earth is better for you than its interior (graves); and when your leaders are corrupt and your rich are misers and your affairs are in the hands of your women, it is better that you too should be under the earth".[125]

"The Almighty has said: "This is a religion which I have chosen for Myself and nothing becomes it except generoisty and good manners. So long as you are by its side honour it by means of these two".[126]

Imam Ali, peace be on him, says: "The greatest persons among the people in this world are the geneorus and in the Hereafter the pious".[127]

SALUTATION

Imam Ja'far Sadiq, peace be on him, says: "To salute is recommended and its reply is obligatory".[128]

"If a person talks without having saluted first, do not give a reply to him".[129]

"Perfect salutation for a resident of the place is shaking hands with him and complete salutation for a traveller who has arrived is embracing him".[130]

ILL NATURE

The Holy Prophet, peace be on him and his progeny, says: "It is necessary for you that you should be truthful and nothing false should ever come out of your lips. Never pick up courage to commit breach of trust. Fear Allah as if you were seeing Him and sacrifice your property and life for the sake of your religion. Adopt good manners and shun bad ones".[131]

Imam Ja'far Sdiq, peace be on him, says: "Whoever is ill-natured tortures himself".[132]

"Ill-nature entails adversity and indigence".[133]

EVIL DEEDS

The Holy Prophet, peace be on him and his progeny, says: "Indeed Allah has made and moulded the hearts of His slaves in such a way that they love a person who treats them well and hate one who harms them".[134]

THANKSGIVING

The Holy Prophet said to Imam Ali (P): "Ali! The Islam of one who possesses these four qualities is perfect: (i) Truthfulness (ii) Thankfulness (iii) Modesty and (iv) Good behaviour.[135]

The Holy Prophet, peace be on him and his progeny, says: "Whoever eats and thanks Allah is better than one who fasts and remains silent (does not thank Allah)".[135]

Imam Ali, peace be on him, says: "During indigence the right of Allah is submission to His Will, and patience; and during affluence His right is that He should be praised and thanked".[137]

PATIENCE

The Holy Prophet, peace be on him and his progeny, says: "Faith consists of two halves. One half of its is patience and the other is thanksgiving".[138]

"Three things form the key to goodness: (i) Possessing a generous heart (ii) Being sweet-spoken (iii) Remaining patient on being harmed".[139]

Imam Musa Kazim, peace be on him, says: "Adversity is single for one, who is patient and double for one who is impatient".[140]

TRUTH

The Holy Prophet, peace be on him and his progeny, says: "There are four signs of one who is truthful: (i) Truthfulness (ii) Believing in the promises and threats of Allah (iii) Being faithful to one's promises (iv) Remaining aloof from treachery".[141]

"On the Day of Judgement from amongst you, he, who is most truthful, most honest, most good-natured and nearest to the people, will be nearest to me".[142]

Imam Ali, peace be on him, says: "The substance of faith is that a slave of Allah should make truthfulness his habit so that he may hate falsehood even when he stands to gain by it. And one should not consider one's speech to be one's distinction".[143]

ALMS

"Do not refuse the request of one who begs, and give him something even though it may be a piece of a grape or a palm-date, because alms increases before Allah".[144]

Imam Muhammad Baqir, peace be on him, says: "Four things form part of the treasures of goodness:
(i) Keeping one's need hidden
(ii) Giving the alms secretly
(iii) Keeping one's pain hidden and
(iv) Keeping one's suffering hidden".[145]

Imam Muhammad Baqir, peace be on him, said: "May I tell you about a thing which, if practised by you, will keep the mischief of the king and Satan away from you?

Abu Hamza said: Yes. Please tell us about it so that we may practise it.

The Imam said: You should give alms in the morning because they blacken the face of Satan and keep the mischief of the king away from you on that day".[146]

OBSERVATION OF RELATIONSHIP

The Holy Prophet, peace be on him and his progeny, says: "Observation of relationship increases one's life".[147]

"Punishment for the following four things is awarded quickly: (i) When you do good to a person and he in return does you harm. (ii) When you do not oppress a person and he oppresses you. (iii) When you make an agreement with a person and intend to be faithful to it, but this intention is otherwise, and (iv) When you observe relationship with a person but he breaks it off".[148]

Imam Riza, peace be on him, said: "Observe relationship although it may be by means of a gulp of water and the best observance of it is that you should refrain from doing harm to your relative". He added: "The Almighty Allah says in the Holy Qur'an: *Do not render your charity useless with taunts*". (Surah al-Baqarah, 2:264).[146]

FEAST

Imam Ali, peace be on him, says: "Invite others to food and do not withhold it from them, becuase you do not at all provide sustenance to anyone and Allah will reward you suitably for this deed. Behave well towards your friend and vacate the seat for him and do not be suspicious about your servant".[150]

COVETOUSNESS

Imam Ali, peace be on him, says: "O people! The wonderful thing in the body of man is his heart. Heart has stocks of wisdom as well as of things which are its opposite. If hopefulness affords it an opportunity, covetousness humiliates it, and if its covetousness increases, its greed kills it".[151]

"Covetousness plucks the hearts of the ignorant and they become pledged to desire, and deceit prevails in them".[152]

OPPRESSION

Imam Ali, peace be on him, says: "The oppressor, his associate, and the one who is agreeable to be oppressed, are all partners of one another".[153]

"May it not be that you should oppress a person who has

none to assist him against you except Allah".[154]

WELFARE

Imam Ali, peace be on him, says: "O people! Pray to Allah for conviction and resort to welfare, because the greatest blessing and the best thing which is firmly rooted in the heart is conviction. The cheated one is he, whose faith is injured, and he, who possesses perfect conviction, should be envied".[155]

Imam Ja'far Sadiq, peace be on him, says: "Welfare is a light blessing which is forgotten when it is in one's possession and is missed when it is lost".[156]

SELF-CONCEIT

Imam Ali, peace be on him, said: "Whoever is able to protect himself from four things deserves that he should not suffer any harm at all. On having been asked as to what those things are he replied: They are: Hastiness, obstinacy, self-conceit and laziness".[157]

Imam Ja'far Sadiq, peace be on him, says: "Three things cause enmity viz. hypocrisy, oppression and self-conceit".[158]

"Allah knows that for a believer there is no sin worse than self-conceit, and if it had not been so no believer would have been polluted with sin".[159]

JUSTICE

Imam Ali, peace be on him, says: "give your blood and wealth to your brother and be just to your enemy and deal with the people with cheerfulness and kindness and salute others so that they may salute you".[160]

Imam Muhammad Baqir, peace be on him, says: "The saddest person on the Day of Judgement will be one who praises justice but himself acts against it".[161]

Imam Ja'far Sadiq, peace be on him, says: "Indeed, the person, who orders others to do good and restrains them from evil, possesses three qualities: (i) He knows what he is ordering others to do and what he is asking them not to do. (ii) He is just in what he is ordering others what to do and is also just in what he is asking them not to do. (iii) He orders others (to do good deeds) gently and also restrains them (from doing bad deeds) gently".[162]

HONOUR

Imam Ali, peace be on him, says: "Do not display your indigence to the people and in order to please Allah bear it patiently with honour and secrecy".[163]

Imam Hasan, peace be on him, was asked: "Do you find a place in greatness?" He replied: Rather (you should say) is there honour in me? Allah says: *Honour belongs to Allah and to His Prophet and to the believers.* (Surah al-Munafiqun, 63:8)[164]

CHASTITY

Imam Ali, peace be on him, says: "Indeed the best thing which the human beings will take before Allah as specimen (of their conduct) besides belief in Allah and His pious slaves, is preservation of their honour, forbearance and patience".[165]

Imam Zaynul 'Ābidin, peace be on him, says: "After recognizing Allah there is nothing that Allah likes more than piety in the matter of one's womb and private parts and there is nothing that Allah likes more than that you should make request to Him".[166]

Imam Ali, peace be on him, says: "Sadness is better than begging from the people. Observing piety in privation is better than rejoicing in debauchery".[167]

Imam Muhammad Baqir, peace be on him, says: "Best worship is the chastity of womb and private parts".[168]

FORGIVENESS

The Holy Prophet, peace be on him and his progeny, says: "My Lord has recommended to me that I should forgive one who has oppressed me".[169]

"The dignity of our family lies in forgiving one who oppresses us and bestowing upon him who deprives us".[170]

"May I guide you to the manners which are best in this world as well as in the Hereafter? You should associate with one, who severs his connection with you; give to one, who deprives you; and forgive one, who oppresses you".[171]

FORGIVENESS AND REMISSION

A companion of the Holy Prophet says that the Holy Prophet addressed him and said: "May I inform you about the worst human being?" I said: "Yes, O Prophet of Allah!" He said: "It is one who does not forgive and does not overlook a lapse". Then he added: "May I inform you about one who is even worse than him?" I said: "Yes O Prophet of Allah!" He said: "It is he, from whose mischief the people are not safe, and who is good-for-nothing".[172]

The Holy Prophet, peace be on him and his progeny, says: "If Allah promises spiritual reward to anyone He honours the promise and if He theatens punishment for a deed He possesses the authority to forgive it".[173]

KNOWLEDGE AND LEARNING

The Holy Prophet, peace be on him and his progeny, says: "Confine your knowledge in writing".[174]

"Knowledge is not taken away from the people, but the scholars are taken away, till not even one of them remains. The people then select ignorant chiefs. They are asked to give judgements and they give judgment without requisite knowledge. They are misled themselves and also mislead others".[175]

"Make enquiries from the learned persons and talk with the sages and associate with the poor".[176]

"The treasures of knowledge are opened by asking questions. May Allah bless you. Ask questions because four persons are rewarded; the questioner, the speaker, the hearer and their friends".[177]

"I consider knowledge to be more valuable than worship and your best religion is humbleness and piety".[178]

Imam Ali, peace be on him, says: "If the bearers of knowledge bear it properly, Allah, the angels and those, who obey Allah, love them. However, if they acquire knowledge for worldly gains, Allah hates them and they become abject and despicable in the eyes of the people".[179]

Imam Muhammad Baqir, peace be on him, says: "A learned person, from whose knowledge others profit, is better than 70,000 worshippers".[180]

Imam Musa Kazim, peace be on him, says: "A small deed by a wise person is accepted and is twice as much, and a good deal of deeds done by an egotistic and ignorant person is rejected".[181]

TABLE MANNERS

The Holy Prophet, peace be on him and his progeny, says: "Allah keeps seventy diseases away from a person who begins his meals with salt, the most minor of them being leprosy".[182]

Imam Ali, peace be on him, says: "do not finish your meals hurriedly so that your companions may also eat their fill and also enjoy the food".[183]

"When you have finished your meals thank Allah for His having given you your daily bread and thank Him loudly so that another person may also thank Him and your spiritual reward may increase".[184]

"Do not fill your belly with food but stop eating while you are still a little hungry. If you do so the food will become wholesome for you. In fact good health lies in eating less and drinking less".[185]

VANITY

Imam Ali, peace be on him, says: "Those who are enamoured of the world are like the people who are residing in a land of affluence (this world) and wish to go to a place of famine and suffering (grave) and suffering (grave) and there is nothing more obnoxious and dreadful for them than separation from the place where they are and from where they are proceeding to another place".[186]

ANGER

The Holy Prophet, peace be on him and his progeny, says: "Do not be angry, and when you are angry sit down and think about the Power, which the Lord has over His slaves, and how much forbearing He is with regard to them. And when you are asked to obey Allah discard your anger and return to forbearance".[187]

A man requested the Holy Prophet to recommend him something. He said: "Don't be angry". The man repeated his request and the Holy Prophet gave him the same reply. Then he added: "Braveness does not lie in making your adversary fall on the ground. On the contrary a brave is one who can control himself while he is angry".[188]

Imam Ali, peace be on him, says: "There are four pillars of infidelity: (i) To be enamoured of the world (ii) To be timid (iii) To be filled with fury and (iv) Anger".[189]

NEGLIGENCE

The Holy Prophet, peace be on him and his progeny, says: "There are four signs of a negligent person: (i) Blindness (ii) Oversight (iii) Sportiveness and (iv) Forgetfulness".[190]

Imam Ali, peace be on him, says: "Dear son, pondering brings light and negligence brings darkness and dispute brings deviation".[191]

Imam Ja'far Sadiq, peace be on him, says: "O believers and confidants! Remind yourselves and think when the forgetful are negligent".[192]

WORRYING FOR SUSTENANCE

The Holy Prophet, peace be on him and his progeny, says: "Do not worry about tomorrow's sustenance for the daily share for every following day is destined".[193]

BACK-BITING

The Holy Prophet, peace be on him and his progeny, says: "When a person co-operates with the people, does not oppress them, tells them the truth, does not tell lies and makes promise with them and does not violate it, his manliness is perfect, his righteousness is evident, his spiritual reward is recorded and it is unlawful to speak ill of him in his absence".[194]

Imam Ali, peace be on him, says: "Let it not be that you should indulge in backbiting, becuase a Muslim does not speak ill of his brother in his absence when the Almighty Allah has forbidden it".[195]

CORRUPTION

Imam Ali, peace be on him, says: "The lapse of one who is being protected is the most serious lapse, and falsehood is an aching malady and corruption destroys much".[196]

WICKEDNESS

The Holy Prophet, peace be on him and his progeny, says: "There are four signs of a libertine: (i) Buffoonery (ii) Idle talk (iii) Aggression and (iv) Calumny".[197]

Imam Ali, peace be on him, says: "Speak the truth in all circumstances, befriend the pious, shun the wicked, keep aloof from the hypocrites and do not associate with the treacherous".[198]

"Do not be one of them about whom Allah has said: *They forgot Allah with the result that He made them forget themselves. It is they who are wicked.* (Surah al-Hashr, 59:19)".[199]

HARD-HEARTEDNESS

The Holy Prophet, peace be on him and his progeny, says: "Four characteristics bring about adversity:
(i) Dryness of the eyes (ii) Hard-heartedness (iii) Prolonged desire and (iv) Love for worldly things".[200]

Imam Muhammad Baqir, peace be on him, says: "Allah awards spiritual and corporeal punishment to His slaves like indigence, and laziness in the matter of worship and no punishment is worse than hard-heartedness".[201]

RETALIATION

Imam Ali, peace be on him, says: "Whoever fears retaliation refrains from oppressing the people".[202]

CONTENTMENT

Imam Ali, peace be on him, says: "Be contented so that you may become respectable".[203]

FALSEHOOD

Imam Ali, peace be on him, says: "Allah's slave cannot relish the taste of faith unless he gives up telling lies whether by way of jest or in earnest".[204]

"A Muslim should not befriend a liar".[205]

Imam Zaynun 'Ābidin, peace be on him, says: "Refrain from falsehood, whether it is small or big and whether it is spoken by way of jest or in earnest, because when a person tells a small lie he picks up courage to tell a big one".[206]

LAWFUL EARNING

The Holy Prophet, peace be on him and his progeny, says: "Whorship consists of seven parts and the highest of all is lawful earning".[207]

CURBING ONE'S ANGER

Imam Ali, peace be on him, says: "I rncommend to you to fear Allah, to offer prayers at the appropriate time, and to pay zakat, and I recommend to you to forgive the wrongdoings of others, and to curb your anger".[208]

Imam Ja'far Sadiq, peace be on him, says: "One who possesses three things is the master: (i) Curbing one's anger (ii) Forgiving an evil-doer (iii) Rendering assistance and observing relationship by means of life and wealth".[209]

"Three things are the proof of the magnanimity of a person: (i) Good nature (ii) Curbing one's anger and (iii) Keeping one's eyes downwards".[210]

INGRATITUDE

The Holy Prophet, peace be on him and his progeny, says: "Whichever habit a believer may acquire he does not acquire the habit of falsehood and treachery".[211]

Imam Ali, peace be on him, says: "Not being thankful for a blessing is meanness and associating oneself with an ignorant person is inauspicious".[212]

"Do not be ungrateful to your benefactor because not being grateful for a blessing is the worst blasphemy".[213]

BEGGING

Imam Muhammad Baqir, peace be on him, says: "If the beggar knew what is in begging, he whould not have begged at all, and if the person from whom the beggars beg knew what is in refusing a requnst, he would not have refused their request at all".[214]

OBSTINACY

The Holy Prophet, peace be on him and his progeny, says: "Refrain from obstinacy, for it begins with ingorance and ends in remorse".[215]

MANLINESS

Imam Ali, peace be on him, says: "The manliness of a person is not perfect unless he understands his religion, leads his life moderately, bears the hardships patiently and tolerates bitterness of his friends".[216]

Imam Ali, peace be on him, was asked: "What is manliness?" He replied: "That you should not do a thing secretly if you feel ashamed while doing it publicly".[217]

Imam Hasan, peace be on him, was asked as to what is

manliness. He replied: "To be anxious for religion and to reform wealth and to rise for the sake of rights".[218]

TO BRUSH THE TEETH

The Holy Prophet, peace be on him and is progeny, says: "It is necessary for you to brush your teeth regularly because brushing the teeth is a means of purity of mouth and pleasure of the Lord and light of the eyes. And your tooth-picking makes you dear to the angels, because the angels are annoyed with a man with stinking mouth, who does not pick his teeth after eating".[219]

CONSULTATION

Imam Ali, peace be on him, says: "A person, who thinks about or seeks good, is not distressed and one, who consults others in his affairs, does not have to regret".[220]

Imam Hasan, peace be on him, says: "People are rightly guided by holding mutual consultations".[221]

Imam Ja'far Sadiq, peace be on him, says: "A person has no excuse to offer in the matter of three things:
(i) Consultation with a benevolent person.
(ii) Dealing leniently with a jealous person.
(iii) Finding friends out of the people".[222]

KNOWLEDGE

Imam Muhammad Baqir, peace be on him, says: "No action is acceptable unless it is based on knowledge, and knowledge is useless unless it is accompanied by action. When a person acquires knowledge, it guides him to action and he, who is ignorant, does not perform any action".[223]

Imam Ja'far Sadiq, peace be on him, says: "The best worship is to recognize Allah and to be humble before Him".[224]

DECEIT

The Holy Prophet, pace be on him and his progeny, says:

"Let it not be that you should practise deceit, for the Almighty Allah has said: Deceit does not fall except upon one who practises it".[225]

HYPOCRISY

The Holy Prophet, peace be on him and his progeny, says: "There are four signs of a hypocrite: (i) He is of dissolute nature (ii) His tongue and heart differ from each other (iii) His words are not accompanied by action (iv) His interior is different from his exterior. Woe betide the hypocrite for he will burn in the Fire of Hell".[226]

Imam Ja'far Sadiq, peace be on him, says: "In whomsoever these three qualities are found is a hypocrite although he may fast and offer prayers: (i) When he speaks he tells a lie (ii) When he makes a promise he violates it (iii) When something is entrusted to him he commits breach of trust".[227]

TALE-BEARING

The Holy Prophet, peace be on him and his progeny, says: "Telling truth in the following three matters is bad: (i) Tale-bearing. (ii) Communicating information to a man about his wife. (iii) Refuting a person who claims to be pious".[228]

"Refrain from backbiting and tale-bearing, because backbiting nullifies the fast and tale-bearing is the cause of torture in the grave".[229]

DECEIT AND FRAUD

The Holy Prophet, peace be on him and his progeny, says: "One who defrauds or harms or deceives a Muslim is not one of us".[230]

KEEPING ONE'S PROMISE

The Holy Prophet, peace be on him and his progeny, says: "Whoever believes in Allah and in the Day of Judgement keeps his promise".[231]

Imam Ali, peace be on him, says: "There are certain signs of the pious by means of which they are identified: Truthfulness, repayment of trust, keeping the promise, observation of relationship, taking pity on the weak, associating less with women, being kind, good-naturedness, perfect forbearance and following knowledge, which is the source of proximity to Allah. How happy they are and how good is their end![232]

Imam Riza, peace be on him, says: "We are a family who consider our promise to be our debt, as was done by the Holy Prophet".[233]

GIFT

The Holy Prophet, peace be on him and his progeny, says: "Gift is of three kinds: (i) Gift for which something is given in return (ii) Gift for affinity and (iii) Gift for the sake of Allah".[234]

Imam Ja'far Sadiq, peace be on him, says: "My dearest friend is he, who gives a gift of my faults to me".[235]

NEIGHBOUR

Imam Ali, peace be on him, says: "Remember Allah in the matter of your neighbours, becuase the Holy Prophet, peace be on him and his progeny, made such continuous recommendations about them that we began to think that he might make them heirs".[236]

Imam Musa Kazim, peace be on him, says: "Good neighbourhood is not only harmlessness, but it is observing patience on being harmed by the neighbour".[237]

Imam Hasan Askari, peace be on him, says: "One of the onerous misfortunes is a neighbour who hides his neighbour's good acts but divulges his bad ones".[238]

DESPAIR

Imam Ali, peace be on him, says: "O people! The most wonderful thing in the body of man is his heart. Heart has stocks of wisdom as well as of things which are its opposite.

If hopefulness affords it an opportunity, covetousness humiliates it, and if its covetousness increases, greed kills it. And if despair seizes it, regret kills it. And if its anger arises, its indignation is severe. And if it prospers, it forgets self-control".[239]

* * * * *

Appendix-I

Hujajul Islam:
1. Husayn Āle Muhammad Talaqāni
2. Asadullah Khurāsāni
3. Muhammad Ja'fari
4. Husayn Haqqāni
5. Ahmad Muhaqqiq Rafsanjāni
6. Hasan Tāhiri Khurramābādi
7. Muhammad Imāmi Shirāzi
8. Muhammad Husayn Furqāni
9. Abdul Rahim Khalkhāli
10. Abbas Ali Amid Zanāni
11. Hasan Umidwār
12. Na'matullah Khādimi
13. Ahmad Mar'ashi
14. Mohsin Mujtahidi Shabistari
15. Husayn Wā'izy Arāki
16. Muhammad Khalkhāli
17. Mustafā Zamāni
18. Abdul Karim Qureshi
19. Hasan Sādiqi Arāki
20. Ata'ullāh Ma'navi
21. Muhammad Ali Girāmi
22. Ali Hujjati Kirmāni
23. Muhiyuddin Fazal
24. Mahdi Ibnur Rizā
25. Zaynul 'Ābidin Qurbāni
26. Ibrāhim Shabbiri
27. Abbās Majdul Husayni
28. Muhammad Ibāhim Haqdān
29. Muhammad Husayn Ranjbar
30. Ghulām Husayn Rahimi

Appendix-II

1. Usūlul Kāfi, p. 20
2. Muniatul Murīd, p. 9
3. Usūlul Kāfi, p. 15
4. Bihārul Anwār, vol. I, p. 55
5. Muniatul Murīd, p. 9
6. Surah al-Baqarah, 2:272
7. Bihārul Anwār, vol. I, p. 59
8. Muniatul Murīd, p. 11
9. Muniatul Murīd, p. 11
10. Bihārul Anwār, vol. I, p. 57
11. Bihārul Anwār, vol. I, p. 57
12. Nahjul Balaghah, p. 1113
13. Usūlul Kāfi, p. 15
14. Usūlul Kāfi, p. 22
15. Bihārul Anwār, vol. I, p. 111
16. Makārimul Akhlāq, p. 484
17. Bihārul Anwār, vol. I, p. 76
18. Surah al-Zumar, 39:9
19. Surah al-Mujadilah, 58:11
20. Nahjul Balaghah, p. 1146
21. Bihārul Anwār, vol. I, p. 76
22. Bihārul Anwār, vol. I, p. 82
23. Bihārul Anwār, vol. I, p. 65
24. Bihārul Anwār, vol. I, p. 64
25. Bihārul Anwār, vol. I, p. 61
26. Bihārul Anwār, vol. I, p. 64
27. Bihārul Anwār, vol. I, p. 82
28. Wasā'ilush Shi'ah, vol. II, p. 214
29. Wasā'ilush Shi'ah, vol. II, p. 214
30. Wasā'ilush Shi'ah, vol. II, p. 215
31. Usūlul Kāfi, p. 451
32. Usūlul Kāfi, p. 451
33. Bihārul Anwār, vol. I, p. 103
34. Nahjul Balaghah, p. 1245
35. Usūlul Kāfi, p. 452
36. Safinatul Bihār, vol. II, p. 532
37. Wasā'ilush Shi'ah, vol. II, p. 232
38. Tehzib, vol. I, p. 531
39. Surah Ale Imran, 3: 109
40. Surah Ale Imran, 3:113
41. Surah Luqman, 31:16
42. Surah al-Tawbah, 9:70
43. Furu'ul Kāfi, vol. I, p. 343
44. Furu'ul Kāfi, vol. I, p. 343
45. Tehzib, vol. II, p. 58
46. Furu'ul Kāfi, vol. I, p. 343
47. Furu'ul Kāfi, vol. I, p. 344
48. Usūlul Kāfi, p. 414
49. Usūlul Kāfi, p. 414
50. Usūlul Kāfi, p. 414
51. Bihārul Anwār, vol. XV, p. 136
52. Furu'ul Kāfi, vol. II, p. 94
53. Furu'ul Kāfi, vol. II, p. 94
54. Nahjul Balaghah, p. 1264
55. Nahjul Balaghah, p. 903
56. Furu'ul Kāfi, vol. II, p. 94
57. Furu'ul Kāfi, vol. II, p. 86
58. Furu'ul Kāfi, vol. II, p. 87
59. Wasā'ilush Shi'ah, vol. III, p. 123
60. Nahjul Balaghah, p. 1264
61. Makārimul Akhlāq, p. 252
62. Furu'ul Kāfi, vol. II, p. 94
63. Furu'ul Kāfi, vol. II, p. 94
64. Furu'ul Kāfi, vol. II, p. 88
65. Makārimul Akhlāq, p. 255
66. Furu'ul Kāfi, vol. II, p. 95
67. Furu'ul Kāfi, vol. II, p. 95
68. Wasā'ilush Shi'ah, vol. III, p. 130
69. Wasā'ilush Shi'ah, vol. III, p. 130
70. Makārimul Akhlāq, p. 256

71. Makārimul Akhlāq, p. 261
72. Makārimul Akhlāq, p. 260
73. Makārimul Akhlāq, p. 252
74. Makārimul Akhlāq, p. 254
75. Surah Bani Isra'il, 17:23 — 24
76. Surah Luqman, 31:14
77. Jāme'us Sa'ādāt, vol. II, p. 259
78. Jāme'us Sa'ādāt, vol. II, p. 259
79. Jāme'us Sa'ādāt, vol. II, p. 260
80. Jāme'us Sa'ādāt, vol. II, p. 261
81. Jāme'us Sa'ādāt, p. 260
82. Jāme'us Sa'ādāt, p. 260
83. Jāme'us Sa'ādāt, p. 257
84. Jāme'us Sa'ādāt, p. 257
85. Jāme'us Sa'ādāt, p. 258
86. Jāme'us Sa'ādāt, p. 262
87. Usūlul Kāfi, p. 390
88. Usūlul Kāfi, p. 476
89. Usūlul Kāfi, p. 476
90. Bihārul Anwār, vol. XVI, p. 80
91. Wasā'ilush Shi'ah, vol. II, p. 523
92. Wasā'ilush Shi'ah, vol. II, p. 523
93. Usūlul Kāfi, p. 390
94. Bihārul Anwār, vol. XV, p. 89
95. Mustadrakul Wasā'il, v. II, p. 407
96. Wasā'ilush Shi'ah, vol. II, p. 523
97. Wasā'ilush Shi'ah, p. 223
98. Usūlul Kāfi, p. 410
99. Usūlul Kāfi, p. 409
100. Usūlul Kāfi, p. 409
101. Wasā'ilush Shi'ah, vol. II, p. 524
102. Wasā'ilush Shi'ah, vol. II, p. 523
103. Bihārul Anwār, vol. XV, p. 90
104. Durarul Hikam, p. 496
105. Usūlul Kāfi, p. 390
106. Usūlul Kāfi, p. 391
107. Bihārul Anwār, vol. XV, p. 124

108. Bihārul Anwār, vol. III, p. 175
109. Surah al-Kahf, 18:44
110. Wasā'ilush Shi'ah, vol. I, p. 304
111. Surah Tawbah, 9:18
112. Bihārul Anwār, vol. XV, p. 131
113. Bihārul Anwār, vol. XV, p. 131
114. Bihārul Anwār, vol. XV, p. 131
115. Bihārul Anwār, vol. XV, p. 123
116. Nahjul Balaghah, p. 986
117. Jāme'us Sa'ādāt, vol. II, p. 221
118. Bihārul Anwār, vol. XV, p. 123
119. Usūlul Kāfi, p. 403
120. Bihārul Anwār, vol. XV, p. 123
121. Surah al-Hujrat, 49:10
122. Nahjul Balaghah, p. 968
123. Usūlul Kāfi, p. 414
124. Bihārul Anwār, vol. XV, p. 65
125. Bihārul Anwār, vol. XV, p. 61
126. Usūlul Kafi, p. 393
127. Usūlul Kāfi, p. 392
128. Bihārul Anwār, vol. XV, p. 41
129. Bihārul Anwār, vol. XV, p. 41
130. Bihārul Anwār, vol. XV, p. 41
131. Bihārul Anwār, vol. XV, p. 41
132. Bihārul Anwār, vol. XV, p. 41
133. Bihārul Anwār, vol. XV, p. 41
134. Nahjul Balaghah, p. 930
135. Rawzatul Kāfi, p. 87
136. Surah al-Baqarah, 2:104
137. Man la Yahzuruhul Faqih, p.151
138. Furu'ul Kāfi, vol. I, p. 140
139. Man la Yahzuruhul Faqih, p.151
140. Wasā'ilush Shi'ah, vol. II, p. 4
141. Nahjul Balaghah, p. 635
142. Kitāb Salim bin Qays, p. 15
143. Furu'ul Kāfi, vol. I, p. 142
144. Wasā'ilush Shi'ah, vol. II, p. 5

145. Man la Yahzuruhul Faqih, p. 152
146. Wasa'ilush Shi'ah, vol. II, p. 4
147. Surah al-Ma'arij, 70:25 — 26
148. Furu'ul Kafi, vol. I, p. 140
149. Furu'ul Kafi, vol. I, p. 156
150. Furu'ul Kafi, vol. I, p. 140
151; Furu'ul Kafi, vol. I, p. 140
152. Jame'us Sa'adat, vol. II, p. 143
153. Jame'us Sa'adat, vol. II, p. 144
154. Usulul Kafi, p. 412
155. Jame'us Sa'adat, vol. II, p. 144
156. Jame'us Sa'adat, vol. II, p. 144
157. Jame'us Sadat, vol. II, p. 145
158. Surah al-Baqarah, 2:262
159. Surah al-Baqarah, 2:264 — 265
160 Wasa'ilush Shi'ah, vol. II, p. 55
161. Majma'ul Bayan, vol. I, p. 375
162. Jame'us Sa'adat, vol. II, 131
163. Majma'ul Bayan, vol. I, p. 385
164. Surah al-Furqan, 25:67.
165. Wasa'ilush Shi'ah, vol. II, p. 534
166. Wasa'ilush Shi'ah, vol. II, p. 534
167. Surah Bani Isra'il, 17:26
168. Surah al-Baqarah, 2:275
169. Wasa'ilush Shi'ah, vol. II, p. 621
170. Mustadrakul Wasa'il, v. II, p. 490
171. Mustadrakul Wasa'il, v. II, p. 488
172. Mustadrakul Wasa'il, v. II, p. 488
173. Wasa'ilush Shi'ah, vol. II, p. 620
174. Furu'ul Kafi, vol. I, p. 353
175. Mustadrakul Wasa'il, v. II, p. 489
176. Furu'ul Kafi, vol. I, p. 353
177. Furu'ul Kafi, vol. I, p. 353
178. Mustadrakul Wasa'il, v. II, p. 489
179. Wasa'ilush Shi'ah, vol. II, p. 621
180. Mustadrakul Wasa'il, v. II, p. 489
181. Wasa'ilush Shi'ah, vol. II, p. 622

182. Wasa'ilush Shi'ah, vol. II, p. 621
183. Mustadrakul Wasa'il, v. II, p. 490
184 Surah al-Baqrah, 2:280
185. Furu'ul Kafi, vol. I, p. 354
186. Wasa'ilush Shi'ah, vol. II, p. 622
187. Mustadrakul Wasa'il, vol. II, p.491
188. Wasa'ilush Shi'ah, vol. II, p. 623
189. Mustadrakul Wasa'il, v. II, p. 491
190. Nahjul Balaghah, p. 1155
191. Surah Ale Imran, 3:134
192. Surah al-Nur, 24:22
193. Surah al-Shura, 26:40
194. Usulul Kafi, p. 361
195. Usulul Kafi, p. 361
196. Nahjul Balaghah, p.1082.
197. Nahjul Balaghah, p. 1102
198. Wasa'ilush Shi'ah, v. II, p. 224
199. Safinatul Bihar, vol. II, p. 207
200. Surah al-Baqarah, 2:8 — 20
201. Surah al-Nisa, 4:138 — 140
202. Surah Tawbah, 9:68
203. Usulul Kafi, p. 485
204. Usulul Kafi, p. 485
205. Biharul Anwar, vol. XV, p. 30
206. Biharul Anwar, vol. XV, p. 30
207. Biharul Anwar, vol. XV, p. 172
208. Biharul Anwar, vol. XV, p. 173
209.Surah al-Hujurat, 49:12
210. Ghurarul Hikam, vol. I, p. 433
211. Nahjul Balaghah, p. 1174
212. Nahjul Balaghah, p. 1244
213. Usulul Kafi, p. 394
214. Ghurarul Hikam, vol. I, p. 80
215. Jame'us Sa'adat, vol. I, p. 283
216. Surah Maryam, 19:41
217. Surah Yusuf, 12:46
218. Surah Maryam, 19:54

219. Surah Maryam, 19:56
220. Surah Maryam, 19:59
221. Usulul Kafi, p. 360
222. Usulul Kafi, p. 360
223. Wasa'ilush Shi'ah, vol. II, p. 222
224. Wasa'ilush Shi'ah, vol. II, p. 222
225. Wasa'ilush Shi'ah, vol. II, p. 222
226. Biharul Anwar, vol. XV, p. 125
227. Surah al-Nahl, 16:107
228. Surah al-Zumar, 39:3
229. Surah al-Zumar, 39:60
230. Wasa'ilush Shi'ah, vol. II, p. 233
231. Wasa'ilush Shi'ah, vol. II, p. 233
232. Jame'us Sa'adat, vol. II, p. 318
233. Jame'us Sa'adat, vol. II, p. 234
234. Wasa'ilush Shi'ah, vol. II, p. 234
235. Wasa'ilush Shi'ah, vol. II, p. 233
236. Jame'us Sa'adat, vol. II, p. 317
237. Safinatul Bihar, vol. II, p. 473
238. Mustadrakul Wasa'il, v. II, p. 100
239. Wasa'ilush Shi'ah, vol. II, p. 233
240. Biharul Anwar, vol. XV, p. 57
241. Surah al-Nisa, 4:58
242. Surah al-Mo'minun, 23:8
243. Surah al-Shu'ara, 26:107, 125 143, 163 and 178 and Surah al-Dukhan, 44:18
244. Biharul Anwar, vol. XV, p. 149
245. Wasa'ilush Shi'ah, vol. II, p. 203
246. Biharul Anwar, vol. XV, p. 148
247. Furu'ul Kafi, vol. I, p. 365
248. Biharul Anwar, vol. I, p. 41
249. Safinatul Bihar, vol. I, p. 41
250. Biharul Anwar, vol. XV, p. 148
251. Biharul Anwar, v. XVIII, p. 146
252. Biharul Anwar, v. XVIII, p. 145
253. Wasa'ilush Shi'ah, vol. I, p. 122
254. Biharul Anwar, v. XVIII, p. 146
255. Biharul Anwar, v. XVIII, p. 146
256. Furu'ul Kafi, vol. I, p..33
257. Furu'ul Kafi, vol. I, p. 33
258. Biharul Anwar, v. XVIII, p. 144
259. Wasa'ilush Shi'ah, vol. I, p. 166
260. Wasa'ilush Si'ah, vol. I, p. 169
261. Wasa'ilush Shi'ah, vol. I, p. 169
262. Surah al-Fatah, 48:29
263. Surah al-Balad, 90:17
264. Biharul Anwar, vol. XV, p. 112
265. Biharul Anwar, vol. XV, p. 51
266. Surah al-Kahf, 18:28
267. Biharul Anwar, vol. XV, p. 52
268. Biharul Anwar, vol. XV, p. 51
269. Safinatul Bihar, vol. I, p. 168
270. Biharul Anwar, vol. XV, p. 51
271. Wasa'ilush Shi'ah, vol. II, p. 205
272. Biharul Anwar, vol. XV, p. 52
273. Biharul Anwar, vol. XV, p. 51
274. Biharul Anwar, vol. XV, p. 52
275. Biharul Anwar, vol. XV, p. 52
276. Biharul Anwar, vol. XV, p. 52
277. Biharul Anwar, vol. XV, p. 52
278. Biharul Anwar, vol. XV, p. 52
279. Wasa'ilush Shi'ah, vol. II, p. 220
280. Mustadrakul Wasa'il, v. II, p. 83
281. Surah al-Qalam, 68:4
282. Surah Ale Imran, 3:159
283. Wasa'ilush Shi'ah, vol. II, p. 220
284. Wasa'ilush Shi'ah, vol. II, p. 221
285. Wasa'ilush Shi'ah, vol. II, p. 445
286. Wasa'ilush Shi'ah, vol. II, p. 221
287. Wasa'ilush Shi'ah, vol. II, p. 221
288. Wasa'ilush Shi'ah, vol. II, p. 221
289. Wasa'ilush Shi'ah, vol. II, p. 221
290. Wasa'ilush Shi'ah, vol. II, p. 221

291. Wasā'ilush Shi'ah, vol. II, p. 485
292. Wasā'ilush Shi'ah, vol. II, p. 221
293. Wasā'ilush Shi'ah, vol. II, p. 475
294. Wasā'ilush Shi'ah, vol. II, p. 222
295. Wasā'ilush Shi'ah, vol. II, p. 222
296. Surah al-Baqrah, 2:177
297. Surah Bani Isra'il, 17:34
298. Surah Maryam, 19:54
299. Safinatul Bihār, vol. II, p. 675
300. Safinatul Bihār, vol. II, p. 295
301. Jāme'us Sa'ādāt, vol. II, p. 327
302. Mustadrakul Wasā'il, v. II, p. 60
303. Bihārul Anwār, vol. XV, p. 143
304. Bihārul Anwār, vol. XV, p. 144
305. Bihārul Anwār, vol. XV, p. 144
306. Wasā'ilush Shi'ah, vol. II, p. 207
307. Wasā'ilush Shi'ah, vol. II, p. 207
308. Wasā'ilush Shi'ah, vol. II, p. 207
309. Bihārul Anwār, vol. XV, p. 146
310. Surah Ale Imran, 3:160
311. Surah Al-Shura, 42:38
312. Nahjul Balaghah, p. 1155
313. Bihārul Anwār, vol. XV, p. 146
314. Wasā'ilush Shi'ah, vol. II, p. 208
315. Wasā'ilush Shi'ah, vol. II, p 207
316. Wasāilush Shi'ah, vol. II, p. 207
317. Wasā'ilush Sh'ah, vol. II, p. 208
318. Wasā'ilush Shi'ah, vol. II, p. 207
319. Wasā'ilush Shi'ah, vol. II, p. 208
320. Wasā'ilush Shi'ah, vol. II, p. 208
321. Bihārul Anwār, vol. XV, p. 144
322. Wasā'ilush Shi'ah, vol. II, p. 208
323. Bihārul Anwār, vol. XVI, p. 57
324. Bihārul Anwār, vol. XV, p. 41
325. Wasā'ilush Shi'ah, vol. II, p. 182
326. Furu'ul Kāfi, vol. I, p. 244
327. Furu'ul Kāfi, vol. I, p. 244

328. Wasā'ilush Shi'ah, vol. II, p. 182
329. Bihārul Anwār, vol. XVI, p. 75
330. Bihārul Anwār, vol. SVI, p. 75
331. Bihārul Anwār, vol. XVI, p. 75
332. Bihārul Anwār, vol. XVI, p. 76
333. Bihārul Anwār, vol. XVI, p. 77
334. Bihārul Anwār, vol. XVI, p. 77
335. Wasā'ilush Shi'ah, vol. II, p 189
336. Usūlul Kāfi, p. 625
337. Usūlul Kāfi, p. 626
338. Wasā'ilush Shi'ah, vol. II, p. 193
339. Wasā'ilush Shi'ah, vol. II, p. 189
340. Wasā'ilush Shi'ah, vol. II, p. 191
341. Bihārul Anwār, vol. XV, p. 80
342. Nahjul Balaghah, p. 1187
343. Furu'ul Kāfi, vol. I, p. 329
344. Furu'ul Kāfi, vol. I, p. 327
345. Furu'ul Kāfi, vol. I, p. 329
346. Furu'ul Kāfi, vol. I, p. 327
347. Nahjul Balaghah, p. 85
348. Surah Ale Imran, 3:167
349. Mustadrakul Wasā'il, v. II, p. 242
350. Sharāy'ul Islam, p. 87
351. Wasā'ilush Shi'ah, vol. II, p. 417
352. Wasā'ilush Shi'ah, vol. II, p. 417
353. Mustadrakul Wasā'il, v. II, p. 245
354. Surah al-Baqarah, 2:189
355. Surah al-Baqarah, 2:192
356. Wasā'ilush Shi'ah, vol. II, p. 421
357. Mustadrakul Wasā'il, v. II, p. 265
358. Wasā'ilush Shi'ah, vol. II, p. 425
359. Wasā'ilush Shi'ah, vol. II, p. 424
360. Mustadrakul Wasā'il, v. II, p. 250
361. Wasā'ilush Shi'ah, vol. II, p. 425
362. Wasā'ilush Shi'ah, vol. II, p. 425
363. Wasā'ilush Shi'ah, vol. II, p. 425
364. Usūlul Kāfi, p. 451

365. Biharul Anwar, vol. XXIV, p. 7
366. Nahjul Balaghah, p. 1000
367. Biharul Anwar, vol. XXIV, p. 9
368. Surah al-Ma'ida, 5:47
369. Surah al-Ma'ida, 5:47
370. Surah al-Ma'ida, 5:44
371. Biharul Anwar, vol. XXIV, p. 6
372. Biharul Anwar, vol. XXIV, p. 6
373. Wasa'ilush Shi'ah, vol. III, p. 396
374. Nahul Balaghah, p. 877
375. Jawahirul Kalam, Kitabul Qaza'
376. Mustadrakul Wasa'il, v. III, p. 197
377. Mustadrakul Wasa'il, v. III, p. 195
378. Jawaharul Kalam, Kitabul Qaza'
379. Mustadrakul Wasa'il v. III, p. 197
380. Mustadrakul Wasa'il, v. III, p. 195
381. Jawaharul Kalam, Kitabul Qaza'
382. Jawaharul Kalam, Kitabul Qaza'
383. Wasa'ilush Shi'ah, vol. III, p. 398
384. Biharul Anwar, vol. XXIV, p. 9
385. Biharul Anwar, vol. XXIV, p. 6
386. Biharul Anwar, vol. XXIV, p. 9
387. Nahjul Balaghah, p. 1001
388. Man la Yahzuruhul Faqih, p. 353
389. Man la Yahzuruhul Faqih, p. 353
390. Furu'ul Kafi, vol. I, p. 347
391. Man la Yahzuruhul Faqih, p. 357
392. Ithna 'Ashriyah, p. 107
393. Man La Yahzuruhul Faqih, p. 353
394. Man la Yahzuruhul Faqih, p. 353
395. Wasa'ilush Shi'ah, vol. II, p. 529
396. Wasa'ilush Shi'ah, vol. II, p. 529
397. Biharul Anwar, vol. XXIII, p. 20
398. Furu'ul Kafi, vol. I, p. 404
399. Biharul Anwar, vol. XXIII, p. 19
400. Biharul Anwar, vol. XXIII, p. 19
401. Biharul Anwar, vol. XIV, p. 686
402. Biharul Anwar, vol. XIV, p. 686
403. Biharul Anwar, vol. XIV, p. 684
404. Wasa'ilush Shi'ah, vol. II, p. 193
405. Wasa'ilush Shi'ah, vol. II, p. 193
406. Biharul Anwar, vol. XVI, p. 82
407. Surah al-Zukhruf, 43:12 − 14
408. Biharul Anwar, vol. XXIII, p. 5
409. Ihya'ul 'Ulum, vol. II, p. 45
410. Biharul Anwar, vol. XXIII, p. 5
411. Furu'ul Kafi, vol. I, p. 370
412. Furu'ul Kafi, vol. I, p. 370
413. Furu'ul Kafi, vol. I, p. 370
414. Furu'ul Kafi, vol. I, p. 370
415. Surah al-Nur, 24:37
416. Mustadrakul Wasa'il, v. II, p. 464
417. Biharul Anwar, vol. XXIII, p. 5
418. Furu'ul Kafi, vol. I, p. 321
419. Furu'ul Kafi, vol. I, p. 372
420. Furu'ul Kafi, vol. I, p. 371
421. Mustadrakul Wasa'il, v. II, p. 467
422. Furu'ul Kafi, vol. I, p. 373
423. Wasa'ilush Shi'ah, vol. II, p. 576
424. Wasa'ilush Shi'ah, vol. II, p. 583
425. Wasa'ilush Shi'ah, vol. II, p. 582
426. Wasa'ilush Shi'ah, vol. II, p. 582
427. Furu'ul Kafi, vol. I, p. 372
428. Wasa'ilush Shi'ah, vol. II, p. 583
429. Furu'ul Kafi, vol. I, p. 386
430. Wasa'ilush Shi'ah, vol. II, p. 579
431. Furu'ul Kafi, vol. I, p. 374
432. Furu'ul Kafi, vol. I, p. 371
433. Nahjul Balaghah, p. 1008
434. Wasa'ilush Shi'ah, vol. III, p. 3
435. Wasa'ilush Shi'ah, vol. III, p. 2
436. Safinatul Bihar, vol. I, p. 561
437. Wasa'ilush Shi'ah, vol. III, p. 14
438. Surah al-Rum, 30:20

439. Safinatul Bihār, vol. I, p. 561
440. Wasā'ilush Shi'ah, vol. II, p. 2
441. Wasā'ilush Shi'ah, vol. II, p. 2
442. Man la Yahzuruhul Faqih, p. 410
443. Safinatul Bihār, vol. I, p. 561
444. Wasā'ilush Shi'ah, vol. III, p. 6
445. Wasā'ilush Shi'ah, vol. III, p. 6
446. Wasā'ilush Shi'ah, vol. III, p. 11
447. Safinatul Bihār, vol. II, p. 586
448. Surah al-Nisa, 4:24
449. Wasā'ilush Shi'ah, vol. III, p. 104
450. Wasā'ilush Shi'ah, vol. III, p. 104
451. Wasā'ilush Shi'ah, vol. III, p. 104
452. Furu'ul Kāfi, vol. II, p. 3
453. Furu'ul Kāfi, vol. III, p. 4
454. Furu'ul Kāfi, vol. III, p. 60
455. Furu'ul Kāfi, vol. III, p. 60
456. Makarimul Akhlāq, p. 247
457. Jāme'us Sa'ādāt, vol. II, p. 141
458. Jāme'us Sa'ādāt, vol. II, p. 139
459. Makarimul Akhlāq, p. 250
460. Jāme'us Sa'ādāt, vol. II, p. 141
461. Makarimul Akhlāq, p. 249
462. Jāme'us Sa'ādāt, vol. II, p. 141
463. Jāme'us Sa'ādāt, vol. II, p. 140
464. Makarimul Akhlāq, p. 245
465. Makarimul Akhlāq, p. 248
466. Furu'ul Kāfi, vol. II, p. 61
467. Makarimul Akhlāq, p. 248
468. Jāme'us Sa'ādāt, vol. II, p. 139
469. Makarimul Akhlāq, p. 246
470. Makarimul Akhlāq, p. 246
471. Makarimul Akhlāq, p. 107
472. Makarimul Akhlāq, p. 101
473. Makarimul Akhlāq, p. 91
474. Surah al-Mursalat, 77:37
475. Wasā'ilush Shi'ah, vol. III, p. 310

476. Mustadrakul Wasā'il, v. II, p. 131
477. Wasā'ilush Shi'ah, vol. III, p. 310
478. Wasā'ilush Shi'ah, vol. III, p. 310
479. Wasā'ilush Shi'ah, vol. III, p. 310
480. Man la Yahzuruhul Faqih, p. 467
481. Mustadrakul Wasā'il, v. III, p. 90
482. Mustadrakul Wasā'il, v. III, p. 90
483. Wasā'ilush Shi'ah, vol. I, p. 69
484. Wasā'ilush Shi'ah, vol. I, p. 71
485. Wasā'ilush Shi'ah, vol. I, p. 73
486. Wasā'ilush Shi'ah vol. I, p. 83
487. Wasā'ilush Shi'ah, vol. I, p. 83
488. Wasā'ilush Shi'ah, vol. I, p. 83
489. Wasā'ilush Shi'ah, vol. I, p. 82
490. Wasā'ilush Shi'ah, vol. I, p. 82
491. Wasā'ilush Shi'ah, vol. I, p. 84
492. Wasā'ilush Shi'ah, vol. I, p. 85
493. Wasā'ilush Shi'ah, vol. I, p. 99
494. Wasā'ilush Shi'ah, vol. I, p. 68
495. Wasā'ilush Shi'ah, vol. I, p. 66
496. Wasā'ilush Shi'ah, vol. I, p. 58
497. Wasā'ilush Shi'ah, vol. I, p. 279
498. Wasā'ilush Shi'ah, vol. I, p. 278
499. Wasā'ilush Shi'ah, vol. I, p. 319
500. Wasā'ilush Shi'ah, vol. I, p. 319
501. Wasā'ilush Shi'ah, vol. I, p. 320
502. Wasā'ilush Shi'ah, vol. I, p. 308
503. Wasā'ilush Shi'ah, vol. I, p. 308
504. Wasā'ilush Shi'ah, vol. I, p. 307
505. Wasā'ilush Shi'ah, vol. I, p. 307
506. Wasā'ilush Shi'ah, vol. I, p. 43
507. Wasā'ilush Shi'ah, vol. I, p. 45
508. Surah al-A'raf, 7:32
509. Wasā'ilush Shi'ah, vol. I, p. 277
510. Wasā'ilush Shi'ah, vol. I, p. 277
511. Wasā'ilush Shi'ah, vol. I, p. 283
512. Wasā'ilush Shi'ah, vol. I, p. 284

413. Wasā'ilush Shi'ah, vol. I, p. 278
514. Wasā'ilush Shi'ah, vol. I, p. 278
515. Wasā'ilush Shi'ah, vol. I, p. 281
516. Wasā'ilush Shi'ah, vol. I, p. 282
517. Wasā'ilush Shi'ah, vol. I, p. 284
518. Wasā'ilush Shi'ah, vol. I, p. 280
519. Wasā'ilush Shi'ah, vol. I, p. 279
520. Wasā'ilush Shi'ah, vol. I, p. 281
521. Wasā'ilush Shi'ah, vol. I, p. 283
522. Wasā'ilush Shi'ah, vol. I, p. 282
523. Wasā'ilush Shi'ah, vol. I, p. 280
524. Surah Bani Isra'il, 17:26
525. Surah Rum, 30:38
526. Usūlul Kāfi, p. 383
527. Usūlul Kāfi, p. 384
528. Usūlul Kāfi, p. 384
529. Nahjul Balagah, p. 930
530. Bihārul Anwār, vol. XV, p. 27
531. Usūlul Kāfi, p. 386
532. Usūlul Kāfi, p. 383
533. Bihārul Anwār, vol. XV, p. 242
534. Bihārul Anwār, vol. XV, p. 242
535. Bihārul Anwār, vol. XV, p. 242
536. Bihārul Anwār, vol. XV, p. 242
537. Bihārul Anwār, vol. XV, p. 241
538. Bihārul Anwār, vol. XV, p. 242
539. Furu'ul Kāki, vol. I, p. 176
540. Bihārul Anwār, vol. XV, p. 240
541. Bihārul Anwār, vol. XV, p. 240
542. Bihārul Anwār, vol. XV, p. 240
543. Bihārul Anwār, vol. XV, p. 240
544. Bihārul Anwār, vol. XV, p. 242
545. Bihārul Anwār, vol. XV, p. 241
546. Bihārul Anwār, vol. XV, p. 240
547. Bihārul Anwār, vol. XV, p. 240
548. Surah al-Baqarah, 2:220
549. Bihārul Anwār, vol. XV, p. 120
550. Bihārul Anwār, vol. XV, p. 120
551. Nahjul Balaghah, p. 968
552. Bihārul Anwār, vol. XV, p. 119
553. Bihārul Anwār, vol. XV, p. 119
554. Misbahul Faqih, vol. I, p. 806
555. Mustadrakul Wasā'il, vo. I, p. 117
556. Wasā'ilush Shi'ah, vol. I, p. 128
557. Wasā'ilush Shi'ah, vol. I, p. 134
558. Mustadrakul Wasā'il, v. I, p. 111
559. Mustadrakul Wasā'il, v.I, p. 128
560. Mustadrakul Wasā'il, v.I, p. 119
561. Mustadrakul Wasā'il, v. I, p. 118
562. Mustadrakul Wasā'il, v. I, p. 131
563. Mustadrakul Wasā'il, v. I, p. 147
564. Mustadrakul Wasā'il, v. I, p. 99
565. Mustadrakul Wasā'il, v.I, p. 132
566. Man la Yahzurhul Faqih, p 573
567. Mustadrakul Wasā'il, v. I, p. 129
568. Man la Yahzuruhul Faqih, p. 228
569. Wasā'ilush Shi'ah, vol. II, p. 194
570. Wasā'ilush Shi'ah, vol. II, p. 433
571. Wasā'ilush Shi'ah, vol. II, p. 50
572. Wasā'ilush Shi'ah, vol. II, p. 196
573. Man la Yahzuruhul Faqih, p. 228
574. Wasā'ilush Shi'ah, vol. II, p. 197
575. Man la Yahzuruhul Faqih, p. 229
576. Man la Yahzuruhul Faqih, p. 229
577. Wasā'ilush Shi'ah, vol. III, p. 415
578. Furu'ul Kāfi, vol. II, p. 230
579. Mustadrakul Wasā'il, v. III, p. 58
580. Wasā'ilush Shi'ah, vol. II, p. 203
581. Wasā'ilush Shi'ah, vol. III, p. 239
582. Wasā'ilush Shi'ah, vol. III, p. 247

Appendix-III

النصوص العربيه

١ - قَالَ رَسُولُ اللهِ ﷺ : اِنَّ اللهَ عَزَّ وَجَلَّ يَقُولُ: تَذَاكُرُ الْعِلْمِ بَيْنَ عِبَادِى مِمَّا يُحْيِى عَلَيْهِ الْقُلُوبَ الْمَيِّتَةَ اِذَاهُمْ اِنْتَهَوْا فِيهِ اِلَى اَمْرِى. (اُصُولِ كافى ص ٢٠)

٢ - قَالَ رَسُولُ اللهِ ﷺ : مَنْ جَاءَهُ الْمَوْتُ وَهُوَ يَطْلُبُ الْعِلْمَ لِيُحْيِىَ بِهِ الْاِسْلَامَ كَانَ بَيْنَهُ وَبَيْنَ الْاَنْبِيَاءِ دَرَجَةٌ وَاحِدَةٌ فِى الْجَنَّةِ. (منية المريد ص ٩)

٣ - قَالَ رَسُولُ اللهِ ﷺ : طَلَبُ الْعِلْمِ فَرِيضَةٌ عَلَى كُلِّ مُسْلِمٍ اَلَا اِنَّ اللهَ يُحِبُّ بُغَاةَ الْعِلْمِ. (اُصُول كافى ص ١٥)

٤ - قَالَ رَسُولُ اللهِ ﷺ : طَلَبُ الْعِلْمِ فَرِيضَةٌ عَلَى كُلِّ مُسْلِمٍ فَاطْلُبُوا الْعِلْمَ مِنْ مَظَانِّهِ وَاقْتَبِسُوهُ مِنْ اَهْلِهِ فَاِنَّ تَعْلِيمَهُ لِلهِ حَسَنَةٌ وَطَلَبَهُ عِبَادَةٌ وَ الْمُذَاكَرَةَ بِهِ تَسْبِيحٌ وَالْعَمَلَ بِهِ جِهَادٌ وَتَعْلِيمَهُ مَنْ يُعَلِّمُهُ صَدَقَةٌ وَبَذْلُهُ لِاَهْلِهِ قُرْبَةٌ اِلَى اللهِ..... (بحار الانوار ج ١ ص ٥٥)

٥ - قَالَ رَسُولُ اللهِ ﷺ : مَنْ طَلَبَ الْعِلْمَ فَهُوَ كَالصَّائِمِ

نَهَارَهُ الْقَائِمِ لَيْلَهُ وَاِنَّ بَابًا مِنَ الْعِلْمِ يَتَعَلَّمُهُ الرَّجُلُ خَيْرٌ لَهُ مِنْ اَنْ يَكُونَ اَبُوقُبَيْسٍ ذَهَبًا فَاَنْفَقَهُ فِي سَبِيلِ اللهِ.   (مُنيةُ المريدِ ص ٩)

٦ - قَوْلَهُ تَعَالَى : وَمَنْ يُؤْتَ الْحِكْمَةَ فَقَدْ اُوتِيَ خَيْرًا كَثِيْرًا   (سورةُ بقره: آيت   )

٧ - قَالَ السَّجَّادُ عَلَيْهِ السَّلَامُ : لَوْ يَعْلَمُ النَّاسُ مَا فِي طَلَبِ الْعِلْمِ لَطَلَبُوهُ وَلَوْ بِسَفْكِ الْمُهَجِ وَخَوْضِ اللُّجَجِ.   (بحارُ الانوارِ ج ١ ص ٥٩)

٨ - قَالَ رَسُولُ اللهِ ﷺ : مَنْ سَلَكَ طَرِيقًا يَطْلُبُ فِيهِ عِلْمًا سَهَّلَ اللهُ لَهُ طَرِيقًا اِلَى الْجَنَّةِ.   (مُنيةُ المريدِ ص ١١)

٩ - قَالَ رَسُولُ اللهِ ﷺ : خَيْرُ مَا تَخَلَّفَ الرَّجُلُ مِنْ بَعْدِهِ ثَلٰثٌ : وَلَدٌ صَالِحٌ يَدْعُوْ لَهُ وَصَدَقَةٌ تَجْرِى يَبْلُغُهُ اَجْرُهَا وَعِلْمٌ يُعْمَلُ بِهِ مِنْ بَعْدِهِ.   (مُنيةُ المريدِ ص ١١)

١٠ - قَالَ رَسُولُ اللهِ ﷺ : مَنْ اَحَبَّ اَنْ يَنْظُرَ اِلَى عُتَقَاءِ اللهِ مِنَ النَّارِ فَلْيَنْظُرْ اِلَى الْمُتَعَلِّمِينَ.   (بحارُالانوارِ ج ١ ص ٥٨)

١١ - قَالَ رَسُولُ اللهِ ﷺ : اُطْلُبُوا الْعِلْمَ وَلَوْ بِالصِّيْنِ.   (بحارُ الانوارِ ج ١ ص ٥٧)

١٢ - قَالَ عَلِيٌّ عَلَيْهِ السَّلَامُ : وَلَا يَسْتَحْيِنَّ اَحَدٌ اِذَا لَمْ يَعْلَمِ الشَّئَ اَنْ يَتَعَلَّمَهُ.   (نهجُ البلاغه ص ١١١٣)

١٣- قَالَ عَلِيٌّ ﷺ: أَيُّهَا النَّاسُ اعْلَمُوا أَنَّ كَمَالَ الدِّينِ طَلَبُ الْعِلْمِ وَالْعَمَلُ بِهِ أَلَا وَإِنَّ طَلَبَ الْعِلْمِ أَوْجَبُ عَلَيْكُمْ مِنْ طَلَبِ الْمَالِ ...   (أصول كافى ص ١٥)

١٤- قَالَ الصَّادِقُ ﷺ: الْعِلْمُ مَقْرُونٌ إِلَى الْعَمَلِ فَمَنْ عَلِمَ عَمِلَ وَمَنْ عَمِلَ عَلِمَ وَالْعِلْمُ يَهْتِفُ بِالْعَمَلِ فَإِنْ أَجَابَهُ وَإِلَّا ارْتَحَلَ عَنْهُ.   (اصول كافى ص ٢٢)

١٥- قَالَ الصَّادِقُ ﷺ: مَنْ أَرَادَ الْحَدِيثَ لِمَنْفَعَةِ الدُّنْيَا لَمْ يَكُنْ لَهُ فِي الْآخِرَةِ نَصِيبٌ وَمَنْ أَرَادَ بِهِ خَيْرَ الْآخِرَةِ أَعْطَاهُ خَيْرَ الدُّنْيَا وَالْآخِرَةِ.   (بحار الانوار ج ١ ص ١١١)

١٦- قَالَ السَّجَّادُ ﷺ: حَقُّ سَائِسِكَ بِالْعِلْمِ التَّعْظِيمُ لَهُ وَالتَّوْقِيرُ لِمَجْلِسِهِ وَحُسْنُ الِاسْتِمَاعِ إِلَيْهِ وَالْإِقْبَالُ عَلَيْهِ وَأَنْ لَا تَرْفَعَ عَلَيْهِ صَوْتَكَ وَلَا تُجِيبَ أَحَدًا يَسْأَلُهُ عَنْ شَيْءٍ حَتَّى يَكُونَ هُوَ الَّذِي يُجِيبُ وَلَا تُحَدِّثَ فِي مَجْلِسِهِ أَحَدًا وَلَا تَغْتَابَ عِنْدَهُ أَحَدًا وَأَنْ تَدْفَعَ عَنْهُ إِذَا ذُكِرَ عِنْدَكَ بِسُوءٍ وَأَنْ تَسْتُرَ عُيُوبَهُ وَتُظْهِرَ مَنَاقِبَهُ وَلَا تُجَالِسَ لَهُ عَدُوًّا وَلَا تُعَادِيَ لَهُ وَلِيًّا فَإِذَا فَعَلْتَ ذَلِكَ شَهِدَ لَكَ مَلَائِكَةُ اللَّهِ تَعَالَى بِأَنَّكَ قَصَدْتَهُ وَتَعَلَّمْتَ عِلْمَهُ لِلَّهِ جَلَّ اسْمُهُ لَا لِلنَّاسِ ......

...... وَأَمَّا حَقُّ رَعِيَّتِكَ بِالْعِلْمِ أَنْ تَعْلَمَ أَنَّ اللَّهَ عَزَّ وَجَلَّ إِنَّمَا جَعَلَكَ قَيِّمًا لَهُمْ فِيمَا آتَاكَ مِنَ الْعِلْمِ وَفَتَحَ لَكَ مِنْ خَزَائِنِهِ فَإِنْ أَحْسَنْتَ فِي تَعْلِيمِ النَّاسِ وَلَمْ تَخْرَقْ

بهم ولم تضجر عليهم (ولم تتجبر عليهم خ ل)
زادك الله من فضله وان انت منعت الناس من علمك
او خرقت بهم عند طلبهم العلم منك كان حقاً على
الله عزوجل ان يسلبك العلم وبهائه ويسقط من
القلوب محلك .   (مكارم الاخلاق ص ٤٨٤)

١٧ - قال رسول الله ﷺ : علماء امتي كانبياء بني اسرائيل
(بحار الانوار ج ١ ص ٧٦)

١٨ - قال الله تعالى : قل هل يستوي الذين يعلمون و
الذين لا يعلمون انما يتذكر اولو الالباب.
(سورة الزمر : آيت ٩)

١٩ - قال الله تعالى : يرفع الله الذين امنوا منكم والذين
اوتوا العلم درجات.   (سوره مجادله : آيت ١١)

٢٠ - قال امير المؤمنين ﷺ : والعلماء باقون ما بقي الدهر
اعيانهم مفقودة وامثالهم في القلوب موجودة.
(نهج البلاغه ص ١١٤٦)

٢١ - قال رسول الله ﷺ : نوم العالم افضل من الف
ركعة يصليها العابد.   (بحار الانوار ج ١ ص ٧٦)

٢٢ - قال رسول الله ﷺ : (في حديث) : والعالم بمنزلة
الصائم القائم المجاهد في سبيل الله واذا مات
العالم انثلم في الاسلام ثلمة لا تنسد الى يوم القيامة
(بحار الانوار ج ١ ص ٨٢)

٢٣ ـ قَالَ أَمِيرُ المُؤْمِنِينَ عَلَيْهِ السَّلامُ: (في حديث): وَرَكْعَتَانِ مِنْ عَالِمٍ خَيْرٌ مِنْ سَبْعِينَ رَكْعَةً مِنْ جَاهِلٍ.

(بحار الانوار ج ١ ص ٧٥)

٢٤ ـ قَالَ رَسُولُ اللهِ صَلَّى اللهُ عَلَيْهِ وَآلِهِ: مُجَانَسَةُ الْعُلَمَاءِ عِبَادَةٌ.

(بحار الانوار ج ١ ص ٦٤)

٢٥ ـ قَالَ رَسُولُ اللهِ صَلَّى اللهُ عَلَيْهِ وَآلِهِ: اَلنَّظَرُ إِلَى وَجْهِ الْعَالِمِ عِبَادَةٌ.

(بحار الانوار ج ١ ص ٦١)

٢٦ ـ قَالَ لُقْمَانُ لِابْنِهِ: يَا بُنَيَّ جَالِسِ الْعُلَمَاءَ وَزَاحِمْهُمْ بِرُكْبَتَيْكَ فَإِنَّ اللهَ عَزَّ وَجَلَّ يُحْيِي الْقُلُوبَ بِنُورِ الْحِكْمَةِ كَمَا يُحْيِي الْأَرْضَ بِوَابِلِ السَّمَاءِ. (بحار الانوار ج ١ ص ٦٤)

٢٧ ـ قَالَ الصَّادِقُ عَلَيْهِ السَّلامُ: مَنْ أَكْرَمَ فَقِيهًا مُسْلِمًا لَقِيَ اللهَ يَوْمَ الْقِيَامَةِ وَهُوَ عَنْهُ رَاضٍ وَمَنْ أَهَانَ فَقِيهًا مُسْلِمًا لَقِيَ اللهَ يَوْمَ الْقِيَامَةِ وَهُوَ عَلَيْهِ غَضْبَانُ.

(بحار الانوار ج ١ ص ٨٢)

٢٨ ـ قَالَ الصَّادِقُ عَلَيْهِ السَّلامُ: إِنَّ مِنْ إِجْلَالِ اللهِ عَزَّ وَجَلَّ إِجْلَالُ الشَّيْخِ الْكَبِيرِ. (وسائل الشيعة ج ٢ ص ٢١٤)

٢٩ ـ قَالَ الصَّادِقُ عَلَيْهِ السَّلامُ: مِنْ إِجْلَالِ اللهِ عَزَّ وَجَلَّ إِجْلَالُ الْمُؤْمِنِ ذِي الشَّيْبَةِ. (وسائل الشيعة ج ٢ ص ٢١٤)

٣٠ ـ قَالَ رَسُولُ اللهِ صَلَّى اللهُ عَلَيْهِ وَآلِهِ: إِذَا أَتَاكُمْ كَرِيمُ قَوْمٍ فَأَكْرِمُوهُ.

(وسائل الشيعة ج ٢ ص ٢١٥)

٣١ ـ قَالَ أَمِيرُ الْمُؤْمِنِينَ عَلَيْهِ السَّلامُ: إِيَّاكُمْ وَالْمِرَاءَ وَالْخُصُومَةَ

فَإِنَّهُمَا يُمرِضَانِ الْقُلُوبَ عَلَى الْإِخْوَانِ وَيُنْبِتُ عَلَيْهِمَا النِّفَاقَ. (أصول كافى ص ٤٥١)

٣٢ - قَالَ الصَّادِقُ عَلَيْهِ السَّلَامُ: إِيَّاكُمْ وَالْمُشَادَّةَ فَإِنَّهَا تُورِثُ الْمَعَرَّةَ وَتُظْهِرُ الْعَوْرَةَ. (أصول كافى ص ٤٥١)

٣٣ - قَالَ الصَّادِقُ عَلَيْهِ السَّلَامُ: مَنْ لَاحَى الرِّجَالَ ذَهَبَتْ مُرُوَّتُهُ. (بحار الانوار ج ١ ص ١٠٣)

٣٤ - قَالَ أَمِيرُ الْمُؤْمِنِينَ عَلَيْهِ السَّلَامُ: مَنْ ضَنَّ بِعِرْضِهِ فَلْيَدَعِ الْمِرَاءَ. (نهج البلاغه ص ١٢٤٥)

٣٥ - قَالَ الصَّادِقُ عَلَيْهِ السَّلَامُ: إِيَّاكُمْ وَالْخُصُومَةَ فَإِنَّهَا تَشْتَغِلُ الْقَلْبَ وَتُورِثُ النِّفَاقَ وَتَكْسِبُ الضَّغَائِنَ. (أصول كافى ص ٤٥٢)

٣٦ - قَالَ الصَّادِقُ عَلَيْهِ السَّلَامُ: لَايَسْتَكْمِلُ عَبْدٌ حَقِيقَةَ الْإِيمَانِ حَتَّى يَدَعَ الْمِرَاءَ وَإِنْ كَانَ مُحِقّاً. (سفينة البحار ج ٢ ص ٥٣٢)

٣٧ - قَالَ رَسُولُ اللهِ صَلَّى اللهُ عَلَيْهِ وَآلِهِ: أَنَا زَعِيمُ بَيْتٍ فِي أَعْلَى الْجَنَّةِ وَبَيْتٍ فِي وَسَطِ الْجَنَّةِ وَبَيْتٍ فِي رِيَاضِ الْجَنَّةِ لِمَنْ تَرَكَ الْمِرَاءَ وَإِنْ كَانَ مُحِقّاً. (وسائل الشيعه ج ٢ ص ٢٣٢)

٣٨ - قَالَ أَبُو عَبْدِ اللهِ عَلَيْهِ السَّلَامُ (فِي حَدِيثٍ): وَالْجِدَالُ قَوْلُ الرَّجُلِ لَا وَاللهِ وَبَلَى وَاللهِ. (تهذيب ج ١ ص ٥٣١)

٣٩ - قَالَ اللهُ تَعَالَى: كُنْتُمْ خَيْرَ أُمَّةٍ أُخْرِجَتْ لِلنَّاسِ تَأْمُرُونَ بِالْمَعْرُوفِ وَتَنْهَوْنَ عَنِ الْمُنْكَرِ. (سورة آل عمران: آيت ١١٠)

٤٠ - قَالَ اللهُ تَعَالَى : يُؤْمِنُونَ بِاللهِ وَالْيَوْمِ الْآخِرِ وَيَأْمُرُونَ بِالْمَعْرُوفِ وَيَنْهَوْنَ عَنِ الْمُنْكَرِ وَيُسَارِعُونَ فِي الْخَيْرَاتِ وَأُولٰٓئِكَ مِنَ الصَّالِحِينَ . (سُورَةُ آلِ عِمْرَانَ: آيَت ١١٤)

٤١ - قَالَ اللهُ تَعَالَى (حِكَايَةً عَنْ لُقْمَانَ) : يَا بُنَيَّ أَقِمِ الصَّلَوٰةَ وَأْمُرْ بِالْمَعْرُوفِ وَانْهَ عَنِ الْمُنْكَرِ وَاصْبِرْ عَلَىٰ مَا أَصَابَكَ إِنَّ ذَٰلِكَ مِنْ عَزْمِ الْأُمُورِ . (سُورَةُ لُقْمَانَ: آيَت ١٧)

٤٢ - قَالَ اللهُ تَعَالَى : وَالْمُؤْمِنُونَ وَالْمُؤْمِنَاتُ بَعْضُهُمْ أَوْلِيَاءُ بَعْضٍ يَأْمُرُونَ بِالْمَعْرُوفِ وَيَنْهَوْنَ عَنِ الْمُنْكَرِ وَيُقِيمُونَ الصَّلَوٰةَ وَيُؤْتُونَ الزَّكَوٰةَ وَيُطِيعُونَ اللهَ وَرَسُولَهُ أُولٰئِكَ سَيَرْحَمُهُمُ اللهُ إِنَّ اللهَ عَزِيزٌ حَكِيمٌ .

(سُورَه تَوبَه: آيَت ٧١)

٤٣ - عَنْ مُحَمَّدِ بْنِ عَرَفَةَ قَالَ : سَمِعْتُ أَبَا الْحَسَنِ عليه السلام يَقُولُ : لَتَأْمُرُنَّ بِالْمَعْرُوفِ وَلَتَنْهُنَّ عَنِ الْمُنْكَرِ أَوْ لَيَسْتَعْمَلَنَّ عَلَيْكُمْ شِرَارُكُمْ فَيَدْعُو خِيَارُكُمْ فَلَا يُسْتَجَابُ لَهُمْ .

(فُرُوعِ كَافِي ج ١ ص ٣٤٣)

٤٤ - قَالَ أَمِيرُ الْمُؤْمِنِينَ عليه السلام (فِي خُطْبَةٍ) : إِنَّمَا هَلَكَ مَنْ كَانَ قَبْلَكُمْ حَيْثُ مَا عَمِلُوا مِنَ الْمَعَاصِي وَلَمْ يَنْهَهُمُ الرَّبَّانِيُّونَ وَالْأَحْبَارُ عَنْ ذَٰلِكَ ......

(فُرُوعِ كَافِي ج ١ ص ٣٤٣)

٤٥ - قَالَ رَسُولُ اللهِ صلى الله عليه وآله : لَا يَزَالُ النَّاسُ (أُمَّتِي) بِخَيْرٍ مَا أَمَرُوا بِالْمَعْرُوفِ وَنَهَوْا عَنِ الْمُنْكَرِ وَتَعَاوَنُوا عَلَى الْبِرِّ

فَاِذَا لَمْ يَفْعَلُوا ذٰلِكَ نُزِعَتْ مِنْهُمُ الْبَرَكَاتُ وَسُلِّطَ بَعْضُهُمْ عَلَى بَعْضٍ وَلَمْ يَكُنْ لَهُمْ نَاصِرٌ فِي الْأَرْضِ وَلَا فِي السَّمَاءِ
(تهذيب ج ٢ ص ٥٨)

٤٦ - قَالَ الْبَاقِرُ عليه السلام (فِي حَدِيثٍ): أَوْحَى اللّٰهُ عَزَّ وَجَلَّ اِلَى شُعَيْبِ النَّبِيِّ اِنِّي مُعَذِّبٌ مِنْ قَوْمِكَ مِائَةَ أَلْفٍ: أَرْبَعِينَ أَلْفًا مِنْ شِرَارِهِمْ وَسِتِّينَ أَلْفًا مِنْ خِيَارِهِمْ. فَقَالَ عليه السلام: يَا رَبِّ هٰؤُلَاءِ الْأَشْرَارُ فَمَا بَالُ الْأَخْيَارِ؟ فَأَوْحَى اللّٰهُ عَزَّ وَجَلَّ اِلَيْهِ: دَاهَنُوا أَهْلَ الْمَعَاصِي وَلَمْ يَغْضَبُوا لِغَضَبِي.
(فروع كافي ج ١ ص ٣٤٣)

٤٧ - قَالَ أَمِيرُ الْمُؤْمِنِينَ عليه السلام أَمَرَنَا رَسُولُ اللّٰهِ صلى الله عليه وآله أَنْ نَلْقَى أَهْلَ الْمَعَاصِي بِوُجُوهٍ مُكْفَهِرَّةٍ.
(فروع كافي ج ١ ص ٣٤٤)

٤٨ - قَالَ رَسُولُ اللّٰهِ صلى الله عليه وآله: اِنَّ أَعْظَمَ النَّاسِ مَنْزِلَةً عِنْدَ اللّٰهِ يَوْمَ الْقِيَامَةِ أَمْشَاهُمْ فِي أَرْضِهِ بِالنَّصِيحَةِ لِخَلْقِهِ.
(أصول كافي ص ٤١٤)

٤٩ - قَالَ رَسُولُ اللّٰهِ صلى الله عليه وآله: لِيَنْصَحِ الرَّجُلُ مِنْكُمْ أَخَاهُ كَنَصِيحَتِهِ لِنَفْسِهِ.
(أصول كافي ص ٤١٤)

٥٠ - عَنْ سُفْيَانَ قَالَ سَمِعْتُ أَبَا عَبْدِ اللّٰهِ عليه السلام يَقُولُ: عَلَيْكَ بِالنُّصْحِ لِلّٰهِ فِي خَلْقِهِ فَلَنْ تَلْقَاهُ بِعَمَلٍ أَفْضَلَ مِنْهُ.
(أصول كافي ص ٤١٤)

٥١ - عَبْدُ الرَّحْمٰنِ بْنُ حَجَّاجٍ قَالَ سَمِعْتُ الصَّادِقَ عليه السلام

يَقُولُ: مَنْ رَأى أخاهُ عَلى أمرٍ يَكْرَهُهُ فَلَمْ يَرُدَّهُ عَنْهُ وَهُوَ يَقْدِرُ عَلَيْهِ فَقَدْ خانَهُ. ... (بحارالانوار ج١٥ كتاب العشرة ص١٣٦)

٥٢ - قَالَ رَسُولُ اللهِ ﷺ: يَلْزَمُ الْوالِدَيْنِ مِنَ الْعُقُوقِ لِوَلَدِهِما ما يَلْزَمُ الْوَلَدَ لَهُما مِنْ عُقُوقِهِما. (فروع كافي ج٢ ص٩٤)

٥٣ - قَالَ رَسُولُ اللهِ ﷺ: رَحِمَ اللهُ وَالِدَيْنِ أعانا وَلَدَهُما عَلى بِرِّهِما. (فروع كافي ج٢ ص٩٤)

٥٤ - قَالَ عَلِيٌّ ﷷ: إنَّ لِلْوَلَدِ عَلَى الْوالِدِ حَقًّا وَإنَّ لِلْوالِدِ عَلَى الْوَلَدِ حَقًّا. (نهج البلاغه ص١٢٦٤)

٥٥ - قَالَ عَلِيٌّ ﷷ: وَإنَّما قَلْبُ الْحَدَثِ كَالْأرْضِ الْخَالِيَةِ ما أُلْقِيَ فِيها مِنْ شَيْءٍ قَبِلَتْهُ. (نهج البلاغه ص٩٠٣)

٥٦ - قَالَ رَجُلٌ يا رَسُولَ اللهِ: ما حَقُّ ابْنِي هذا؟ قَالَ ﷺ: تُحْسِنُ اسْمَهُ وَأدَبَهُ وَضَعْهُ مَوْضِعًا حَسَنًا. (فروع كافي ج٢ ص٩٤)

٥٧ - قَالَ الْبَاقِرُ ﷷ: أصْدَقُ الأسْماءِ ما سُمِّيَ بِالْعُبُودِيَّةِ وَأفْضَلُها أسْماءُ الأنْبِياءِ. (فروع كافي ج٢ ص٨٦)

٥٨ - قَالَ الْبَاقِرُ ﷷ: إنَّ أبْغَضَ الأسْماءِ إلى اللهِ حارِثٌ وَمالِكٌ وَخالِدٌ. (فروع كافي ج٢ ص٨٧)

٥٩ - قَالَ رَسُولُ اللهِ ﷺ: إذا سَمَّيْتُمُ الْوَلَدَ مُحَمَّدًا فَأكْرِمُوهُ وَأوْسِعُوا لَهُ فِي الْمَجْلِسِ وَلا تُقَبِّحُوا لَهُ وَجْهًا. (وسائل الشيعه ج٣ ص١٢٣)

٦٠ - قَالَ عَلِيٌّ ﷷ: وَحَقُّ الْوَلَدِ عَلَى الْوالِدِ أنْ يُحْسِنَ اسْمَهُ

205

وَيُحْسِنَ أَدَبَهُ وَيُعَلِّمَهُ الْقُرْآنَ. (نهج البلاغه ص ١٢٦٤)

٦١ - عَنْ أَحَدِهِمَا عَلَيْهِمَا السَّلامُ قَالَ: ... حَتَّى يَتِمَّ لَهُ خَمْسُ سِنِينَ، ثُمَّ يُقَالُ لَهُ أَيُّهُمَا يَمِينُكَ وَأَيُّهُمَا شِمَالُكَ فَإِذَا عَرَفَ ذَلِكَ حَوَّلَ وَجْهَهُ إِلَى الْقِبْلَةِ وَيُقَالُ لَهُ: اسْجُدْ ثُمَّ يُتْرَكُ حَتَّى يَتِمَّ لَهُ سِتُّ سِنِينَ فَإِذَا تَمَّ لَهُ سِتُّ سِنِينَ عَلِّمَ الرُّكُوعَ وَالسُّجُودَ حَتَّى يَتِمَّ لَهُ سَبْعُ سِنِينَ فَإِذَا تَمَّ لَهُ سَبْعُ سِنِينَ قِيلَ لَهُ: اغْسِلْ وَجْهَكَ وَكَفَّيْكَ فَإِذَا غَسَلَهُمَا قِيلَ لَهُ: صَلِّ، ثُمَّ يُتْرَكُ حَتَّى يَتِمَّ لَهُ تِسْعٌ فَإِذَا تَمَّتْ لَهُ عُلِّمَ الْوُضُوءَ وَضُرِبَ عَلَيْهِ وَأُمِرَ بِالصَّلَوةِ وَضُرِبَ عَلَيْهَا. (مكارم الأخلاق ص ٢٥٤)

٦٢ - قَالَ أَمِيرُ الْمُؤْمِنِينَ عَلَيْهِ السَّلامُ: قَالَ رَسُولُ اللهِ صَلَّى اللهُ عَلَيْهِ وَآلِهِ: عَلِّمُوا أَوْلَادَكُمُ السِّبَاحَةَ وَالرِّمَايَةَ. (فروع كافى ج ٢ ص ٩٤)

٦٣ - قَالَ أَبُو عَبْدِ اللهِ عَلَيْهِ السَّلامُ: الْغُلَامُ يَلْعَبُ سَبْعَ سِنِينَ وَيَتَعَلَّمُ الْكِتَابَ سَبْعَ سِنِينَ وَيَتَعَلَّمُ الْحَلَالَ وَالْحَرَامَ سَبْعَ سِنِينَ. (فروع كافى ج ٢ ص ٩٤)

٦٤ - قَالَ رَسُولُ اللهِ صَلَّى اللهُ عَلَيْهِ وَآلِهِ: مَنْ وُلِدَ لَهُ مَوْلُودٌ فَلْيُؤَذِّنْ فِى أُذُنِهِ الْيُمْنَى بِأَذَانِ الصَّلَوةِ وَلْيُقِمْ فِى الْيُسْرَى فَإِنَّهَا عِصْمَةٌ مِنَ الشَّيْطَانِ الرَّجِيمِ. (فروع كافى ج ٢ ص ٨٨)

٦٥ - قَالَ رَسُولُ اللهِ صَلَّى اللهُ عَلَيْهِ وَآلِهِ: الْوَلَدُ سَيِّدٌ سَبْعَ سِنِينَ وَعَبْدٌ سَبْعَ سِنِينَ وَوَزِيرٌ سَبْعَ سِنِينَ. (مكارم الأخلاق ص ٢٥٥)

٦٦ - قَالَ رَسُولُ اللهِ صَلَّى اللهُ عَلَيْهِ وَآلِهِ: مَنْ قَبَّلَ وَلَدَهُ كَتَبَ اللهُ لَهُ حَسَنَةً. (فروع كافى ج ٢ ص ٩٥)

٦٧ـ قَالَ الصَّادِقُ عَلَيْهِ السَّلَامُ: جَاءَ رَجُلٌ إِلَى النَّبِيِّ صَلَّى اللهُ عَلَيْهِ وَآلِهِ فَقَالَ مَا قَبَّلْتُ صَبِيًّا قَطُّ فَلَمَّا وَلَّى قَالَ رَسُولُ اللهِ صَلَّى اللهُ عَلَيْهِ وَآلِهِ هٰذَا رَجُلٌ عِنْدِي أَنَّهُ مِنْ أَهْلِ النَّارِ.

(فروع كافي ج٢ ص٩٥)

٦٨ـ قَالَ رَسُولُ اللهِ صَلَّى اللهُ عَلَيْهِ وَآلِهِ: لَا تَضْرِبُوا أَطْفَالَكُمْ عَلَى بُكَائِهِمْ فَإِنَّ بُكَاءَهُمْ أَرْبَعَةَ أَشْهُرٍ: شَهَادَةُ أَنْ لَا إِلٰهَ إِلَّا اللهُ وَأَرْبَعَةَ أَشْهُرٍ: اَلصَّلَوَةُ عَلَى النَّبِيِّ، وَأَرْبَعَةَ أَشْهُرٍ: اَلدُّعَاءُ لِوَالِدَيْهِ.

(وسائل الشيعة ج٣ ص١٣٠)

٦٩ـ قَالَ رَسُولُ اللهِ صَلَّى اللهُ عَلَيْهِ وَآلِهِ: طَهِّرُوا أَوْلَادَكُمْ يَوْمَ السَّابِعِ فَإِنَّهُ أَطْيَبُ وَأَسْرَعُ لِنَبَاتِ اللَّحْمِ.

(وسائل الشيعة ج٣ ص١٢٨)

٧٠ـ قَالَ رَسُولُ اللهِ صَلَّى اللهُ عَلَيْهِ وَآلِهِ: تَوَقَّوْا عَلَى أَوْلَادِكُمْ مِنْ لَبَنِ البَغِيَّةِ وَالْمَجْنُونَةِ فَإِنَّ اللَّبَنَ يُعَدِّي.

(مكارم الأخلاق ص٢٥٦)

٧١ـ قَالَ الصَّادِقُ عَلَيْهِ السَّلَامُ: اَلْمَوْلُودُ إِذَا وُلِدَ يُؤَذَّنُ فِي أُذُنِهِ الْيُمْنَى وَيُقَامُ فِي الْيُسْرَى. (مكارم الأخلاق ص٢٦١)

٧٢ـ قَالَ الصَّادِقُ عَلَيْهِ السَّلَامُ: اَلْعَقِيقَةُ لَازِمَةٌ لِمَنْ كَانَ غَنِيًّا وَمَنْ كَانَ فَقِيرًا إِذَا أَيْسَرَ فَعَلَ فَإِنْ لَمْ يَقْدِرْ عَلَى ذٰلِكَ فَلَيْسَ عَلَيْهِ ... وَكُلُّ مَوْلُودٍ يُرْتَهَنُ بِعَقِيقَتِهِ.

(مكارم الأخلاق ص٢٦٠)

٧٣ـ قَالَ رَسُولُ اللهِ صَلَّى اللهُ عَلَيْهِ وَآلِهِ: اِعْدِلُوا بَيْنَ أَوْلَادِكُمْ كَمَا تُحِبُّونَ

اَنْ يَعْدِلُوا بَيْنَكُمْ فِى البِرِّ وَ اللُّطْفِ.

(مكارم الاخلاق ص ٢٥٢)

٧٤ ـ قَالَ رَسُولُ اللهِ ﷺ: مَنْ دَخَلَ السُّوقَ فَاشْتَرَىٰ تُحْفَةً فَحَمَلَهَا اِلىٰ عِيَالِهِ كَانَ كَحَامِلِ صَدَقَةٍ اِلىٰ قَوْمٍ مَحَاوِيجَ، وَلْيَبْدَأْ بِالْإِنَاثِ قَبْلَ الذُّكُورِ فَاِنَّهُ مَنْ فَرَّحَ اِبْنَتَهُ فَكَاَنَّمَا اَعْتَقَ رَقَبَةً مِنْ وُلْدِ اِسْمَاعِيلَ ﷺ.

(مكارم الاخلاق ص ٢٥٤)

٧٥ ـ قَالَ اللهُ تَعَالىٰ: وَقَضىٰ رَبُّكَ اَلَّا تَعْبُدُوا اِلَّا اِيَّاهُ وَ بِالْوَالِدَيْنِ اِحْسَانًا اِمَّا يَبْلُغَنَّ عِنْدَكَ الْكِبَرَ اَحَدُهُمَا اَوْ كِلَاهُمَا فَلَا تَقُلْ لَهُمَا اُفٍّ وَلَا تَنْهَرْهُمَا وَقُلْ لَهُمَا قَوْلًا كَرِيمًا وَاخْفِضْ لَهُمَا جَنَاحَ الذُّلِّ مِنَ الرَّحْمَةِ وَقُلْ رَبِّ ارْحَمْهُمَا كَمَا رَبَّيَانِى صَغِيرًا.

(سورة بنى اسرائيل ـ آيت ٢٣-٢٤)

٧٦ ـ قَالَ اللهُ تَعَالىٰ: وَوَصَّيْنَا الْإِنْسَانَ بِوَالِدَيْهِ حَمَلَتْهُ اُمُّهُ وَهْنًا عَلىٰ وَهْنٍ وَفِصَالُهُ فِى عَامَيْنِ اَنِ اشْكُرْ لِى وَلِوَالِدَيْكَ اِلَىَّ الْمَصِيرُ. (سوره لقمان ـ آيت ١٤)

٧٧ ـ قَالَ رَسُولُ اللهِ ﷺ: بِرُّ الْوَالِدَيْنِ اَفْضَلُ مِنَ الصَّلوٰةِ وَالصَّوْمِ وَالْحَجِّ وَالْعُمْرَةِ وَالْجِهَادِ فِى سَبِيلِ اللهِ.

(جامع السعادات ج ٢ ص ٢٥٩)

٧٨ ـ قَالَ رَسُولُ اللهِ ﷺ: مَنْ اَصْبَحَ مَرْضِيًّا لِاَبَوَيْهِ اَصْبَحَ لَهُ بَابَانِ مَفْتُوحَانِ اِلَى الْجَنَّةِ. (جامع السعادات ج ٢ ص ٢٥٩)

٧٩ - قَالَ الصَّادِقُ عَلَيْهِ السَّلَامُ (فِي حَدِيثٍ): وَأَتَاهُ النَّبِيَّ ﷺ رَجُلٌ آخَرُ وَقَالَ: إِنِّي رَجُلٌ شَابٌّ نَشِيطٌ وَأُحِبُّ الْجِهَادَ وَلِي وَالِدَةٌ تَكْرَهُ ذٰلِكَ. فَقَالَ لَهُ النَّبِيُّ ﷺ: ارْجِعْ فَكُنْ مَعَ وَالِدَتِكَ فَوَالَّذِي بَعَثَنِي بِالْحَقِّ لَأُنْسُهَا بِكَ لَيْلَةً خَيْرٌ مِنْ جِهَادٍ فِي سَبِيلِ اللّٰهِ سَنَةً. (جامع السعادات ج٢ ص٢٦٠)

٨٠ - وَجَاءَ آخَرُ إِلَيْهِ النَّبِيِّ ﷺ لِلْجِهَادِ فَقَالَ ﷺ: أَلَكَ وَالِدَةٌ؟ قَالَ نَعَمْ، قَالَ فَالْزَمْهَا فَإِنَّ الْجَنَّةَ تَحْتَ قَدَمَيْهَا. (جامع السعادات ج٢ ص٢٦١)

٨١ - قَالَ الصَّادِقُ عَلَيْهِ السَّلَامُ: إِنَّ رَسُولَ اللّٰهِ ﷺ أَتَتْهُ أُخْتٌ لَهُ مِنَ الرَّضَاعَةِ فَلَمَّا نَظَرَ إِلَيْهَا سُرَّ بِهَا وَبَسَطَ مِلْحَفَتَهُ لَهَا فَأَجْلَسَهَا عَلَيْهَا ثُمَّ أَقْبَلَ يُحَدِّثُهَا وَيَضْحَكُ فِي وَجْهِهَا ثُمَّ قَامَتْ فَذَهَبَتْ وَجَاءَ أَخُوهَا فَلَمْ يَصْنَعْ بِهِ مَا صَنَعَ بِهَا فَقِيلَ لَهُ يَا رَسُولَ اللّٰهِ صَنَعْتَ بِأُخْتِهِ مَا لَمْ تَصْنَعْ بِهِ وَهُوَ رَجُلٌ فَقَالَ ﷺ: لِأَنَّهَا كَانَتْ أَبَرَّ بِوَالِدَيْهَا مِنْهُ. (جامع السعادات ج٢ ص٢٦٠)

٨٢ - قَالَ لِلصَّادِقِ عَلَيْهِ السَّلَامُ رَجُلٌ: إِنَّ لِي أَبَوَيْنِ مُخَالِفَيْنِ فَقَالَ بَرَّهُمَا كَمَا تَبَرُّ الْمُسْلِمِينَ مِمَّنْ يَتَوَلَّانَا. (جامع السعادات ج٢ ص٢٦٠)

٨٣ - قَالَ رَسُولُ اللّٰهِ ﷺ: مَنْ أَصْبَحَ مُسْخِطًا لِأَبَوَيْهِ أَصْبَحَ لَهُ بَابَانِ مَفْتُوحَانِ إِلَى النَّارِ. (جامع السعادات ج٢ ص٢٥٧)

٨٤ ـ قَالَ رَسُولُ اللهِ ﷺ : اِيَّاكُمْ وَعُقُوقَ الْوَالِدَيْنِ فَاِنَّ رِيحَ الْجَنَّةِ تُوجَدُ مِنْ مَسِيرَةِ اَلْفِ عَامٍ وَلَا يَجِدُهَاعَاقٌّ ...
(جامعُ السعادات ج ٢ ص ٢٥٧)

٨٥ ـ قَالَ الصَّادِقُ ﷻ: لَوْ عَلِمَ اللهُ شَيْئًا هُوَ اَدْنَى مِنْ اُفٍّ لَنَهَى عَنْهُ وَهُوَ اَدْنَى مِنَ الْعُقُوقِ وَمِنَ الْعُقُوقِ اَنْ يَنْظُرَ الرَّجُلُ اِلَى وَالِدَيْهِ فَيُحِدَّ النَّظَرَ اِلَيْهِمَا.
(جامع السعادات ج ٢ ص ٢٥٨)

٨٦ ـ قَالَ رَسُولُ اللهِ ﷺ : حَقُّ كَبِيرِ الْاِخْوَةِ عَلَى صَغِيرِهِمْ كَحَقِّ الْوَالِدِ عَلَى وَلَدِهِ. (جامع السعادات ج ٢ ص ٢٦٢)

٨٧ ـ قَالَ الصَّادِقُ ﷻ: اِنَّ النَّبِيَّ ﷺ قَالَ: مَنْ اَصْبَحَ لَا يَهْتَمُّ بِاُمُورِ الْمُسْلِمِينَ فَلَيْسَ مِنْهُمْ وَمَنْ سَمِعَ رَجُلًا يُنَادِي بِالْمُسْلِمِينَ فَلَمْ يُجِبْهُ فَلَيْسَ بِمُسْلِمٍ.
(اصول كافي ص ٣٩٠)

٨٨ ـ قَالَ الصَّادِقُ ﷻ: اَيُّمَا رَجُلٍ مِنْ شِيعَتِنَا اَتَى رَجُلًا مِنْ اِخْوَانِهِ فَاسْتَعَانَ بِهِ فِي حَاجَتِهِ فَلَمْ يُعِنْهُ وَهُوَ يَقْدِرُ اِلَّا اِبْتَلَاهُ اللهُ تَعَالَى بِاَنْ يَقْضِيَ حَوَائِجَ عِدَّةٍ مِنْ اَعْدَائِنَا يُعَذِّبُهُ اللهُ عَلَيْهَا يَوْمَ الْقِيَامَةِ. (اصول كافي ص ٤٧٦)

٨٩ ـ قَالَ الصَّادِقُ ﷻ: مَنْ كَانَتْ لَهُ دَارٌ فَاحْتَاجَ مُؤْمِنٌ اِلَى سُكْنَاهَا فَمَنَعَهُ اِيَّاهَا قَالَ اللهُ تَعَالَى يَا مَلَائِكَتِي اَبَخِلَ عَبْدِي عَلَى عَبْدِي بِسُكْنَى الدَّارِ ؟ وَعِزَّتِي وَجَلَالِي لَا يَسْكُنُ جَنَّاتِي اَبَدًا. (اصول كافي ص ٤٧٦)

210

٩٠ - قَالَ الصَّادِقُ ﷻ : مَنْ سَأَلَهُ أَخُوهُ الْمُؤْمِنُ حَاجَةً مِنْ ضُرٍّ فَمَنَعَهُ مِنْ سَعَةٍ وَهُوَ يَقْدِرُ عَلَيْهَا مِنْ عِنْدِهِ أَوْ مِنْ غَيْرِهِ حَشَرَهُ اللهُ يَوْمَ الْقِيَامَةِ مَغْلُولَةً يَدُهُ إِلَى عُنُقِهِ حَتَّى يَفْرَغَ اللهُ مِنْ حِسَابِ الْخَلْقِ .

(بحار الانوار ج ١٦ ص ٨٠)

٩١ - قَالَ رَسُولُ اللهِ ﷺ : إِنَّ لِلَّهِ عِبَادًا يُحَكِّمُهُمْ فِي جَنَّتِهِ قِيلَ وَمَنْ هُمْ ؟ قَالَ مَنْ قَضَى لِمُؤْمِنٍ حَاجَةً بِنِيَّةٍ .

(وسائل الشيعه ج ٢ ص ٥٢٣)

٩٢ - قَالَ أَمِيرُ الْمُؤْمِنِينَ ﷺ سَمِعْتُ رَسُولَ اللهِ ﷺ يَقُولُ : مَنْ قَضَى لِأَخِيهِ الْمُؤْمِنِ حَاجَةً كَانَ كَمَنْ عَبَدَ اللهَ دَهْرَهُ .

(وسائل الشيعه ج ٢ ص ٥٢٣)

٩٣ - قَالَ رَسُولُ اللهِ ﷺ : مَنْ رَدَّ عَنْ قَوْمٍ مِنَ الْمُسْلِمِينَ عَادِيَةَ مَاءٍ أَوْ نَارٍ وَجَبَتْ لَهُ الْجَنَّةُ .

(اصول کافی ص ٣٩٠)

٩٤ - قَالَ الْبَاقِرُ ﷺ : إِنَّهُ لَيَعْرِضُ لِي صَاحِبُ الْحَاجَةِ فَأُبَادِرُ إِلَى قَضَائِهَا مَخَافَةَ أَنْ يَسْتَغْنِيَ عَنْهَا صَاحِبُهَا .

(بحار الانوار ج ١٥ کتاب العشره ص ٨٩)

٩٥ - قَالَ الصَّادِقُ ﷻ : إِنَّ الْمُسْلِمَ إِذَا جَاءَ أَخُوهُ الْمُسْلِمُ فَقَامَ مَعَهُ فِي حَاجَةٍ كَانَ كَالْمُجَاهِدِ فِي سَبِيلِ اللهِ عَزَّ وَجَلَّ .

(مستدرك الوسائل ج ٢ ص ٤٠٧)

٩٦ - قَالَ الصَّادِقُ ﷻ : مَا قَضَى مُسْلِمٌ لِمُسْلِمٍ حَاجَةً إِلَّا

نَادَاهُ اللهُ تَبَارَكَ وَتَعَالَى: عَلَى ثَوَابِكَ وَلَا أَرْضَى لَكَ بِدُونِ الْجَنَّةِ.
(وسائل الشيعة ج ٢ ص ٥٢٣)

٩٧ - قَالَ الصَّادِقُ عليه السلام: وَمَنْ قَضَى لِأَخِيهِ الْمُؤْمِنِ حَاجَةً قَضَى اللهُ لَهُ يَوْمَ الْقِيَامَةِ مِائَةَ أَلْفِ حَاجَةٍ مِنْ ذَلِكَ أَوَّلُهَا الْجَنَّةُ وَمِنْ ذَلِكَ أَنْ يُدْخِلَ قَرَابَتَهُ وَمَعَارِفَهُ وَإِخْوَانَهُ الْجَنَّةَ بَعْدَ أَنْ لَا يَكُونُوا أَنْصَابًا.
(وسائل الشيعة ج ٢ ص ٢٢٣)

٩٨ - قَالَ الصَّادِقُ عليه السلام: أَيُّمَا مُؤْمِنٍ نَفَّسَ عَنْ مُؤْمِنٍ كُرْبَةً وَهُوَ مُعْسِرٌ يَسَّرَ اللهُ لَهُ حَوَائِجَهُ فِي الدُّنْيَا وَالْآخِرَةِ وَمَنْ سَتَرَ عَلَى مُؤْمِنٍ عَوْرَةً يَخَافُهَا سَتَرَ اللهُ عَلَيْهِ سَبْعِينَ عَوْرَةً مِنْ عَوْرَاتِ الدُّنْيَا وَالْآخِرَةِ قَالَ: وَاللهُ فِي عَوْنِ الْمُؤْمِنِ مَا كَانَ الْمُؤْمِنُ فِي عَوْنِ أَخِيهِ فَانْتَفِعُوا بِالْعَظَمَةِ وَارْغَبُوا فِي الْخَيْرِ.
(أصول كافي ص ٤١٠)

٩٩ - قَالَ صَفْوَانُ الْجَمَّالُ: كُنْتُ جَالِسًا مَعَ أَبِي عَبْدِ اللهِ عليه السلام إِذْ دَخَلَ عَلَيْهِ رَجُلٌ مِنْ أَهْلِ مَكَّةَ يُقَالُ لَهُ: مَيْمُونٌ، فَشَكَا إِلَيْهِ تَعَذُّرَ الْكِرَاءِ عَلَيْهِ. فَقَالَ لِي: قُمْ فَأَعِنْ أَخَاكَ فَقُمْتُ مَعَهُ فَيَسَّرَهُ اللهُ كِرَاءَهُ فَرَجَعْتُ إِلَى مَجْلِسِي فَقَالَ أَبُو عَبْدِ اللهِ عليه السلام: مَا صَنَعْتَ فِي حَاجَةِ أَخِيكَ ؟ فَقُلْتُ: قَضَاهَا (ه - خل) اللهُ - بِأَبِي أَنْتَ وَأُمِّي - فَقَالَ: أَمَا أَنْتَ أَنْ تُعِينَ أَخَاكَ الْمُسْلِمَ أَحَبُّ إِلَيَّ مِنْ طَوَافِ أُسْبُوعٍ بِالْبَيْتِ مُبْتَدِيًا...
(أصول كافي ص ٤٠٩)

١٠٠- قَالَ الصَّادِقُ علیه السلام: قَالَ اللهُ عَزَّ وَجَلَّ: الْخَلْقُ عِيَالِي فَأَحَبُّهُمْ إِلَيَّ أَلْطَفُهُمْ بِهِمْ وَأَسْعَاهُمْ فِي حَوَائِجِهِمْ...
(أصول كافي ص ٤٠٩)

١٠١- قَالَ الكَاظِمُ علیه السلام: إِنَّ لِلهِ عِبَادًا فِي الأَرْضِ يَسْعَوْنَ فِي حَوَائِجِ النَّاسِ، هُمُ الآمِنُونَ يَوْمَ القِيَامَةِ وَمَنْ أَدْخَلَ عَلَى مُؤْمِنٍ سُرُورًا فَرَّحَ اللهُ قَلْبَهُ يَوْمَ القِيَامَةِ.
(وسائل الشيعة ج ٢ ص ٥٢٤)

١٠٢- قَالَ البَاقِرُ علیه السلام: إِنَّ المُؤْمِنَ لَتَرِدُ عَلَيْهِ الحَاجَةُ لِأَخِيهِ فَلَا تَكُونُ عِنْدَهُ، نِيَّتُهُ بِهِمَّهَا قَلْبُهُ، فَيُدْخِلُهُ اللهُ تَبَارَكَ وَتَعَالَى بِهَمِّهِ الجَنَّةَ. (وسائل الشيعة ج ٢ ص ٥٢٣)

١٠٣- قَالَ حُسَيْنُ بْنُ عَلِيٍّ علیه السلام: إِنَّ حَوَائِجَ النَّاسِ إِلَيْكُمْ مِنْ نِعَمِ اللهِ عَلَيْكُمْ فَلَا تَمَلُّوا النِّعَمَ.
(بحار الانوار ج ١٥ كتاب العشرة ص ٩٠)

١٠٤- قَالَ عَلِيٌّ علیه السلام: عَجِبْتُ لِرَجُلٍ يَأْتِيهِ أَخُوهُ المُسْلِمُ فِي حَاجَةٍ فَيَمْتَنِعُ عَنْ قَضَائِهَا وَلَا يَرَى نَفْسَهُ لِلْخَيْرِ أَهْلًا! فَهَبْ أَنَّهُ لَا ثَوَابَ يُرْجَى وَلَا عِقَابَ يُتَّقَى أَفَتَزْهَدُونَ فِي مَكَارِمِ الأَخْلَاقِ؟
(درر الحكم ص ٤٩٦)

١٠٥- قَالَ رَسُولُ اللهِ صلى الله عليه وآله: مَنْ أَصْبَحَ لَا يَهْتَمُّ بِأُمُورِ المُسْلِمِينَ فَلَيْسَ بِمُسْلِمٍ.
(أصول كافي ص ٣٩٠)

١٠٦- سُئِلَ رَسُولُ اللهِ صلى الله عليه وآله: مَنْ أَحَبُّ النَّاسِ إِلَى اللهِ؟ قَالَ: أَنْفَعُ النَّاسِ لِلنَّاسِ..
(أصول كافي ص ٣٩١)

١٠٧- قَالَ رَسُولُ اللهِ ﷺ : خَيْرُ النَّاسِ مَنِ انْتَفَعَ بِهِ النَّاسُ
(بحار الانوار ج ١٥ كتاب العشرة ص ١٢٤)

١٠٨- قَالَ الصَّادِقُ ﷻ : لَيْسَ يَتْبَعُ الرَّجُلَ بَعْدَ مَوْتِهِ مِنَ الْأَجْرِ إِلَّا ثَلَاثُ خِصَالٍ : صَدَقَةٌ أَجْرَاهَا فِي حَيَاتِهِ فَهِيَ تَجْرِي بَعْدَ مَوْتِهِ ، وَسُنَّةُ هُدًى سَنَّهَا فَهِيَ يُعْمَلُ بِهَا بَعْدَ مَوْتِهِ ، وَوَلَدٌ صَالِحٌ يَسْتَغْفِرُ لَهُ.
(بحار الانوار ج ٣ ص ١٧٥)

١٠٩- قَوْلُهُ تَعَالَى : الْمَالُ وَالْبَنُونَ زِينَةُ الْحَيَوةِ الدُّنْيَا وَالْبَاقِيَاتُ الصَّالِحَاتُ خَيْرٌ عِنْدَ رَبِّكَ ثَوَابًا وَخَيْرٌ أَمَلًا.
(سورة كهف - آية ٤٦)

١١٠- عَنْ عُبَيْدَةَ الْحَذَّاءِ قَالَ : سَمِعْتُ أَبَا عَبْدِ اللهِ ﷻ يَقُولُ : مَنْ بَنَى مَسْجِدًا بَنَى اللهُ لَهُ بَيْتًا فِي الْجَنَّةِ.
(وسائل الشيعه ج ١ ص ٣٠٤)

١١١- قَوْلُهُ تَعَالَى : إِنَّمَا يَعْمُرُ مَسَاجِدَ اللهِ مَنْ آمَنَ بِاللهِ وَالْيَوْمِ الْآخِرِ وَأَقَامَ الصَّلَوةَ وَآتَى الزَّكَوةَ وَلَمْ يَخْشَ إِلَّا اللهَ فَعَسَى أُولَئِكَ أَنْ يَكُونُوا مِنَ الْمُهْتَدِينَ.
(سورة توبه - آيت ١٨)

١١٢- قَالَ رَسُولُ اللهِ ﷺ : مَنْ أَمَاطَ عَنْ طَرِيقِ الْمُسْلِمِينَ مَا يُؤْذِيهِمْ كَتَبَ اللهُ لَهُ أَجْرَ قِرَاءَةِ أَرْبَعِمِائَةِ آيَةٍ كُلُّ حَرْفٍ مِنْهَا بِعَشْرِ حَسَنَاتٍ.
(بحار الانوار ج ١٥ كتاب العشرة ص ١٣١)

١١٣- قَالَ الصَّادِقُ عَلَيْهِ السَّلَامُ: لَقَدْ كَانَ عَلِيُّ بْنُ الْحُسَيْنِ عَلَيْهِ السَّلَامُ يَمُرُّ عَلَى الْمُدْرَةِ فِي وَسَطِ الطَّرِيقِ فَيَنْزِلُ عَنْ دَابَّتِهِ حَتَّى يُنَحِّيَهَا بِيَدِهِ عَنِ الطَّرِيقِ.

(بحار الانوار ج ١٥ كتاب العشرة ص ١٣)

١١٤- قَالَ رَسُولُ اللهِ صَلَّى اللهُ عَلَيْهِ وَآلِهِ (في حديث): قَالَ: اِنَّ عَلَى كُلِّ مُسْلِمٍ فِي كُلِّ يَوْمٍ صَدَقَةً، قِيلَ: مَنْ يُطِيقُ ذَلِكَ؟ قَالَ: اِمَاطَتُكَ الْأَذَى عَنِ الطَّرِيقِ صَدَقَةٌ.

(بحار الانوار ج ١٥ كتاب العشرة ص ١٣١)

١١٥- قَالَ الصَّادِقُ عَلَيْهِ السَّلَامُ: مَا مِنْ مُؤْمِنٍ يَخْذُلُ أَخَاهُ، وَهُوَ يَقْدِرُ عَلَى نُصْرَتِهِ اِلَّا خَذَلَهُ اللهُ فِي الدُّنْيَا وَالْآخِرَةِ.

(بحار الانوار ج ١٥ كتاب العشرة ص ١٢٣)

١١٦- قَالَ عَلِيٌّ عَلَيْهِ السَّلَامُ: وَكُونَا لِلظَّالِمِ خَصْمًا وَلِلْمَظْلُومِ عَوْنًا.

(نهج البلاغه ص ٩٦٨)

١١٧- قَالَ رَسُولُ اللهِ صَلَّى اللهُ عَلَيْهِ وَآلِهِ: مَنْ حَمَى مُؤْمِنًا مِنْ ظَالِمٍ بَعَثَ اللهُ لَهُ مَلَكًا يَوْمَ الْقِيَامَةِ يَحْمِي لَحْمَهُ مِنْ نَارِ جَهَنَّمَ.

(جامع السعادات ج ٢ ص ٢٢١)

١١٨- قَالَ الصَّادِقُ عَلَيْهِ السَّلَامُ: مَا مِنْ مُؤْمِنٍ يُعِينُ مُؤْمِنًا مَظْلُومًا اِلَّا كَانَ أَفْضَلَ مِنْ صِيَامِ شَهْرٍ وَاعْتِكَافِهِ فِي الْمَسْجِدِ الْحَرَامِ...

(بحار الانوار ج ١٥ كتاب العشرة ص ١٢٣)

١١٩- قَالَ الْبَاقِرُ عَلَيْهِ السَّلَامُ: اِنَّ مُؤْمِنًا كَانَ فِي مَمْلَكَةِ جَبَّارٍ فَوَلِعَ بِهِ فَهَرَبَ مِنْهُ اِلَى دَارِ الشِّرْكِ، فَنَزَلَ بِرَجُلٍ مِنْ أَهْلِ

الشِّرْكِ فَأَظَلَّهُ وَأَرْفَقَهُ وَأَضَافَهُ فَلَمَّا حَضَرَهُ الْمَوْتُ أَوْحَى اللهُ إِلَيْهِ: وَعِزَّتِى وَجَلَالِى لَوْ كَانَ لَكَ فِى جَنَّتِى مَسْكَنٌ لَأَسْكَنْتُكَ فِيهَا وَلَكِنَّهَا مُحَرَّمَةٌ عَلَى مَنْ مَاتَ بِى مُشْرِكًا وَلَكِنْ يَا نَارُ هَيِّدِيهِ وَلَا تُؤْذِيهِ...

(اصول كافى ص ٤٠٣)

١٢٠- قَالَ الصَّادِقُ عَلَيْهِ السَّلَامُ (فِى حَدِيثٍ): لِأَنَّ نُصْرَةَ الْمُؤْمِنِ عَلَى الْمُؤْمِنِ فَرِيضَةٌ وَاجِبَةٌ...

(بحار الانوار ج ١٥ كتاب العشرة ص ١٢٣)

١٢١- قَوْلُهُ تَعَالَى: إِنَّمَا الْمُؤْمِنُونَ إِخْوَةٌ فَأَصْلِحُوا بَيْنَ أَخَوَيْكُمْ وَاتَّقُوا اللهَ لَعَلَّكُمْ تُرْحَمُونَ. (سوره حجرات - آيت ١٠)

١٢٢- قَالَ عَلِىٌّ عَلَيْهِ السَّلَامُ فِى وَصِيَّتِهِ عِنْدَ وَفَاتِهِ لِلْحَسَنِ وَالْحُسَيْنِ عَلَيْهِمَا السَّلَامُ: أُوصِيكُمَا وَجَمِيعَ وُلْدِى وَمَنْ بَلَغَهُ كِتَابِى بِتَقْوَى اللهِ وَ نَظْمِ أَمْرِكُمْ وَصَلَاحِ ذَاتِ بَيْنِكُمْ فَإِنِّى سَمِعْتُ جَدَّكُمَا رَسُولَ اللهِ صَلَّى اللهُ عَلَيْهِ وَآلِهِ يَقُولُ: صَلَاحُ ذَاتِ الْبَيْنِ أَفْضَلُ مِنْ عَامَّةِ الصَّلَوةِ وَالصِّيَامِ. (نهج البلاغة ص ٩٦٨)

١٢٣- عَنْ أَبِى حَنِيفَةَ سَائِقِ الْحَاجِّ قَالَ: مَرَّ بِنَا الْمُفَضَّلُ وَأَنَا وَخَتَنِى نَتَشَاجَرُ فِى مِيرَاثٍ فَوَقَفَ عَلَيْنَا سَاعَةً ثُمَّ قَالَ تَعَالَوْا إِلَى الْمَنْزِلِ فَأَتَيْنَاهُ فَأَصْلَحَ بَيْنَنَا بِأَرْبَعِمِائَةِ دِرْهَمٍ فَدَفَعَهَا إِلَيْنَا مِنْ عِنْدِهِ حَتَّى إِذَا اسْتَوْثَقَ كُلُّ وَاحِدٍ مِنَّا مِنْ صَاحِبِهِ قَالَ: أَمَا إِنَّهَا لَيْسَتْ مِنْ مَالِى وَلَكِنْ أَبُو عَبْدِ اللهِ عَلَيْهِ السَّلَامُ أَمَرَنِى إِذَا تَنَازَعَ رَجُلَانِ مِنْ أَصْحَابِنَا فِى

شئٍ اَنْ اَصْلَحَ بَيْنَهُمْ فَافْتَدى بِها مِنْ مالِهِ فَهذا مِنْ مالِ اَبى عَبْدِاللهِ عَلَيْهِ . (اُصولِ كافى ص ٤١٤)

١٢٤- قالَ عَلىٌّ عَلَيْهِ : قالَ رَسُولُ اللهِ صَلَّى اللهُ عَلَيْهِ وَآلِهِ : لِلْمُسْلِمِ عَلى اَخيهِ ثَلاثُونَ حَقّاً لا بَراءَةَ لَهُ مِنْها اِلاّ بِالاَداءِ وَالْعَفْوِ :- يَغْفِرُ زَلَّتَهُ وَيَرْحَمُ عَبْرَتَهُ وَيَسْتُرُ عَوْرَتَهُ وَيُقيلُ عَثْرَتَهُ وَيَقْبَلُ مَعْذِرَتَهُ وَيَرُدُّ غيبَتَهُ وَيُديمُ نَصيحَتَهُ وَيَحْفَظُ خُلَّتَهُ وَيَرْعى ذِمَّتَهُ وَيَعُودُ مَرْضَتَهُ وَيَشْهَدُ مَيِّتَهُ وَيُجيبُ دَعْوَتَهُ وَيَقْبَلُ هَدِيَّتَهُ وَيُكافى صِلَتَهُ وَيَشْكُرُ نِعْمَتَهُ وَيُحْسِنُ نُصْرَتَهُ وَيَحْفَظُ حَليلَتَهُ وَيَقْضى حاجَتَهُ وَيَسْتَنْجِحُ مَسْأَلَتَهُ وَيُشَمِّتُ عَطْسَتَهُ وَيُرْشِدُ ضالَّتَهُ وَيَرُدُّ سَلامَهُ وَيُطيبُ كَلامَهُ وَيَبَرُّ اِنْعامَهُ وَيُصَدِّقُ اَقْسامَهُ وَيُوالى وَلِيَّهُ وَلا يُعاديهِ يَنْصُرُهُ ظالِماً وَمَظْلُوماً فَامّا نَصْرَتُهُ ظالِماً فَيَرُدَّهُ عَنْ ظُلْمِهِ وَامّا نَصْرَتُهُ مَظْلُوماً فَيُعينُهُ عَلى اَخْذِ حَقِّهِ وَلا يُسَلِّمُهُ وَلا يَخْذُلُهُ وَيُحِبُّ لَهُ مِنَ الْخَيْرِ ما يُحِبُّ لِنَفْسِهِ وَيَكْرَهُ لَهُ مِنَ الشَّرِّ ما يَكْرَهُ لِنَفْسِهِ .

(بحارالانوار ج١٥ كتاب العشرة ص٦٥)

١٢٥- عَنِ الصّادِقِ عَلَيْهِ عَنْ آبائِهِ عَلَيْهِ قالَ رَسُولُ اللهِ صَلَّى اللهُ عَلَيْهِ وَآلِهِ : لِلْمُؤْمِنِ عَلَى الْمُؤْمِنِ سَبْعَةُ حُقُوقٍ واجِبَةٍ مِنَ اللهِ عَزَّوَجَلَّ عَلَيْهِ : اَلْاِجْلالُ لَهُ فى عَيْنِهِ وَالْوُدُّ لَهُ فى صَدْرِهِ وَالْمُواساةُ لَهُ فى مالِهِ وَاَنْ يُحَرِّمَ غيبَتَهُ وَاَنْ يَعُودَهُ فى مَرَضِهِ وَاَنْ

يُشَيِّعَ جَنَازَتَهُ وَاَنْ لَا يَقُولَ بَعْدَ مَوْتِهِ الْاَخِيرَا.

(بحارالانوار ج ۱۵ کتاب العشرة ص ٦١)

۱۲٦ - قَالَ الْبَاقِرُ عَلَيْهِ السَّلَامُ: مِنْ حَقِّ الْمُؤْمِنِ عَلَى اَخِيهِ الْمُؤْمِنِ اَنْ يُشَيِّعَ جَوْعَتَهُ وَيُوَارِيَ عَوْرَتَهُ وَيُفَرِّجَ عَنْهُ كُرْبَتَهُ وَ يَقْضِيَ دَيْنَهُ فَاِذَا مَاتَ خَلَفَهُ فِي اَهْلِهِ وَ وُلْدِهِ.

(اصول کافی ص ۳۹۳)

۱۲۷ - قَالَ الصَّادِقُ عَلَيْهِ السَّلَامُ: الْمُؤْمِنُ اَخُو الْمُؤْمِنِ عَيْنُهُ وَ دَلِيلُهُ لَا يَخُونُهُ وَلَا يَظْلِمُهُ وَلَا يَغُشُّهُ وَلَا يَعِدُهُ عِدَةً فَيُخْلِفَهُ

(اصول کافی ص ۳۹۲)

۱۲۸ - قَالَ رَسُولُ اللهِ صَلَّى اللهُ عَلَيْهِ وَآلِهِ: اِخْوَانُكُمْ جَعَلَهُمُ اللهُ تَحْتَ اَيْدِيكُمْ فَمَنْ كَانَ اَخُوهُ تَحْتَ يَدِهِ فَلْيُطْعِمْهُ مِمَّا يَأْكُلُ وَلْيَكْسِهِ مِمَّا يَلْبَسُ وَلَا يُكَلِّفُهُ مَا يَغْلِبُهُ.

(بحارالانوار ج ۱۵ کتاب العشرة ص ٤١)

۱۲۹ - قَالَ اَبُو عَبْدِ اللهِ عَلَيْهِ السَّلَامُ فِي كِتَابِ رَسُولِ اللهِ صَلَّى اللهُ عَلَيْهِ وَآلِهِ: اِذَا اسْتَعْمَلْتُمْ مَا مَلَكَتْ اَيْمَانُكُمْ فِي شَيْءٍ يَشُقُّ عَلَيْهِمْ فَاعْمَلُوا مَعَهُمْ فِيهِ

(بحارالانوار ج ۱۵ کتاب العشرة ص ٤١)

۱۳۰ - قَالَ رَسُولُ اللهِ صَلَّى اللهُ عَلَيْهِ وَآلِهِ: اَلَا اَنَبِّئُكُمْ بِشَرِّ النَّاسِ؟ قَالُوا بَلَى يَا رَسُولَ اللهِ. فَقَالَ: مَنْ سَافَرَ وَحْدَهُ وَمَنَعَ رِفْدَهُ وَ ضَرَبَ عَبْدَهُ.   (بحارالانوار ج ۱۵ کتاب العشرة ص ٤١)

۱۳۱ - عَنْ يَاسِرٍ الْخَادِمِ وَ نَادِرٍ قَالَا : قَالَ لَنَا اَبُو الْحَسَنِ عَلَيْهِ السَّلَامُ: اِنْ قُمْتُ عَلَى رُؤُوسِكُمْ وَاَنْتُمْ تَاْكُلُونَ فَلَا تَقُومُوا حَتَّى

تَفَرَّعُوا ... (بحارالانوار ج١٥ كتاب العشرة ص ١٤)

١٣٢- اَتى اَميرُ الْمُؤْمِنينَ عَلَيْهِ السَّلامُ سُوقَ الْكَرابيسِ فَاشْتَرى ثَوْبَيْنِ اَحَدُهُما بِثَلاثَةِ دَراهِمَ وَالْآخَرَ بِدِرْهَمَيْنِ، فَقالَ: يا قَنْبَرُ خُذِ الَّذى بِثَلاثَةٍ. قالَ: اَنْتَ اَوْلى بِهِ يا اَميرَ الْمُؤْمِنينَ! تَصْعَدُ الْمِنْبَرَ وَتَخْطُبُ النّاسَ، قالَ: يا قَنْبَرُ اَنْتَ شابٌّ وَلَكَ سُرَّةُ الشَّبابِ وَاَنَا اَسْتَحْيى مِنْ رَبّى اَنْ اَتَفَضَّلَ عَلَيْكَ لِاَنّى سَمِعْتُ رَسُولَ اللهِ صَلَّى اللهُ عَلَيْهِ وَآلِهِ اَلْبِسُوهُمْ مِمّا تَلْبَسُونَ وَاَطْعِمُوهُمْ مِمّا تَأْكُلُونَ.

(بحارالانوار ج١٥ كتاب العشرة ص ١٤)

١٣٣- قالَ رَسُولُ اللهِ صَلَّى اللهُ عَلَيْهِ وَآلِهِ: عَلَيْكُمْ بِغِضارِ الْخَدَمِ فَاِنَّهُ اَقْوى لَكُمْ فيما تُريدُونَ. (بحارالانوار ج١٥ كتاب العشرة ص ١٤)

١٣٤- قالَ اَميرُ الْمُؤْمِنينَ عَلَيْهِ السَّلامُ فى وَصِيَّتِهِ لِابْنِهِ الْحَسَنِ عَلَيْهِ السَّلامُ: وَاجْعَلْ لِكُلِّ اِنْسانٍ مِنْ خَدَمِكَ عَمَلاً تَأْخُذُهُ بِهِ فَاِنَّهُ اَحْرى اَنْ لا يَتَواكَلُوا فى خِدْمَتِكَ. (نهج البلاغة ص ٩٣٠)

١٣٥- بَعَثَ اَبُو عَبْدِاللهِ عَلَيْهِ السَّلامُ غُلاماً لَهُ فى حاجَةٍ فَاَبْطَأَ فَخَرَجَ اَبُو عَبْدِاللهِ عَلَيْهِ السَّلامُ عَلى اَثَرِهِ لِما اَبْطَأَ عَلَيْهِ فَوَجَدَهُ نائِماً فَجَلَسَ عِنْدَ رَأْسِهِ يُرَوِّحُهُ حَتّى انْتَبَهَ، قالَ لَهُ اَبُو عَبْدِاللهِ عَلَيْهِ السَّلامُ: يا فُلانُ وَاللهِ ما ذاكَ لَكَ تَنامُ اللَّيْلَ وَالنَّهارَ، لَكَ اللَّيْلُ وَلَنا مِنْكَ النَّهارُ.

(روضة كافى طبع تهران ص ٨٧ حديث ٥٠)

١٣٦- قالَ اللهُ تَعالى: اَقيمُوا الصَّلوةَ وَ اتُوا الزَّكوةَ وَما تُقَدِّمُوا

219

لِاَنْفُسِكُمْ مِنْ خَيْرٍ تَجِدُوهُ عِنْدَ اللهِ.

(سوره بقره - آيت ١٠٤)

١٣٧ - قَالَ الصَّادِقُ عليه السلام: اِنَّمَا وُضِعَتِ الزَّكوةُ اخْتِبَاراً لِلْاَغْنِيَاءِ وَمَعُونَةً لِلْفُقَرَاءِ وَلَوْ اَنَّ النَّاسَ اَدَّوْا زَكوةَ اَمْوَالِهِمْ مَا بَقِيَ مُسْلِمٌ فَقِيراً مُحْتَاجاً وَلَاسْتَغْنى بِمَا فَرَضَ اللهُ لَهُ وَاِنَّ النَّاسَ مَا افْتَقَرُوا وَلَا احْتَاجُوا وَلَا جَاعُوا وَلَا عَرُوا اِلَّا بِذُنُوبِ الْاَغْنِيَاءِ وَحَقِيقٌ عَلَى اللهِ اَنْ يَمْنَعَ رَحْمَتَهُ مِمَّنْ مَنَعَ حَقَّ اللهِ فِي مَالِهِ ....

(من لايحضره الفقيه ص ١٥١)

١٣٨ - قَالَ الصَّادِقُ عليه السلام: اِنَّ اللهَ عَزَّ وَجَلَّ فَرَضَ لِلْفُقَرَاءِ فِي اَمْوَالِ الْاَغْنِيَاءِ فَرِيضَةً لَا يُحْمَدُونَ اِلَّا بِاَدَائِهَا وَهِيَ الزَّكوةُ، بِهَا حَقَنُوا دِمَائَهُمْ وَبِهَا سُمُّوا مُسْلِمِينَ.

(فروع كافى ج ١ ص ١٤٠)

١٣٩ - قَالَ الصَّادِقُ عليه السلام: اِنَّمَا جَعَلَ اللهُ تَبَارَكَ وَتَعَالى الزَّكوةَ فِي كُلِّ اَلْفٍ خَمْسَةً وَعِشْرِينَ دِرْهَماً لِاَنَّهُ عَزَّ وَجَلَّ خَلَقَ الْخَلْقَ فَعَلِمَ غَنِيَّهُمْ وَفَقِيرَهُمْ وَقَوِيَّهُمْ وَضَعِيفَهُمْ فَجَعَلَ مِنْ كُلِّ اَلْفٍ خَمْسَةً وَعِشْرِينَ مِسْكِيناً لَوْلَا ذلِكَ لَزَادَهُمُ اللهُ لِاَنَّهُ خَالِقُهُمْ وَهُوَ اَعْلَمُ بِهِمْ.

(من لايحضره الفقيه ص ١٥١)

١٤٠ - قَالَ رَسُولُ اللهِ صلى الله عليه وآله (فِي حَدِيثٍ): حَصِّنُوا اَمْوَالَكُمْ بِالزَّكوةِ (وَمِثْلُهُ عَنْ اَبِي عَبْدِ اللهِ عليه السلام فِي ضِمْنِ رِوَايَةٍ،

وَعَنْ مُوسَى بْنِ جَعْفَرٍ عَلَيْهِمَا فِي رِوَايَةٍ أُخْرَى)

(وسائل الشيعه ج٢ ص ٤)

١٤١ - قَالَ عَلِيٌّ عَلَيْهِ السَّلَامُ : ثُمَّ إِنَّ الزَّكوةَ جُعِلَتْ مَعَ الصَّلوةِ قُرْبَانًا لِأَهْلِ الإِسْلَامِ فَمَنْ أَعْطَاهَا طَيِّبَ النَّفْسِ بِهَا فَإِنَّهَا تُجْعَلُ لَهُ كَفَّارَةً وَمِنَ النَّارِ حِجَازًا وَوِقَايَةً فَلَا يَتْبَعَنَّهَا أَحَدٌ نَفْسَهُ وَلَا يُكْثِرَنَّ عَلَيْهَا لَهْفَهُ.

(نهج البلاغه ص ٦٣٥)

١٤٢ - قَالَ عَلِيٌّ عَلَيْهِ السَّلَامُ : اللهَ اللهَ فِي الزَّكوةِ فَإِنَّهَا تُطْفِئُ غَضَبَ رَبِّكُمْ. (كتاب سليم بن قيس طبع نجف ص ١٥)

١٤٣ - قَالَ الْبَاقِرُ عَلَيْهِ السَّلَامُ : وَجَدْنَا فِي كِتَابِ عَلِيٍّ عَلَيْهِ السَّلَامُ قَالَ رَسُولُ اللهِ صَلَّى اللهُ عَلَيْهِ وَآلِهِ : إِذَا مُنِعَتِ الزَّكوةُ مُنِعَتِ الأَرْضُ بَرَكَاتِهَا.

(فروع كافي ج ١ ص ١٤٢)

١٤٤ - قَالَ الصَّادِقُ عَلَيْهِ السَّلَامُ : مَنْ مَنَعَ قِيرَاطًا مِّنَ الزَّكوةِ فَلَيْسَ بِمُؤْمِنٍ وَّلَا مُسْلِمٍ. (وسائل الشيعه ج٢ ص ٥)

١٤٥ - قَالَ الْبَاقِرُ عَلَيْهِ السَّلَامُ : بَيْنَمَا رَسُولُ اللهِ صَلَّى اللهُ عَلَيْهِ وَآلِهِ فِي الْمَسْجِدِ إِذْ قَالَ : قُمْ يَا فُلَانُ قُمْ يَا فُلَانُ قُمْ يَا فُلَانُ حَتَّى أَخْرَجَ خَمْسَةَ نَفَرٍ فَقَالَ : اُخْرُجُوا مِنْ مَّسْجِدِنَا لَا تُصَلُّوا فِيهِ وَأَنْتُمْ لَا تُزَكُّونَ. (من لايحضره الفقيه ص ١٥٢)

١٤٦ - سُئِلَ أَبُو جَعْفَرٍ عَلَيْهِ السَّلَامُ عَنِ الدَّنَانِيرِ وَالدَّرَاهِمِ وَمَا عَمِلَ النَّاسُ فِيهَا فَقَالَ أَبُو جَعْفَرٍ عَلَيْهِ السَّلَامُ : هِيَ خَوَاتِيمُ اللهِ فِي أَرْضِهِ جَعَلَهَا اللهُ مَصْلَحَةً لِّخَلْقِهِ وَبِهَا تَسْتَقِيمُ

221

شُؤُونُهُمْ وَمَطَالِبُهُمْ فَمَنْ اَكْثَرَ لَهُ مِنْهَا فَقَامَ بِحَقِّ اللهِ فِيهَا وَاَدَّى زَكُوتَهَا فَذَاكَ الَّذِي طَابَتْ وَخَلَصَتْ لَهُ وَمَنْ اَكْثَرَ لَهُ مِنْهَا فَبَخِلَ بِهَا وَلَمْ يُؤَدِّ حَقَّ اللهِ فِيهَا وَاتَّخَذَ مِنْهَا الْاٰنِيَةَ فَذَاكَ الَّذِي حَقَّ عَلَيْهِ وَعِيدُ اللهِ عَزَّ وَجَلَّ فِي كِتَابِهِ يَقُولُ اللهُ تَعَالَى: يَوْمَ يُحْمَى عَلَيْهَا فِي نَارِ جَهَنَّمَ فَتُكْوَى بِهَا جِبَاهُهُمْ وَجُنُوبُهُمْ وَظُهُورُهُمْ هٰذَا مَا كَنَزْتُمْ لِاَنْفُسِكُمْ فَذُوقُوا مَا كُنْتُمْ تَكْنِزُونَ.

(وسائل الشيعة ج ٢ ص ٤)

١٤٧ـ قَالَ اللهُ تَعَالَى: وَالَّذِينَ فِي اَمْوَالِهِمْ حَقٌّ مَعْلُومٌ لِلسَّائِلِ وَالْمَحْرُومِ. (سوره معارج ـ آيت ٢٥-٢٦)

١٤٨ـ قَالَ الصَّادِقُ عَلَيْهِ السَّلَامُ (فِي حَدِيثٍ) وَلٰكِنَّ اللهَ عَزَّ وَجَلَّ فَرَضَ فِي اَمْوَالِ الْاَغْنِيَاءِ حُقُوقًا غَيْرَ الزَّكَوٰةِ فَقَالَ عَزَّ وَجَلَّ: وَالَّذِينَ فِي اَمْوَالِهِمْ حَقٌّ مَعْلُومٌ فَالْحَقُّ الْمَعْلُومُ غَيْرُ الزَّكَوٰةِ وَهُوَ شَيْءٌ يَفْرِضُهُ الرَّجُلُ عَلَى نَفْسِهِ فِي مَالِهِ يَجِبُ عَلَيْهِ اَنْ يَفْرِضَهُ عَلَى قَدْرِ طَاقَتِهِ وَسِعَةِ مَالِهِ فَيُؤَدِّ الَّذِي فَرَضَ عَلَى نَفْسِهِ اِنْ شَاءَ فِي كُلِّ يَوْمٍ وَاِنْ شَاءَ فِي كُلِّ جُمْعَةٍ وَاِنْ شَاءَ فِي كُلِّ شَهْرٍ وَقَدْ قَالَ اللهُ عَزَّ وَجَلَّ اَيْضًا: يُنْفِقُونَ مِمَّا رَزَقْنَاهُمْ سِرًّا وَعَلَانِيَةً وَالْمَاعُونُ اَيْضًا هُوَ الْقَرْضُ يُقْرِضُهُ وَالْمَتَاعُ يُعِيرُهُ وَالْمَعْرُوفُ يَصْنَعُهُ وَمِمَّا فَرَضَ اللهُ عَزَّ وَجَلَّ اَيْضًا فِي الْمَالِ مِنْ غَيْرِ الزَّكَوٰةِ قَوْلُهُ عَزَّ وَجَلَّ: اَلَّذِينَ يَصِلُونَ مَا اَمَرَ اللهُ بِهِ

اَنْ يُوصَلَ . وَمَنْ اَدَّى مَا فَرَضَ اللهُ عَلَيْهِ فَقَدْ قَضَى مَا عَلَيْهِ ...
(فروع كافى ج ١ ص ١٤٠)

١٤٩- قَالَ الصَّادِقُ علیه‌السلام : اَتَرَوْنَ اِنَّمَا فِى الْمَالِ زَكوةٌ وَحْدَهَا مَا فَرَضَ اللهُ فِى الْمَالِ مِنْ غَيْرِ الزَّكوةِ اَكْثَرُ تُعْطِى مِنْهُ الْقَرَابَةَ وَالْمُعْتَرِضَ لَكَ مِمَّنْ يَسْاَلُكَ.
(فروع كافى ج ١ ص ١٥٦)

١٥٠- عَنِ الصَّادِقِ علیه‌السلام فِى قَوْلِ اللهِ عَزَّ وَجَلَّ : وَالَّذِينَ فِى اَمْوَالِهِمْ حَقٌّ مَعْلُومٌ لِلسَّائِلِ وَالْمَحْرُومِ اَهُوَ سِوَى الزَّكوةِ ؟ فَقَالَ علیه‌السلام : هُوَ الرَّجُلُ يُؤْتِيهُ اللهُ الثَّرْوَةَ مِنَ الْمَالِ فَيُخْرِجُ مِنْهُ (مِنَ) الْاَلْفِ وَالْاَلْفَيْنِ وَ الثَّلَاثَةَ الْاَلَافِ وَالْاَقَلَّ وَالْاَكْثَرَ فَيَصِلُ بِهِ رَحِمَهُ وَيَحْمِلُ بِهِ الْكَلَّ عَنْ قَوْمِهِ .
(فروع كافى ج ١ ص ١٤٠)

١٥١- عَنْ عَمَّارٍ السَّابَاطِىّ اَنَّ الصَّادِقَ علیه‌السلام قَالَ لَهُ : يَا عَمَّارُ اَنْتَ رَبُّ مَالٍ كَثِيرٍ ؟ قَالَ نَعَمْ جُعِلْتُ فِدَاكَ . قَالَ : فَتُؤَدِّى مَا افْتَرَضَ اللهُ عَلَيْكَ مِنَ الزَّكوةِ ؟ فَقَالَ نَعَمْ قَالَ : فَتُخْرِجُ الْحَقَّ الْمَعْلُومَ مِنْ مَالِكَ ؟ قَالَ نَعَمْ قَالَ : فَتَصِلُ قَرَابَتَكَ ؟ قَالَ نَعَمْ قَالَ : فَتَصِلُ اِخْوَانَكَ ؟ قَالَ نَعَمْ فَقَالَ علیه‌السلام : يَا عَمَّارُ! اِنَّ الْمَالَ يَفْنَى وَالْبَدَنَ يَبْلَى وَالْعَمَلَ يَبْقَى وَالدَّيَّانَ حَىٌّ لَا يَمُوتُ . يَا عَمَّارُ اِنَّهُ مَا قَدَّمْتَ فَلَنْ يَسْبِقَكَ وَمَا اَخَّرْتَ فَلَنْ يَلْحَقَكَ.
(فروع كافى ج ١ ص ١٤١)

١٥٢- قَالَ رَسُولُ اللهِ ﷺ: كُلُّ امْرِءٍ فِي ظِلِّ صَدَقَتِهِ حَتَّى يُقْضَى بَيْنَ النَّاسِ. (جامع السعادات ج ٢ ص ١٤٣)

١٥٣- قَالَ رَسُولُ اللهِ ﷺ: صَدَقَةُ السِّرِّ تُطْفِئُ غَضَبَ الرَّبِّ. (جامع السعادات ج ٢ ص ١٤٤)

١٥٤- قَالَ أَبُو عَبْدِ اللهِ ﷺ: مَنْ كَسَا مُؤْمِنًا ثَوْبًا مِنْ غِنًى لَمْ يَزَلْ فِي سِتْرٍ مِنَ اللهِ مَا بَقِيَ مِنَ الثَّوْبِ خِرْقَةٌ. (اصول كافى ص ٤١٢)

١٥٥- قَالَ الصَّادِقُ ﷺ: دَاوُوا مَرْضَاكُمْ بِالصَّدَقَةِ ...... اِسْتَنْزِلُوا الرِّزْقَ بِالصَّدَقَةِ .... وَهِيَ تَقَعُ فِي يَدِ الرَّبِّ تَعَالَى قَبْلَ أَنْ تَقَعَ فِي يَدِ الْعَبْدِ. (جامع السعادات ج ٢ ص ١٤٤)

١٥٦- قَالَ الْبَاقِرُ ﷺ: اَلْبِرُّ وَالصَّدَقَةُ يَنْفِيَانِ الْفَقْرَ وَيَزِيدَانِ فِي الْعُمُرِ وَيَدْفَعَانِ عَنْ صَاحِبِهِمَا سَبْعِينَ مِيتَةَ سُوءٍ. (جامع السعادات ج ٢ ص ١٤٤)

١٥٧- سُئِلَ رَسُولُ اللهِ ﷺ أَيُّ الصَّدَقَةِ أَفْضَلُ؟ قَالَ ﷺ: أَنْ تَتَصَدَّقَ وَأَنْتَ صَحِيحٌ شَحِيحٌ، تَأْمَلُ الْبَقَاءَ وَتَخْشَى الْفَاقَةَ وَلَا تُمْهِلْ حَتَّى إِذَا بَلَغَتِ الْحُلْقُومَ قُلْتَ لِفُلَانٍ كَذَا وَلِفُلَانٍ كَذَا. (جامع السعادات ج ٢ ص ١٤٥)

١٥٨- قَالَ اللهُ تَعَالَى: اَلَّذِينَ يُنْفِقُونَ أَمْوَالَهُمْ فِي سَبِيلِ اللهِ ثُمَّ لَا يُتْبِعُونَ مَا أَنْفَقُوا مَنًّا وَلَا أَذًى لَهُمْ أَجْرُهُمْ عِنْدَ رَبِّهِمْ وَلَا خَوْفٌ عَلَيْهِمْ وَلَا هُمْ يَحْزَنُونَ. (سوره بقره آيت ٢٦٢)

۱۵۹ - قَوْلُهُ تَعَالَى : يَا أَيُّهَا الَّذِينَ آمَنُوا لَا تُبْطِلُوا صَدَقَاتِكُمْ بِالْمَنِّ وَالْأَذَى كَالَّذِي يُنْفِقُ مَالَهُ رِئَاءَ النَّاسِ وَلَا يُؤْمِنُ بِاللَّهِ وَالْيَوْمِ الْآخِرِ فَمَثَلُهُ كَمَثَلِ صَفْوَانٍ عَلَيْهِ تُرَابٌ فَأَصَابَهُ وَابِلٌ فَتَرَكَهُ صَلْدًا لَا يَقْدِرُونَ عَلَى شَيْءٍ مِمَّا كَسَبُوا وَاللَّهُ لَا يَهْدِي الْقَوْمَ الْكَافِرِينَ. وَمَثَلُ الَّذِينَ يُنْفِقُونَ أَمْوَالَهُمُ ابْتِغَاءَ مَرْضَاتِ اللَّهِ وَتَثْبِيتًا مِنْ أَنْفُسِهِمْ كَمَثَلِ جَنَّةٍ بِرَبْوَةٍ أَصَابَهَا وَابِلٌ فَآتَتْ أُكُلَهَا ضِعْفَيْنِ فَإِنْ لَمْ يُصِبْهَا وَابِلٌ فَطَلٌّ وَاللَّهُ بِمَا تَعْمَلُونَ بَصِيرٌ.

(سوره بقره - آیت ۲۶۴ - ۲۶۵)

۱۶۰ - قَالَ رَسُولُ اللَّهِ ﷺ: مَنْ أَسْدَى إِلَى مُؤْمِنٍ مَعْرُوفًا ثُمَّ آذَاهُ بِالْكَلَامِ أَوْ مَنَّ عَلَيْهِ فَقَدْ أَبْطَلَ اللَّهُ صَدَقَتَهُ.

(وسائل الشیعه ج ۲ ص ۵۵)

۱۶۱ - قَالَ رَسُولُ اللَّهِ ﷺ: الْمَنَّانُ بِمَا يُعْطِي لَا يُكَلِّمُهُ اللَّهُ وَلَا يَنْظُرُ إِلَيْهِ وَلَا يُزَكِّيهِ ....

(مجمع البیان چاپ صیدا ج۱ ص ۳۷۵)

۱۶۲ - قَالَ عَلِيٌّ ؏: إِذَا نَاوَلْتُمُ السَّائِلَ فَلْيَرُدَّ الَّذِي نَاوَلَهُ يَدَهُ إِلَى فِيهِ فَيُقَبِّلُهَا فَإِنَّ اللَّهَ عَزَّ وَجَلَّ يَأْخُذُ الصَّدَقَاتِ

(جامع السعادات ج ۲ ص ۱۳۱)

۱۶۳ - قَالَ رَسُولُ اللَّهِ ﷺ: سَبْعَةٌ يُظِلُّهُمُ اللَّهُ فِي ظِلِّهِ يَوْمَ لَا ظِلَّ إِلَّا ظِلُّهُ (وَعَدَّ مِنْهَا) وَرَجُلٌ تَصَدَّقَ بِصَدَقَةٍ فَأَخْفَاهَا حَتَّى لَمْ تَعْلَمْ يَمِينُهُ مَا تُنْفِقُ

شِمالُهُ. (مجمع البيان ج ١ ص ٣٨٥)

١٦٤- قَوْلُهُ تَعَالَى: وَالَّذِينَ إِذَا أَنْفَقُوا لَمْ يُسْرِفُوا وَلَمْ يَقْتُرُوا وَكَانَ بَيْنَ ذَلِكَ قَوَامًا. (سوره فرقان آيت ٦٧)

١٦٥- قَالَ الصَّادِقُ عَلَيْهِ السَّلَامُ: الْكَمَالُ كُلُّ الْكَمَالِ فِي ثَلَاثَةٍ فَذَكَرَ فِي الثَّالِثَةِ التَّقْدِيرَ فِي الْمَعِيشَةِ.

(وسائل الشيعة ج ٢ ص ٥٣٤)

١٦٦- قَالَ أَبُو جَعْفَرٍ عَلَيْهِ السَّلَامُ: مَا خَيْرٌ فِي رَجُلٍ لَا يَقْتَصِدُ فِي مَعِيشَتِهِ مَا يَصْلُحُ لَا لِدُنْيَاهُ وَلَا لِآخِرَتِهِ.

(وسائل الشيعة ج ٢ ص ٥٣٤)

١٦٧- قَوْلُهُ تَعَالَى: وَلَا تُبَذِّرْ تَبْذِيرًا إِنَّ الْمُبَذِّرِينَ كَانُوا إِخْوَانَ الشَّيَاطِينِ. (سوره اسراء آيت ٢٦)

١٦٨- قَوْلُهُ تَعَالَى: وَأَحَلَّ اللهُ الْبَيْعَ وَحَرَّمَ الرِّبَا.

(سوره بقره آيت ٢٧٥)

١٦٩- قَالَ الصَّادِقُ عَلَيْهِ السَّلَامُ: مَا مِنْ مُسْلِمٍ أَقْرَضَ مُسْلِمًا قَرْضًا حَسَنًا يُرِيدُ بِهِ وَجْهَ اللهِ إِلَّا حَسِبَ لَهُ أَجْرَهَا كَحِسَابِ الصَّدَقَةِ حَتَّى يَرْجِعَ إِلَيْهِ. (وسائل الشيعة ج ٢ ص ٦٢١)

١٧٠- قَالَ رَسُولُ اللهِ صَلَّى اللهُ عَلَيْهِ وَآلِهِ: رَأَيْتُ مَكْتُوبًا عَلَى بَابِ الْجَنَّةِ: الصَّدَقَةُ بِعَشَرَةٍ وَالْقَرْضُ بِثَمَانِيَةَ عَشَرَ. فَقُلْتُ يَا جِبْرِيلُ وَلِمَ ذَلِكَ وَالَّذِي يَتَصَدَّقُ لَا يُرِيدُ الرُّجُوعَ وَالَّذِي يُقْرِضُ يُعْطِي لِأَنْ يُرْجِعَهُ؟ فَقَالَ نَعَمْ هُوَ كَذَلِكَ وَلَكِنْ كُلُّ مَنْ يَأْخُذُ الصَّدَقَةَ لَهُ بِهَا حَاجَةٌ فَالصَّدَقَةُ قَدْ تَصِلُ إِلَى غَيْرِ الْمُسْتَحِقِّ

226

وَالْقَرْضُ لَا يَصِلُ اِلَّا اِلَى الْمُسْتَحِقِّ وَلِذَا صَارَ الْقَرْضُ اَفْضَلَ مِنَ الصَّدَقَةِ. (مستدرك الوسائل ج ٢ ص ٤٩٠)

١٧١ - قَالَ رَسُولُ اللهِ ﷺ: اِيَّاكُمْ وَالدَّيْنَ فَاِنَّهُ شَيْنٌ لِلدِّينِ وَهُوَ هَمٌّ بِاللَّيْلِ وَذُلٌّ بِالنَّهَارِ.

(مستدرك الوسائل ج ٢ ص ٤٨٨)

١٧٢ - قَالَ الصَّادِقُ عَلَيْهِ السَّلامُ: خَفِّفُوا الدَّيْنَ فَاِنَّ فِي خِفَّةِ الدَّيْنِ زِيَادَةَ الْعُمُرِ. (مستدرك الوسائل ج ٢ ص ٤٨٨)

١٧٣ - قَالَ رَسُولُ اللهِ ﷺ: اَعُوذُ بِاللهِ مِنَ الْكُفْرِ وَالدَّيْنِ قِيلَ يَا رَسُولَ اللهِ اَتَعْدِلُ الدَّيْنَ بِالْكُفْرِ؟ قَالَ نَعَمْ.

(وسائل الشيعة ج ٢ ص ٦٢٠)

١٧٤ - قَالَ اَبُو الْحَسَنِ عَلَيْهِ السَّلامُ: مَنْ طَلَبَ هَذَا الرِّزْقَ مِنْ حِلِّهِ لِيَعُودَ بِهِ عَلَى نَفْسِهِ وَعِيَالِهِ كَانَ كَالْمُجَاهِدِ فِي سَبِيلِ اللهِ عَزَّ وَجَلَّ. فَاِنْ غُلِبَ عَلَيْهِ فَلْيَسْتَدِنْ عَلَى اللهِ وَرَسُولِهِ مَا يَقُوتُ بِهِ عِيَالَهُ. فَاِنْ مَاتَ وَلَمْ يَقْضِهِ كَانَ عَلَى الْاِمَامِ عَلَيْهِ السَّلامُ قَضَاؤُهُ. (فروع كافي ج ١ ص ٣٥٣)

١٧٥ - قَالَ رَسُولُ اللهِ ﷺ: اِنَّ اللهَ مَعَ الدَّايِنِ مَا لَمْ يَكُنْ دَيْنُهُ فِي اَمْرٍ يَكْرَهُهُ اللهُ. (مستدرك الوسائل ج ٢ ص ٤٨٩)

١٧٦ - عَنْ مُعَاوِيَةَ بْنِ وَهَبٍ قَالَ: قُلْتُ لِاَبِي عَبْدِ اللهِ عَلَيْهِ السَّلامُ اِنَّهُ ذَكَرَ لَنَا اَنَّ رَجُلًا مِنَ الْاَنْصَارِ مَاتَ وَعَلَيْهِ دِينَارَانِ دَيْنًا فَلَمْ يُصَلِّ عَلَيْهِ النَّبِيُّ ﷺ وَقَالَ صَلُّوا عَلَى صَاحِبِكُمْ حَتَّى ضَمِنَهَا بَعْضُ قَرَابَتِهِ فَقَالَ اَبُو عَبْدِ اللهِ

ﷺ: ذلِكَ الْحَقُّ. ثُمَّ قَالَ: اِنَّ رَسُولَ اللّٰهِ ﷺ اِنَّمَا فَعَلَ ذٰلِكَ لِيَتَّعِظُوا وَلِيَرُدَّ بَعْضُهُمْ عَلٰى بَعْضٍ وَلِئَلَّا يَسْتَخِفُّوا بِالدَّيْنِ... (فروع كافى ج ١ ص ٣٥٣)

١٧٧- قَالَ الْبَاقِرُ ؏: كُلُّ ذَنْبٍ يُكَفِّرُهُ الْقَتْلُ فِى سَبِيلِ اللّٰهِ اِلَّا الدَّيْنَ، لَاكَفَّارَةَ لَهُ اِلَّا اَدَاءُهُ اَوْيَقْضِى صَاحِبُهُ اَوْيَعْفُوَ الَّذِى لَهُ الْحَقُّ. (فروع كافى ج ١ ص ٣٥٤)

١٧٨- قَالَ رَسُولُ اللّٰهِ ﷺ: لَيْسَ ذَنْبٌ اَعْظَمَ عِنْدَ اللّٰهِ بَعْدَ الْكَبَائِرِ مِنْ رَجُلٍ يَمُوتُ وَعَلَيْهِ دَيْنٌ لِرِجَالٍ وَلَيْسَ لَهُ مَا يَقْضِى عَنْهُ. (مستدرك الوسائل ج ٢ ص ٤٨٩)

١٧٩- قَالَ الصَّادِقُ ؏: مَنِ اسْتَدَانَ دَيْنًا فَلَمْ يَنْوِ قَضَاءَهُ كَانَ بِمَنْزِلَةِ السَّارِقِ. (وسائل الشيعة ج ٢ ص ٦٢١)

١٨٠- قَالَ عَلِىُّ بْنُ الْحُسَيْنِ ؏ فِى وَصِيَّتِهِ لِابْنِهِ: اِعْلَمْ يَا بُنَىَّ اِنَّهُ مَنِ اسْتَدَانَ دَيْنًا وَنَوٰى قَضَاءَهُ فَهُوَ فِى اَمَانِ اللّٰهِ حَتّٰى يَقْضِيَهُ وَاِنْ لَمْ يَنْوِ قَضَاءَهُ فَهُوَ سَارِقٌ. (مستدرك الوسائل ج ٢ ص ٤٨٩)

١٨١- قَالَ رَسُولُ اللّٰهِ ﷺ: وَمَنْ مَطَلَ عَلٰى ذِى حَقٍّ حَقَّهُ وَهُوَ يَقْدِرُ عَلٰى اَدَاءِ حَقِّهِ فَعَلَيْهِ كُلَّ يَوْمٍ خَطِيئَةُ عِشَارٍ. (وسائل الشيعة ج ٢ ص ٦٢٢)

١٨٢- قَالَ الْبَاقِرُ ؏: مَنْ حَبَسَ حَقَّ امْرِئٍ مُسْلِمٍ وَهُوَ يَقْدِرُ عَلٰى اَنْ يُعْطِيَهُ اِيَّاهُ مَخَافَةَ اَنَّهُ اِذَا خَرَجَ ذٰلِكَ الْحَقُّ مِنْ يَدِهِ اَنْ يَفْتَقِرَ كَانَ اللّٰهُ عَزَّ وَجَلَّ اَقْدَرَ اَنْ يُفْقِرَهُ

مِنْهُ عَلَى أَنْ يُغْنِى نَفْسَهُ بِحَبْسِ ذَلِكَ الْحَقِّ .

(وسائل الشيعة ج ٢ ص ٦٢١)

١٨٣ ـ فِقْهُ الرِّضَا رُوِىَ : كَمَا لَا يَحِلُّ لِلْغَرِيمِ الْمَطْلُ وَهُوَ مُوسِرٌ كَذَلِكَ لَا يَحِلُّ لِصَاحِبِ الْمَالِ أَنْ يُعْسِرَ الْمُعْسَرَ .

(مستدرك الوسائل ج ٢ ص ٣٩٠)

١٨٤ ـ قَوْلُهُ تَعَالَى : وَإِنْ كَانَ ذُو عُسْرَةٍ فَنَظِرَةٌ إِلَى مَيْسَرَةٍ وَأَنْ تَصَدَّقُوا خَيْرٌ لَكُمْ إِنْ كُنْتُمْ تَعْلَمُونَ .

(سوره بقره ـ آيت ٢٨٠)

١٨٥ ـ قَالَ أَبُو عَبْدِ اللهِ (ع) : لَا تُبَاعُ الدَّارُ وَلَا الْجَارِيَةُ فِى الدَّيْنِ وَذَلِكَ أَنَّهُ لَا بُدَّ لِلرَّجُلِ مِنْ ظِلٍّ يَسْكُنُهُ ......

(فروع كافى ج ١ ص ٣٥٤)

١٨٦ ـ عَنْ إِبْرَاهِيمَ بْنِ هَاشِمٍ : أَنَّ مُحَمَّدَ بْنَ أَبِى عُمَيْرٍ كَانَ رَجُلًا بَزَّازًا فَذَهَبَ مَالُهُ وَافْتَقَرَ وَكَانَ لَهُ عَلَى رَجُلٍ عَشَرَةُ آلَافِ دِرْهَمٍ فَبَاعَ دَارًا لَهُ كَانَ يَسْكُنُهَا بِعَشَرَةِ آلَافِ دِرْهَمٍ وَحَمَلَ الْمَالَ إِلَى بَابِهِ فَخَرَجَ إِلَيْهِ مُحَمَّدُ بْنُ عُمَيْرٍ فَقَالَ مَا هَذَا ؟ فَقَالَ هَذَا مَالُكَ الَّذِى لَكَ عَلَىَّ . قَالَ وَرِثْتَهُ ؟ قَالَ : لَا . قَالَ وُهِبَ لَكَ قَالَ : لَا . فَقَالَ : هُوَ مِنْ ثَمَنِ ضَيْعَةٍ بِعْتَهَا ؟ فَقَالَ : لَا . فَقَالَ : مَا هُوَ ؟ فَقَالَ بِعْتُ دَارِى الَّتِى أَسْكُنُهَا لِأَقْضِىَ دَيْنِى. فَقَالَ مُحَمَّدُ بْنُ عُمَيْرٍ : حَدَّثَنِى زُرَيْعٌ الْمُحَارِبُ عَنْ أَبِى عَبْدِ اللهِ (ع) قَالَ : لَا يُخْرِجُ الرَّجُلُ

مِنْ مَسْقَطِ رَأْسِهِ بِالدَّيْنِ. اِدْفَعْهَا فَلَا حَاجَةَ لِي فِيهَا وَإِنِّي لَمُحْتَاجٌ فِي وَقْتِي هَذَا إِلَى دِرْهَمٍ وَمَا يَدْخُلُ مِلْكِي مِنْ هَذَا الدِّرْهَمِ. (وسائل الشیعه ج ۲ ص ۶۲۲)

۱۸۷- قَالَ رَسُولُ اللهِ ﷺ: أَوَّلُ شَيْءٍ يُبْدَأُ بِهِ مِنَ الْمَالِ: الْكَفَنُ ثُمَّ الدَّيْنُ ثُمَّ الْوَصِيَّةُ ثُمَّ الْمِيرَاثُ.

(مستدرك الوسائل ج ۲ ص ۴۹۱)

۱۸۸- قَالَ الْبَاقِرُ ﷺ: إِذَا كَانَ عَلَى الرَّجُلِ دَيْنٌ إِلَى أَجَلٍ وَّ مَاتَ الرَّجُلُ حَلَّ الدَّيْنُ. (وسائل الشیعه ج۲ ص ۶۲۳)

۱۸۹- قَالَ الرِّضَا ﷺ: وَإِنْ كَانَ لَكَ عَلَى رَجُلٍ مَّالٌ وَضَمِنَهُ رَجُلٌ عِنْدَ مَوْتِهِ وَقَبِلْتَ ضَمَانَتَهُ فَالْمَيِّتُ قَدْ بَرِئَ مِنْهُ وَقَدْ لَزِمَ الضَّامِنَ رَدُّهُ عَلَيْكَ.

(مستدرك الوسائل ج ۲ ص ۴۹۱)

۱۹۰- قَالَ عَلِيٌّ ﷺ: عَاقِبْ أَخَاكَ بِالْإِحْسَانِ إِلَيْهِ وَارْدُدْ شَرَّهُ بِالْإِنْعَامِ عَلَيْهِ. (نهج البلاغة ص ۱۱۵۵)

۱۹۱- قَوْلُهُ تَعَالَى: اَلَّذِينَ يُنْفِقُونَ فِي السَّرَّاءِ وَالضَّرَّاءِ وَالْكَاظِمِينَ الْغَيْظَ وَالْعَافِينَ عَنِ النَّاسِ وَاللهُ يُحِبُّ الْمُحْسِنِينَ. (سوره آل عمران آیت ۱۳۴)

۱۹۲- قَوْلُهُ تَعَالَى: وَلْيَعْفُوا وَلْيَصْفَحُوا أَلَا تُحِبُّونَ أَنْ يَّغْفِرَ اللهُ لَكُمْ وَاللهُ غَفُورٌ رَّحِيمٌ. (سوره نور آیت ۲۲)

۱۹۳- قَوْلُهُ تَعَالَى: فَمَنْ عَفَا وَأَصْلَحَ فَأَجْرُهُ عَلَى اللهِ ... (سوره شوری آیت ۴۰)

١٩٤- قَالَ رَسُولُ اللهِ ﷺ: اَلاَ اَدُلُّكُم عَلَى خَيرِ اَخلاَقِ الدُّنيَا وَالآخِرَةِ ؛ تَصِلُ مَن قَطَعَكَ وَتُعطِى مَن حَرَمَكَ وَتَعفُو عَمَّن ظَلَمَكَ.   (اصول كافى ، ص ٣٦١)

١٩٥- قَالَ الصَّادِقُ ﷷ: قَالَ رَسُولُ اللهِ ﷺ: عَلَيكُم بِالعَفوِ فَاِنَّ العَفوَ لاَ يَزِيدُ العَبدَ اِلاَّ عِزًّا فَتَعَافُوا يُعِزَّكُمُ اللهُ.   (اصول كافى ، ص ٣٦١)

١٩٦- قَالَ عَلِىٌّ ﷷ: اِذَا قَدَرتَ عَلَى عَدُوِّكَ فَاجعَلِ العَفوَ عَنهُ شُكرًا لِلقُدرَةِ عَلَيهِ.   (نهج البلاغه ص ١٠٨٢)

١٩٧- قَالَ عَلِىٌّ ﷷ: اَولَى النَّاسِ بِالعَفوِ اَقدَرُهُم عَلَى العُقُوبَةِ.   (نهج البلاغه ص ١١٠٢)

١٩٨- قَالَ الصَّادِقُ ﷷ: اِنَّا اَهلُ بَيتٍ مُرُوَّتُنَا العَفوُ عَمَّن ظَلَمَنَا.   (وسائل الشيعه ج ٢ ص ٢٢٤)

١٩٩- قَالَ الصَّادِقُ ﷷ: العَفوُ عِندَ القُدرَةِ مِن سُنَنِ المُرسَلِينَ وَالمُتَّقِينَ.   (سفينة البحار ج ٢ ص ٢٠٧)

٢٠٠- قَولُهُ تَعَالَى: وَمِنَ النَّاسِ مَن يَقُولُ آمَنَّا بِاللهِ وَبِاليَومِ الآخِرِ وَمَا هُم بِمُؤمِنِينَ. يُخَادِعُونَ اللهَ وَالَّذِينَ آمَنُوا وَمَا يَخدَعُونَ اِلاَّ اَنفُسَهُم وَمَا يَشعُرُونَ. فِى قُلُوبِهِم مَرَضٌ فَزَادَهُمُ اللهُ مَرَضًا وَلَهُم عَذَابٌ اَلِيمٌ بِمَا كَانُوا يَكذِبُونَ. وَاِذَا قِيلَ لَهُم لاَ تُفسِدُوا فِى الاَرضِ قَالُوا اِنَّمَا نَحنُ مُصلِحُونَ. اَلاَ اِنَّهُم هُمُ المُفسِدُونَ وَلَكِن لاَ يَشعُرُونَ. وَاِذَا قِيلَ لَهُم آمِنُوا كَمَا آمَنَ

231

النَّاسُ قَالُوا أَنُؤْمِنُ كَمَا آمَنَ السُّفَهَاءُ أَلَا إِنَّهُمْ هُمُ السُّفَهَاءُ وَلَكِنْ لَا يَعْلَمُونَ. وَإِذَا لَقُوا الَّذِينَ آمَنُوا قَالُوا آمَنَّا وَإِذَا خَلَوْا إِلَى شَيَاطِينِهِمْ قَالُوا إِنَّا مَعَكُمْ إِنَّمَا نَحْنُ مُسْتَهْزِئُونَ. اللهُ يَسْتَهْزِئُ بِهِمْ وَيَمُدُّهُمْ فِي طُغْيَانِهِمْ يَعْمَهُونَ. أُولَئِكَ الَّذِينَ اشْتَرَوُا الضَّلَالَةَ بِالْهُدَى فَمَا رَبِحَتْ تِجَارَتُهُمْ وَمَا كَانُوا مُهْتَدِينَ. مَثَلُهُمْ كَمَثَلِ الَّذِي اسْتَوْقَدَ نَارًا فَلَمَّا أَضَاءَتْ مَا حَوْلَهُ ذَهَبَ اللهُ بِنُورِهِمْ وَتَرَكَهُمْ فِي ظُلُمَاتٍ لَا يُبْصِرُونَ. صُمٌّ بُكْمٌ عُمْيٌ فَهُمْ لَا يَرْجِعُونَ. أَوْ كَصَيِّبٍ مِنَ السَّمَاءِ فِيهِ ظُلُمَاتٌ وَرَعْدٌ وَبَرْقٌ يَجْعَلُونَ أَصَابِعَهُمْ فِي آذَانِهِمْ مِنَ الصَّوَاعِقِ حَذَرَ الْمَوْتِ وَاللهُ مُحِيطٌ بِالْكَافِرِينَ. يَكَادُ الْبَرْقُ يَخْطَفُ أَبْصَارَهُمْ كُلَّمَا أَضَاءَ لَهُمْ مَشَوْا فِيهِ وَإِذَا أَظْلَمَ عَلَيْهِمْ قَامُوا وَلَوْ شَاءَ اللهُ لَذَهَبَ بِسَمْعِهِمْ وَأَبْصَارِهِمْ إِنَّ اللهَ عَلَى كُلِّ شَيْءٍ قَدِيرٌ. (سوره بقره آيت ٨ـ٢٠)

٢٠١ـ قَوْلُهُ تَعَالَى: بَشِّرِ الْمُنَافِقِينَ بِأَنَّ لَهُمْ عَذَابًا أَلِيمًا. الَّذِينَ يَتَّخِذُونَ الْكَافِرِينَ أَوْلِيَاءَ مِنْ دُونِ الْمُؤْمِنِينَ أَيَبْتَغُونَ عِنْدَهُمُ الْعِزَّةَ فَإِنَّ الْعِزَّةَ لِلَّهِ جَمِيعًا. وَقَدْ نَزَّلَ عَلَيْكُمْ فِي الْكِتَابِ أَنْ إِذَا سَمِعْتُمْ آيَاتِ اللهِ يُكْفَرُ بِهَا وَيُسْتَهْزَأُ بِهَا فَلَا تَقْعُدُوا مَعَهُمْ حَتَّى يَخُوضُوا فِي حَدِيثٍ غَيْرِهِ إِنَّكُمْ إِذًا مِثْلُهُمْ إِنَّ اللهَ جَامِعُ

الْمُنَافِقِينَ وَالْكَافِرِينَ فِي جَهَنَّمَ جَمِيعًا.

(سوره نساء ـ آيت ١٣٧-١٤٠)

٢٠٢ - قَوْلُهُ تَعَالَى : وَعَدَ اللهُ الْمُنَافِقِينَ وَالْمُنَافِقَاتِ وَالْكُفَّارَ نَارَ جَهَنَّمَ خَالِدِينَ فِيهَا وَلَهُمْ عَذَابٌ مُقِيمٌ.

(سوره توبه ـ آيت ٦٨)

٢٠٣ - قَالَ رَسُولُ اللهِ ﷺ: مَثَلُ الْمُنَافِقِ مَثَلُ جِذْعِ النَّخْلِ أَرَادَ صَاحِبُهُ أَنْ يَنْتَفِعَ بِهِ فِي بَعْضِ بِنَائِهِ فَلَمْ يَسْتَقِمْ لَهُ فِي الْمَوْضِعِ الَّذِي أَرَادَ فَحَوَّلَهُ فِي مَوْضِعٍ آخَرَ فَلَمْ يَسْتَقِمْ لَهُ فَكَانَ آخِرُ ذَلِكَ أَنْ أَحْرَقَهُ بِالنَّارِ.

(اصول كافي ص ٤٨٥)

٢٠٤ - قَالَ رَسُولُ اللهِ ﷺ : مَازَادَ خُشُوعُ الْجَسَدِ عَلَى مَا فِي الْقَلْبِ فَهُوَ عِنْدَنَا نِفَاقٌ. (اصول كافي ص ٤٨٥)

٢٠٥ - قَالَ رَسُولُ اللهِ ﷺ : وَلِلْمُنَافِقِ ثَلَاثُ عَلَامَاتٍ : إِذَا حَدَّثَ كَذَبَ وَإِذَا وَعَدَ أَخْلَفَ وَإِذَا اؤْتُمِنَ خَانَ.

(بحار الانوار ج ١٥ ـ جزء ٣ ص ٣٠)

٢٠٦ - قَالَ أَبُو عَبْدِ اللهِ ﷻ : قَالَ لُقْمَانُ لِابْنِهِ : .... وَلِلْمُنَافِقِ ثَلَاثُ عَلَامَاتٍ : يُخَالِفُ لِسَانُهُ قَلْبَهُ وَقَلْبُهُ فِعْلَهُ وَعَلَانِيَتُهُ سَرِيرَتَهُ.

(بحار الانوار ج ١٥ ـ جزء ٣ ص ٣٠)

٢٠٧ - عَنِ الْبَاقِرِ ﷻ قَالَ : بِئْسَ الْعَبْدُ عَبْدٌ يَكُونُ ذَا وَجْهَيْنِ وَذَا لِسَانَيْنِ يُطْرِي أَخَاهُ شَاهِدًا وَيَأْكُلُهُ غَائِبًا، إِنْ

اُعطِيَ حِسَدَهُ وَاِنِ ابْتُلِيَ خَذَلَهُ .

(بحار الانوار ج ١٥ كتاب العشرة ص ١٧٣)

٢٠٨ـ قَالَ رَسُولُ اللهِ ﷺ : مَنْ كَانَ لَهُ وَجْهَانِ فِى الدُّنْيَا كَانَ لَهُ يَوْمَ الْقِيَامَةِ لِسَانَانِ مِنْ نَارٍ .

(بحار الانوار ج ١٥ كتاب العشرة ص ١٧٣)

٢٠٩ـ قَوْلُهُ تَعَالَى : يَا أَيُّهَا الَّذِينَ آمَنُوا اجْتَنِبُوا كَثِيرًا مِنَ الظَّنِّ إِنَّ بَعْضَ الظَّنِّ إِثْمٌ . (سوره حجرات آيت ١٢)

٢١٠ـ قَالَ عَلِىٌّ ﷿ : سُوءُ الظَّنِّ بِالْمُحْسِنِ شَرُّ الْإِثْمِ وَأَقْبَحُ الظُّلْمِ .

(غرر الحكم ج ١ ص ٤٣٣)

٢١١ـ قَالَ عَلِىٌّ ﷿ : لَيْسَ مِنَ الْعَدْلِ الْقَضَاءُ عَلَى الثِّقَةِ بِالظَّنِّ .

(نهج البلاغه ص ١٢٤٤)

٢١٢ـ قَالَ عَلِىٌّ ﷿ : لَا تَظُنَّنَّ بِكَلِمَةٍ خَرَجَتْ مِنْ أَحَدٍ سُوءًا وَ أَنْتَ تَجِدُ لَهَا فِى الْخَيْرِ مُحْتَمَلًا .

(نهج البلاغه ص ١٢٤٤)

٢١٣ـ قَالَ أَبُو عَبْدِ اللهِ ﷿ : مِنْ حَقِّ الْمُؤْمِنِ عَلَى الْمُؤْمِنِ .... وَأَنْ لَا يُكَذِّبَهُ .   (اصول كافى ص ٣٩٤)

٢١٤ـ قَالَ عَلِىٌّ ﷿ : الشِّرِّيرُ لَا يَظُنُّ بِأَحَدٍ خَيْرًا لِأَنَّهُ لَا يَرَاهُ إِلَّا بِطَبْعِ نَفْسِهِ .   (غرر الحكم ج ١ ص ٨٠)

٢١٥ـ رُوِىَ أَنَّهُ ﷺ كَانَ يُكَلِّمُ زَوْجَتَهُ صَفِيَّةَ بِنْتَ حُيَىّ ابْنِ أَخْطَبَ فَمَرَّ بِهِ رَجُلٌ مِنَ الْأَنْصَارِ فَدَعَاهُ رَسُولُ اللهِ ﷺ وَقَالَ : يَا فُلَانُ هذِهِ زَوْجَتِى صَفِيَّةُ. فَقَالَ:

يَا رَسُولَ اللهِ أَفَظَنَنْتَ بِكَ الْأَخِيرَ قَالَ: إِنَّ الشَّيْطَانَ يَجْرِي مِنِ ابْنِ آدَمَ مَجْرَى الدَّمِ فَخَشِيتُ أَنْ يَدْخُلَ عَلَيْكَ.
(جامع السعادات ج ١ ص ٢٨٣)

٢١٦- قَوْلُهُ تَعَالَى: وَاذْكُرْ فِي الْكِتَابِ إِبْرَاهِيمَ إِنَّهُ كَانَ صِدِّيقًا نَبِيًّا.
(سوره مريم آيت ٤١)

٢١٧- قَوْلُهُ تَعَالَى: (حِكَايَةً عَنْ رَسُولِ مَلِكِ مِصْرَ) أَيُّهَا الصِّدِّيقُ أَفْتِنَا...
(سوره يوسف آيت ٤٦)

٢١٨- قَوْلُهُ تَعَالَى: وَاذْكُرْ فِي الْكِتَابِ إِسْمَاعِيلَ إِنَّهُ كَانَ صَادِقَ الْوَعْدِ وَكَانَ رَسُولًا نَبِيًّا.
(سوره مريم آيت ٥٤)

٢١٩- قَوْلُهُ تَعَالَى: وَاذْكُرْ فِي الْكِتَابِ إِدْرِيسَ إِنَّهُ كَانَ صِدِّيقًا نَبِيًّا.
(سوره مريم آيت ٥٦)

٢٢٠- قَوْلُهُ تَعَالَى: وَجَعَلْنَا لَهُمْ لِسَانَ صِدْقٍ عَلِيًّا.
(سوره مريم آيت ٥٠)

٢٢١- قَالَ أَبُو عَبْدِ اللهِ عليه السلام: إِنَّ اللهَ عَزَّ وَجَلَّ لَمْ يَبْعَثْ نَبِيًّا إِلَّا بِصِدْقِ الْحَدِيثِ وَأَدَاءِ الْأَمَانَةِ إِلَى الْبِرِّ وَالْفَاجِرِ.
(اصول كافى ص ٣٦٠)

٢٢٢- قَالَ أَبُو عَبْدِ اللهِ عليه السلام: لَا تَغْتَرُّوا بِصَلَاتِهِمْ وَلَا صِيَامِهِمْ فَإِنَّ الرَّجُلَ رُبَّمَا لَهِجَ بِالصَّلَاةِ وَالصَّوْمِ حَتَّى لَوْ تَرَكَهُ اسْتَوْحَشَ وَلَكِنِ اخْتَبِرُوهُمْ عِنْدَ صِدْقِ الْحَدِيثِ وَأَدَاءِ الْأَمَانَةِ.
(اصول كافى ص ٣٦٠)

٢٢٣- قَالَ أَبُوعَبْدِاللهِ عَلَيْهِ السَّلامُ : مَنْ صَدَقَ لِسَانُهُ زَكَى عَمَلُهُ .
(وسائل الشيعه ج ٢ ص ٢٢٢)

٢٢٤- قَالَ رَسُولُ اللهِ صَلَّى اللهُ عَلَيْهِ وَآلِهِ : إِنَّ أَقْرَبَكُمْ مِنِّي غَدًا وَأَوْجَبَكُمْ عَلَيَّ شَفَاعَةً أَصْدَقُكُمْ لِلْحَدِيثِ وَآدَاكُمْ لِلْأَمَانَةِ ...
(وسائل الشيعه ج ٢ ص ٢٢٢)

٢٢٥- قَالَ رَسُولُ اللهِ صَلَّى اللهُ عَلَيْهِ وَآلِهِ : أُوصِيكَ يَاعَلِيُّ فِي نَفْسِكَ بِخِصَالٍ اللَّهُمَّ أَعِنْهُ ... الْأُولَى : اَلصِّدْقُ وَلَا يَخْرُجَنَّ مِنْ فِيكَ كِذْبَةٌ أَبَدًا .
(وسائل الشيعه ج ٢ ص ٢٢٢)

٢٢٦- قَالَ عَلِيٌّ عَلَيْهِ السَّلامُ : اَلْزَمُوا الصِّدْقَ فَإِنَّهُ مَنْجَاةٌ .
(بحار الانوار ج ١٥ جزء ٢ ص ١٢٥)

٢٢٧- قَوْلُهُ تَعَالَى : إِنَّمَا يَفْتَرِي الْكَذِبَ الَّذِينَ لَا يُؤْمِنُونَ بِآيَاتِ اللهِ .
(سوره نحل آيت ١٠٦)

٢٢٨- قَوْلُهُ تَعَالَى : إِنَّ اللهَ لَا يَهْدِي مَنْ هُوَ كَاذِبٌ كَفَّارٌ .
(سوره زمر آيت ٣)

٢٢٩- قَوْلُهُ تَعَالَى : وَيَوْمَ الْقِيَامَةِ تَرَى الَّذِينَ كَذَبُوا عَلَى اللهِ وُجُوهُهُمْ مُسْوَدَّةٌ . (سوره زمر آيت ٦٠)

٢٣٠- قَالَ أَبُوعَبْدِاللهِ عَلَيْهِ السَّلامُ : قَالَ عِيسَى بْنُ مَرْيَمَ عَلَيْهِ السَّلامُ : مَنْ كَثُرَ كِذْبُهُ ذَهَبَ بَهَاؤُهُ . (وسائل الشيعه ج ٢ ص ٢٣٣)

٢٣١- قَالَ أَبُوجَعْفَرٍ عَلَيْهِ السَّلامُ : إِنَّ اللهَ جَعَلَ لِلشَّرِّ أَقْفَالًا وَجَعَلَ مَفَاتِيحَ تِلْكَ الْأَقْفَالِ الشَّرَابَ وَالْكَذِبُ شَرٌّ مِنَ الشَّرَابِ .
(وسائل الشيعه ج ٢ ص ٢٣٣)

٢٣٢- قَالَ الْإِمَامُ الْعَسْكَرِيُّ عَلَيْهِ السَّلَامُ: جُعِلَتِ الْخَبَائِثُ كُلُّهَا فِي بَيْتٍ وَجُعِلَ مِفْتَاحُهَا الْكِذْبَ.

(جامع السعادات ج ٢ ص ٣١٨)

٢٣٣- قَالَ أَبُو جَعْفَرٍ عَلَيْهِ السَّلَامُ: اَلْكِذْبُ هُوَ خَرَابُ الْإِيمَانِ.

(جامع السعادات ج ٢ ص ٣١٨)

٢٣٤- قَالَ أَمِيرُ الْمُؤْمِنِينَ عَلَيْهِ السَّلَامُ: لَا يَجِدُ عَبْدٌ طَعْمَ الْإِيمَانِ حَتَّى يَتْرُكَ الْكِذْبَ جِدَّهُ وَهَزْلَهُ.

(وسائل الشيعة ج ٢ ص ٢٣٤)

٢٣٥- قَالَ أَبُو الْحَسَنِ الرِّضَا عَلَيْهِ السَّلَامُ: سُئِلَ رَسُولُ اللهِ صَلَّى اللهُ عَلَيْهِ وَآلِهِ: يَكُونُ الْمُؤْمِنُ جَبَانًا؟ قَالَ نَعَمْ. قِيلَ وَيَكُونُ بَخِيلًا؟ قَالَ نَعَمْ. قِيلَ وَيَكُونُ كَذَّابًا؟ قَالَ لَا.

(وسائل الشيعه ج ٢ ص ٢٣٣)

٢٣٦- قَالَ رَسُولُ اللهِ صَلَّى اللهُ عَلَيْهِ وَآلِهِ: اَلْكِذْبُ يَنْقُصُ الرِّزْقَ.

(جامع السعادات ج ٢ ص ٣١٧)

٢٣٧- قَالَ أَمِيرُ الْمُؤْمِنِينَ عَلَيْهِ السَّلَامُ: إِعْتِيَادُ الْكِذْبِ يُورِثُ الْفَقْرَ.

(سفينة البحار ج ٢ ص ٤٧٣)

٢٣٨- قَالَ رَسُولُ اللهِ صَلَّى اللهُ عَلَيْهِ وَآلِهِ: وَاجْتَنِبُوا الْكِذْبَ وَإِنْ رَأَيْتُمْ فِيهِ النَّجَاةَ فَإِنَّ فِيهِ الْهَلَكَةَ.

(مستدرك الوسائل ج ٢ ص ١٠٠)

٢٣٩- قَالَ أَمِيرُ الْمُؤْمِنِينَ عَلَيْهِ السَّلَامُ: يَنْبَغِي لِلرَّجُلِ الْمُسْلِمِ أَنْ يَجْتَنِبَ مُؤَاخَاةَ الْكَذَّابِ... (وسائل الشيعه ج ٢ ص ٢٣٣)

٢٤٠ـ قَالَ الْبَاقِرُ عَلَيْهِ السَّلَامُ: قَالَ لِي عَلِيُّ بْنُ الْحُسَيْنِ عَلَيْهِ السَّلَامُ: يَابُنَيَّ انْظُرْ خَمْسَةً فَلَا تُصَاحِبْهُمْ وَلَا تُحَادِثْهُمْ وَلَا تُرَافِقْهُمْ فِي طَرِيقٍ. فَقُلْتُ يَا أَبَهْ مَنْ هُمْ؟ قَالَ: إِيَّاكَ وَمُصَاحَبَةَ الْكَذَّابِ فَإِنَّهُ بِمَنْزِلَةِ السَّرَابِ يُقَرِّبُ لَكَ الْبَعِيدَ وَيُبَاعِدُ لَكَ الْقَرِيبَ ...

(بحار الانوار ج ١٥ كتاب العشرة ص ٥٧)

٢٤١ـ قَوْلُهُ تَعَالَى: إِنَّ اللهَ يَأْمُرُكُمْ أَنْ تُؤَدُّوا الْأَمَانَاتِ إِلَى أَهْلِهَا. (سوره نساء آيت ٥٨)

٢٤٢ـ قَوْلُهُ تَعَالَى: وَالَّذِينَ هُمْ لِأَمَانَاتِهِمْ وَعَهْدِهِمْ رَاعُونَ. (سوره مومنون آيت ٨)

٢٤٣ـ قَوْلُهُ تَعَالَى: إِنِّي لَكُمْ رَسُولٌ أَمِينٌ.

(سوره شعراء آيت ١٠٧ ـ ١٢٥ ـ ١٤٣ ـ ١٦٣ و ١٧٨ ـ وسوره دخان آيت ١٨)

٢٤٤ـ قَالَ رَسُولُ اللهِ صَلَّى اللهُ عَلَيْهِ وَآلِهِ: لَا إِيمَانَ لِمَنْ لَا أَمَانَةَ لَهُ.

(بحار الانوار ج ١٥ كتاب العشرة ص ١٤٩)

٢٤٥ـ قَالَ مُعَاوِيَةُ بْنُ وَهْبٍ: قُلْتُ لِأَبِي عَبْدِ اللهِ عَلَيْهِ السَّلَامُ كَيْفَ يَنْبَغِي لَنَا أَنْ نَصْنَعَ فِيمَا بَيْنَنَا وَبَيْنَ قَوْمِنَا وَبَيْنَ خُلَطَائِنَا مِنَ النَّاسِ قَالَ: فَقَالَ عَلَيْهِ السَّلَامُ: تُؤَدُّونَ الْأَمَانَةَ إِلَيْهِمْ...

(وسائل الشيعه ج ٢ ص ٢٠٣)

٢٤٦ـ قَالَ الصَّادِقُ عَلَيْهِ السَّلَامُ: أَدُّوا الْأَمَانَةَ وَلَوْ إِلَى قَاتِلِ الْحُسَيْنِ بْنِ عَلِيٍّ عَلَيْهِ السَّلَامُ. (بحار الانوار ج ١٥ كتاب العشرة ص ١٤٨)

٢٤٧- قَالَ اَبُو عَبدِ اللهِ علیه السلام : اِعلَم اَنَّ ضَارِبَ عَلِیٍّ بِالسَّیفِ وَقَاتِلَهُ لَوِ ائتَمَنَنِی وَاستَنصَحَنِی وَ استَشَارَنِی ثُمَّ قَبِلتُ ذلِكَ مِنهُ لَاَدَّیتُ اِلَیهِ الاَمَانَةَ .

(فروع كافى ج ١ ص ٣٦٥)

٢٤٨- قَالَ الصَّادِقُ علیه السلام لِابنِهِ : یَا بُنَیَّ اَدِّ الاَمَانَةَ یَسلَم لَكَ دُنیَاكَ وَ اخِرَتَكَ وَكُن اَمِینًا تَكُن غَنِیًّا .

(بحارالانوار ج ١٥ كتاب العشرة ص ١٤٩)

٢٤٩- عَن اِسحَاقَ بنِ عَمَّارٍ عَنِ الصَّادِقِ علیه السلام قَالَ مَاوَدَّعَنَا قَطُّ اِلَّا اَوصَانَا بِخَصلَتَینِ : عَلَیكُم بِصِدقِ الحَدِیثِ وَاَدَاءِ الاَمَانَةِ اِلَى البَرِّ وَالفَاجِرِ .

(سفینة البحار ج ١ ص ٤١)

٢٥٠- قَالَ رَسُولُ اللهِ صلى الله علیه وآله : اَلاَمَانَةُ یَجلِبُ الرِّزقَ وَالخِیَانَةُ یَجلِبُ الفَقرَ . (بحارالانوار ج ١٥ كتاب العشرة ص ١٤٨)

٢٥١- قَالَ رَسُولُ اللهِ صلى الله علیه وآله : اَیَّمَا مُؤمِنٍ عَادَ مَرِیضًا خَاضَ الرَّحمَةَ فَاِذَا قَعَدَ عِندَهُ استَنقَعَ فِیهَا فَاِذَا اَعَادَهُ غَدوَةً صَلَّى عَلَیهِ سَبعُونَ اَلفَ مَلَكٍ اِلَى اَن یُمسِىَ وَ اِن عَادَ عَشِیَّةً صَلَّى عَلَیهِ سَبعُونَ اَلفَ مَلَكٍ حَتَّى یُصبِحَ .

(بحارالانوار ج ١٨ ص ١٤٥)

٢٥٢ـ قَالَ الصَّادِقُ عليه السلام: قَالَ رَسُولُ اللهِ صلى الله عليه وآله: عُودُوا الْمَرْضَى وَاتَّبِعُوا الْجَنَائِزَ يُذَكِّرْكُمُ الْآخِرَةَ، وَتَدْعُوا لِلْمَرِيضِ فَتَقُولُ: اَللَّهُمَّ اشْفِهِ بِشِفَائِكَ وَدَاوِهِ بِدَوَائِكَ وَعَافِهِ مِنْ بَلَائِكَ. وَقَالَ: مَنْ أَطْعَمَ مَرِيضًا بِشَهْوَتِهِ أَطْعَمَهُ اللهُ مِنْ ثِمَارِ الْجَنَّةِ. (بحار الانوار ج ١٨ ص ١٤٥)

١٥٣ـ عَنْ مَوْلَى جَعْفَرِ بْنِ مُحَمَّدٍ عليه السلام قَالَ: مَرِضَ بَعْضُ مَوَالِيهِ فَخَرَجْنَا نَعُودُهُ وَنَحْنُ عِدَّةٌ مِنْ مَوَالِي جَعْفَرٍ عليه السلام فَاسْتَقْبَلَنَا جَعْفَرٌ عليه السلام فِي بَعْضِ الطَّرِيقِ فَقَالَ: أَيْنَ تُرِيدُونَ؟ فَقُلْنَا نُرِيدُ فُلَانًا نَعُودُهُ فَقَالَ لَنَا قِفُوا، فَوَقَفْنَا. قَالَ مَعَ أَحَدِكُمْ تُفَّاحَةٌ أَوْ سَفَرْجَلَةٌ أَوْ أُتْرُجَّةٌ أَوْ لَعْقَةٌ مِنْ طِيبٍ أَوْ قِطْعَةٌ مِنْ عُودِ بُخُورٍ؟ فَقُلْنَا مَا مَعَنَا مِنْ هَذَا شَيْءٌ؟ فَقَالَ: أَمَا تَعْلَمُونَ أَنَّ الْمَرِيضَ يَسْتَرِيحُ إِلَى كُلِّ مَا أُدْخِلَ بِهِ عَلَيْهِ؟! (وسائل الشيعة ج ١ ص ١٢٢)

١٥٤ـ قَالَ أَمِيرُ الْمُؤْمِنِينَ عليه السلام: نَهَى رَسُولُ اللهِ صلى الله عليه وآله أَنْ يَأْكُلَ الْعَائِدُ عِنْدَ الْعَلِيلِ فَيُحْبِطَ اللهُ أَجْرَ عِيَادَتِهِ.

(بحار الانوار ج ١٨ ص ١٤٦)

١٥٥ـ قَالَ أَمِيرُ الْمُؤْمِنِينَ عليه السلام: اَلْعِيَادَةُ بَعْدَ ثَلَاثَةِ أَيَّامٍ...

(بحار الانوار ج ١٨ ص ١٤٦)

١٥٦ـ قَالَ أَمِيرُ الْمُؤْمِنِينَ عليه السلام: إِنَّ مِنْ أَعْظَمِ الْعُوَّادِ أَجْرًا عِنْدَ اللهِ عَزَّ وَجَلَّ لَمَنْ إِذَا عَادَ خَفَّفَ الْجُلُوسَ إِلَّا أَنْ يَكُونَ يُحِبُّ ذَلِكَ وَيُرِيدُهُ. (فروع كافي ج ١ ص ٣٣)

٢٥٧- قَالَ الصَّادِقُ عَلَيْهِ السَّلامُ : تَمَامُ الْعِيَادَةِ لِلْمَرِيضِ أَنْ تَضَعَ يَدَكَ عَلَى ذِرَاعِهِ وَ تَعَجَّلَ الْقِيَامَ مِنْ عِنْدِهِ فَإِنَّ عِيَادَةَ النَّوْكَى أَشَدُّ عَلَى الْمَرِيضِ مِنْ وَجَعِهِ .

(فروع كافى ج ١ ص ٣٣)

٢٥٨- قَالَ رَسُولُ اللهِ صَلَّى اللهُ عَلَيْهِ وَآلِهِ : مَنْ سَعَى لِمَرِيضٍ فِي حَاجَةٍ قَضَاهَا أَوْ لَمْ يَقْضِهَا خَرَجَ مِنْ ذُنُوبِهِ ...

(بحار الانوار ج ١٨ ص ١٤٤)

٢٥٩- عَنْ أَبِي عَبْدِ اللهِ عَلَيْهِ السَّلامُ قَالَ : مَنْ عَزَّى مُصَابًا كَانَ لَهُ مِثْلُ أَجْرِهِ غَيْرَ أَنْ يَنْتَقِصَ مِنْ أَجْرِ الْمُصَابِ شَيْءٌ .

(وسائل الشيعه ج ١ ص ١٦٦)

٢٦٠- قَالَ الصَّادِقُ عَلَيْهِ السَّلامُ : يَنْبَغِي لِجِيرَانِ صَاحِبِ الْمُصِيبَةِ أَنْ يُطْعِمُوا الطَّعَامَ عَنْهُ ثَلاثَةَ أَيَّامٍ .

(وسائل الشيعه ج ١ ص ١٦٩)

٢٦١- قَالَ الصَّادِقُ عَلَيْهِ السَّلامُ : الأَكْلُ عِنْدَ أَهْلِ الْمُصِيبَةِ مِنْ عَمَلِ أَهْلِ الْجَاهِلِيَّةِ . وَالسُّنَّةُ الْبَعْثُ إِلَيْهِمْ بِالطَّعَامِ كَمَا أَمَرَ بِهِ النَّبِيُّ صَلَّى اللهُ عَلَيْهِ وَآلِهِ فِي آلِ جَعْفَرِ بْنِ أَبِي طَالِبٍ لَمَّا جَاءَ نَعْيُهُ .

(وسائل الشيعه ج ١ ص ١٦٩)

٢٦٢- قَوْلُهُ تَعَالَى : وَالَّذِينَ مَعَهُ أَشِدَّاءُ عَلَى الْكُفَّارِ رُحَمَاءُ بَيْنَهُمْ .

(سوره فتح آيت ٢٩)

٢٦٣- قَوْلُهُ تَعَالَى : وَتَوَاصَوْا بِالْمَرْحَمَةِ ......

(سوره بلد آيت ١٧)

٢٦٤ - قَالَ الصَّادِقُ عليه السلام: ثَلاثُ دَعَوَاتٍ لا يُحْجَبْنَ عَنِ اللهِ تَعَالَى ... وَرَجُلٌ مُؤْمِنٌ دَعَا لِأَخٍ لَهُ مُؤْمِنٍ وَاسَاهُ فِينَا وَدُعَاؤُهُ عَلَيْهِ إِذَا لَمْ يُوَاسِهِ مَعَ الْقُدْرَةِ عَلَيْهِ وَاضْطِرَارِ أَخِيهِ إِلَيْهِ. (بحار الانوار ج ١٥ كتاب العشرة ص ١١٢)

٢٦٥ - قَالَ رَسُولُ اللهِ صلى الله عليه وآله: إِذَا رَأَيْتُمْ رَوْضَةً مِنْ رِيَاضِ الْجَنَّةِ فَارْتَعُوا فِيهَا. قِيلَ يَا رَسُولَ اللهِ وَمَا رَوْضَةُ الْجَنَّةِ ؟ قَالَ صلى الله عليه وآله: مَجَالِسُ الْمُؤْمِنِينَ.

(بحار الانوار ج ١٥ كتاب العشرة ص ٥١)

٢٦٦ - قَوْلُهُ تَعَالَى: وَاصْبِرْ نَفْسَكَ مَعَ الَّذِينَ يَدْعُونَ رَبَّهُمْ بِالْغَدَاةِ وَالْعَشِيِّ يُرِيدُونَ وَجْهَهُ وَلَا تَعْدُ عَيْنَاكَ عَنْهُمْ تُرِيدُ زِينَةَ الْحَيَوةِ الدُّنْيَا وَلَا تُطِعْ مَنْ أَغْفَلْنَا قَلْبَهُ عَنْ ذِكْرِنَا وَاتَّبَعَ هَوَاهُ وَكَانَ أَمْرُهُ فُرُطًا.

(سوره كهف آيت ٢٨)

٢٦٧ - قَالَ رَسُولُ اللهِ صلى الله عليه وآله: الْجَلِيسُ الصَّالِحُ خَيْرٌ مِنَ الْوَحْدَةِ وَالْوَحْدَةُ خَيْرٌ مِنْ جَلِيسِ السُّوءِ.

(بحار الانوار ج ١٥ كتاب العشرة ص ٥٢)

٢٦٨ - قَالَ رَسُولُ اللهِ صلى الله عليه وآله: أَسْعَدُ النَّاسِ مَنْ خَالَطَ كِرَامَ النَّاسِ. (بحار الانوار ج ١٥ كتاب العشرة ص ٥١)

٢٦٩ - قَالَ رَسُولُ اللهِ صلى الله عليه وآله: الْمَرْءُ عَلَى دِينِ خَلِيلِهِ وَقَرِينِهِ.

(سفينة البحار ج ١ ص ١٦٨)

٢٧٠ - قِيلَ يَا رَسُولَ اللهِ: أَيُّ الْجُلَسَاءِ خَيْرٌ ؟ قَالَ صلى الله عليه وآله: مَنْ

ذَكَّرَكُمْ بِاللهِ رُؤْيَتُهُ وَزَادَكُمْ فِي عَمَلِكُمْ مَنْطِقُهُ وَزَادَكُمْ بِالْآخِرَةِ عَمَلُهُ. (بحار الانوار ج ١٥ كتاب العشرة ص ٥١)

٢٧١ - قَالَ الصَّادِقُ عليه السلام: أَحَبُّ إِخْوَانِي إِلَيَّ مَنْ أَهْدَى إِلَيَّ عُيُوبِي.
(وسائل الشيعه ج ٢ ص ٢٠٥)

٢٧٢ - قَالَ الصَّادِقُ عليه السلام: مَنْ رَأَى أَخَاهُ عَلَى أَمْرٍ يَكْرَهُهُ فَلَمْ يَرُدَّهُ عَنْهُ وَهُوَ يَقْدِرُ فَقَدْ خَانَهُ ...
(بحار الانوار ج ١٥ كتاب العشرة ص ٥٢)

٢٧٣ - قَالَ الصَّادِقُ عليه السلام: مَنْ لَمْ يَكُنْ لَهُ وَاعِظٌ مِنْ قَلْبِهِ وَزَاجِرٌ مِنْ نَفْسِهِ وَلَمْ يَكُنْ لَهُ قَرِينٌ مُرْشِدٌ اسْتَمْكَنَ عَدُوُّهُ مِنْ عُنُقِهِ. (بحار الانوار ج ١٥ كتاب العشرة ص ٥١)

٢٧٤ - قَالَ النَّبِيُّ صلى الله عليه وآله: أَحْكَمُ النَّاسِ مَنْ فَرَّ مِنْ جُهَّالِ النَّاسِ.
(بحار الانوار ج ١٥ كتاب العشرة ص ٥٢)

٢٧٥ - قَالَ أَمِيرُ الْمُؤْمِنِينَ عليه السلام: مُجَالَسَةُ الْأَشْرَارِ تُورِثُ الظَّنَّ بِالْأَخْيَارِ. (بحار الانوار ج ١٥ كتاب العشرة ص ٥٢)

٢٧٦ - سُئِلَ أَمِيرُ الْمُؤْمِنِينَ عليه السلام: أَيُّ صَاحِبٍ شَرٌّ؟ قَالَ: الْمُزَيِّنُ لَكَ مَعْصِيَةَ اللهِ. (بحار الانوار ج ١٥ كتاب العشرة ص ٥٢)

٢٧٧ - قَالَ أَبُو جَعْفَرٍ عليه السلام: لَا تُقَارِنْ وَلَا تُوَاخِ أَرْبَعَةً: الْأَحْمَقَ وَالْبَخِيلَ وَالْجَبَانَ وَالْكَذَّابَ. أَمَّا الْأَحْمَقُ فَإِنَّهُ يُرِيدُ أَنْ يَنْفَعَكَ فَيَضُرُّكَ وَأَمَّا الْبَخِيلُ فَإِنَّهُ يَأْخُذُ مِنْكَ وَلَا يُعْطِيكَ وَأَمَّا الْجَبَانُ فَإِنَّهُ يَهْرُبُ عَنْكَ وَعَنْ وَالِدَيْهِ وَأَمَّا الْكَذَّابُ فَإِنَّهُ يَصْدُقُ وَلَا يُصَدَّقُ.
(بحار الانوار ج ١٥ كتاب العشرة ص ٥٢)

٢٧٨- قَالَ رَسُولُ اللهِ ﷺ: أَرْبَعَةٌ مُفْسِدَةٌ لِلْقُلُوبِ: ... وَمُجَالَسَةُ الْمَوْتَى. قِيلَ يَا رَسُولَ اللهِ وَمَا مُجَالَسَةُ الْمَوْتَى ؟ قَالَ مُجَالَسَةُ كُلِّ ضَالٍّ عَنِ الْإِيمَانِ وَجَائِرٍ عَنِ الْأَحْكَامِ.

(بحار الانوار ج ١٥ كتاب العشرة ص ٥٢)

٢٧٩- قَالَ الصَّادِقُ ﷺ: اخْتَبِرُوا إِخْوَانَكُمْ بِخَصْلَتَيْنِ؛ فَإِنْ كَانَتَا فِيهِمْ وَإِلَّا فَاعْزُبْ عَنْهُ ثُمَّ اعْزُبْ اعْزُبْ: اَلْمُحَافَظَةُ عَلَى الصَّلَوَاتِ فِي مَوَاقِيتِهَا وَالْبِرُّ فِي الْإِخْوَانِ فِي الْعُسْرِ وَالْيُسْرِ.

(وسائل الشيعة ج ٢ ص ٢٢٠)

٢٨٠- قَالَ الصَّادِقُ ﷺ: مِنْ سَعَادَةِ الرَّجُلِ حُسْنُ الْخُلُقِ.

(مستدرك الوسائل ج ٢ ص ٨٣)

٢٨١- قَوْلُهُ تَعَالَى: وَإِنَّكَ لَعَلَى خُلُقٍ عَظِيمٍ. (سورة قلم ـ آية ٤)

٢٨٢- قَوْلُهُ تَعَالَى: فَبِمَا رَحْمَةٍ مِنَ اللهِ لِنْتَ لَهُمْ وَلَوْ كُنْتَ فَظًّا غَلِيظَ الْقَلْبِ لَانْفَضُّوا مِنْ حَوْلِكَ ....

(سورة آل عمران ـ آية ١٥٩)

٢٨٣- قَالَ الْبَاقِرُ ﷺ: إِنَّ أَكْمَلَ الْمُؤْمِنِينَ إِيمَانًا أَحْسَنُهُمْ خُلُقًا.

(وسائل الشيعة ج ٢ ص ٢٢٠)

٢٨٤- قَالَ الصَّادِقُ ﷺ: أَكْمَلُ النَّاسِ عَقْلًا أَحْسَنُهُمْ خُلُقًا.

(وسائل الشيعة ج ٢ ص ٢٢١)

٢٨٥- قَالَ الصَّادِقُ ﷺ: إِنَّ اللهَ عَزَّ وَجَلَّ ارْتَضَى لَكُمُ الْإِسْلَامَ دِينًا فَأَحْسِنُوا صُحْبَتَهُ بِالسَّخَاءِ وَحُسْنِ الْخُلُقِ.

(وسائل الشيعة ج ٢ ص ٤٤٥)

٢٨٦- قَالَ الصَّادِقُ ﷷ: قَالَ رَسُولُ اللهِ ﷺ: اِنَّ صَاحِبَ الْخُلُقِ الْحَسَنِ لَهُ مِثْلُ أَجْرِ الصَّائِمِ الْقَائِمِ.

(وسائل الشيعة ج ٢ ص ٢٢١)

٢٨٧- قَالَ الصَّادِقُ ﷷ: قَالَ رَسُولُ اللهِ ﷺ: اَكْثَرُ مَا تَلِجُ بِهِ اُمَّتِى الْجَنَّةَ تَقْوَى اللهِ وَحُسْنُ الْخُلُقِ.

(وسائل الشيعة ج ٢ ص ٢٢١)

٢٨٨- قَالَ الصَّادِقُ ﷷ: اِنَّ اللهَ تَعَالَى لَيُعْطِى الْعَبْدَ مِنَ الثَّوَابِ عَلَى حُسْنِ الْخُلُقِ كَمَا يُعْطِى الْمُجَاهِدَ فِى سَبِيلِ اللهِ يَغْدُو عَلَيْهِ وَيَرُوحُ. (وسائل الشيعة ج ٢ ص ٢٢١)

٢٨٩- قَالَ الصَّادِقُ ﷷ: اِنَّ الْخُلُقَ الْحَسَنَ يَمِيثُ الْخَطِيئَةَ كَمَا تَمِيثُ الشَّمْسُ الْجَلِيدَ. (وسائل الشيعة ج ٢ ص ٢٢١)

٢٩٠- قَالَ الصَّادِقُ ﷷ: اِنَّ سُوءَ الْخُلُقِ لَيُفْسِدُ الْعَمَلَ كَمَا يُفْسِدُ الْخَلُّ الْعَسَلَ. (وسائل الشيعة ج ٢ ص ٤٧٥)

٢٩١- قَالَ الصَّادِقُ ﷷ: قَالَ النَّبِىُّ ﷺ: اَبَى اللهُ لِصَاحِبِ الْخُلُقِ السَّيِّئِ بِالتَّوْبَةِ. قِيلَ وَكَيْفَ ذَاكَ يَا رَسُولَ اللهِ؟ قَالَ اِذَا تَابَ مِنْ ذَنْبٍ وَقَعَ فِى ذَنْبٍ اَعْظَمَ مِنْهُ.

(وسائل الشيعة ج ٢ ص ٤٨٥)

٢٩٢- قَالَ الصَّادِقُ ﷷ: اَلْبِرُّ وَحُسْنُ الْخُلُقِ يُعَمِّرَانِ الدِّيَارَ وَيَزِيدَانِ فِى الْاَعْمَارِ. (وسائل الشيعة ج ٢ ص ٢٢١)

٢٩٣- قَالَ الصَّادِقُ ﷷ: مَنْ سَاءَ خُلُقُهُ عَذَّبَ نَفْسَهُ.

(وسائل الشيعة ج ٢ ص ٤٧٥)

٢٩٤ـ قَالَ رَسُولُ اللهِ ﷺ: يَا بَنِي عَبدِ الْمُطَّلِبِ اِنَّكُمْ لَمْ تَسَعُوا النَّاسَ بِاَمْوَالِكُمْ فَالْقُوهُمْ بِطَلَاقَةِ الْوَجْهِ وَحُسْنِ الْبِشْرِ. (وسائل الشيعة ج ٢ ص ٢٢٢)

٢٩٥ـ عَنْ بَعْضِ اَصْحَابِ الصَّادِقِ ﷺ قَالَ: قُلْتُ مَا حَدُّ حُسْنِ الْخُلُقِ؟ قَالَ: تُلَيِّنُ جَنَاحَكَ وَتُطَيِّبُ كَلَامَكَ وَتَلْقَى اَخَاكَ بِبِشْرٍ حَسَنٍ. (وسائل الشيعه ج ٢ ص ٢٢٢)

٢٩٦ـ قَوْلُهُ تَعَالَى: ..... وَالْمُوفُونَ بِعَهْدِهِمْ اِذَا عَاهَدُوا ..... (سوره بقره ـ آيت ١٧٧)

٢٩٧ـ قَوْلُهُ تَعَالَى: وَاَوْفُوا بِالْعَهْدِ اِنَّ الْعَهْدَ كَانَ مَسْئُولًا. (سوره بني اسرائيل آيت ٣٤)

٢٩٨ـ قَوْلُهُ تَعَالَى: وَاذْكُرْ فِي الْكِتَابِ اِسْمَعِيلَ اِنَّهُ كَانَ صَادِقَ الْوَعْدِ وَكَانَ رَسُولًا نَبِيًّا. (سوره مريم آيت ٥٢)

٢٩٩ـ قَالَ عَلِيٌّ ﷺ: اِنَّ الْوَفَاءَ بِالْعَهْدِ مِنْ عَلَامَاتِ اَهْلِ الدِّينِ. (سفينة البحار ج ٢ ص ٦٧٥)

٣٠٠ـ قَالَ رَسُولُ اللهِ ﷺ: لَا دِينَ لِمَنْ لَا عَهْدَ لَهُ. (سفينة البحار ج ٢ ص ٢٩٤)

٣٠١ـ قَالَ رَسُولُ اللهِ ﷺ: مَنْ كَانَ يُؤْمِنُ بِاللهِ وَالْيَوْمِ الْاخِرِ فَلْيَفِ اِذَا وَعَدَ. (جامع السعادات ج ٢ ص ٣٢٧)

٣٠٢ـ قَالَ اَمِيرُ الْمُؤْمِنِينَ ﷺ: مِنْ دَلَائِلِ الْاِيمَانِ الْوَفَاءُ بِالْعَهْدِ. (مستدرك الوسائل ج ٢ ص ٦٠)

٣٠٣ـ قَالَ النَّبِيُّ ﷺ: اَرْبَعٌ مَنْ كُنَّ فِيهِ فَهُوَ مُنَافِقٌ وَاِنْ كَانَتْ

فيهِ واحِدَةٌ مِنهُنَّ كانَتْ فيهِ خَصلَةٌ مِنَ النِّفاقِ حَتَّى يَدَعَها: مَنْ اِذا حَدَّثَ كَذَبَ وَاِذا وَعَدَ خَلَفَ وَاِذا عاهَدَ غَدَرَ وَاِذا خاصَمَ فَجَرَ.

بحار الانوار ج ١٥ كتاب العشرة ص ١٤٣

٣٠٤ - قالَ الصّادِقُ عليه السلام: اِنَّ اِسماعيلَ نَبِيَّ اللهِ وَعَدَ رَجُلًا بِالصَّفاحِ فَمَكَثَ بِهِ سَنَةً مُقيمًا وَ اَهلُ مَكَّةَ يَطلُبونَهُ لا يَدرونَ اَينَ هُوَ حَتّى وَقَعَ عَلَيهِ رَجُلٌ فَقالَ يا نَبِيَّ اللهِ ضَعُفنا بَعدَكَ وَهَلَكنا، فَقالَ اِنَّ فُلانَ الظّاهِرَ وَعَدَنى اَنْ اَكُنْ هُنا وَلَمْ اَبرَحْ حَتَّى يَجيءَ فَقالَ فَخَرَجوا اِلَيهِ حَتَّى قالوا لَهُ يا عَدوَّ اللهِ وَعَدتَّ النَّبِيَّ فَاَخلَفتَهُ فَجاءَ وَهُوَ يَقولُ لِاِسماعيلَ عليه السلام يا نَبِيَّ اللهِ ما ذَكَرتُ وَلَقَدْ نَسيتُ ميعادَكَ. فَقالَ: اَما وَاللهِ لَوْ لَمْ تَجِئْنى لَكانَ مِنهُ المَحشَرُ. فَاَنزَلَ اللهُ تَعالى: وَاذكُرْ فِي الكِتابِ اِسمعيلَ اِنَّهُ كانَ صادِقَ الوَعدِ.

(بحار الانوار ج ١٥ كتاب العشره ص ١٤٤)

٣٠٥ - عَبدُ اللهِ بنُ سِنانٍ قالَ سَمِعتُ اَبا عَبدِ اللهِ عليه السلام يَقولُ: اِنَّ رَسولَ اللهِ صلى الله عليه وآله وَعَدَ رَجُلًا اِلى صَخرَةٍ فَقالَ: اَنا لَكَ هَهُنا حَتّى تَأتِىَ قالَ: فَاشتَدَّتِ الشَّمسُ عَلَيهِ، فَقالَ اَصحابُهُ يا رَسولَ اللهِ لَوْ اَنَّكَ تَحَوَّلتَ اِلَى الظِّلِّ قالَ قَدْ وَعَدتُهُ اِلى هَهُنا وَاِنْ لَمْ يَجِئْ كانَ مِنهُ اِلَى المَحشَرِ. (بحار الانوار ج ١٥ كتاب العشرة ص ١٤٤)

247

٣٠٦ - قَالَ أَمِيرُ الْمُؤْمِنِينَ عَلَيْهِ السَّلَامُ : ..... وَلَا ظَهِيرَ كَالْمُشَاوَرَةِ.
(وسائل الشيعة ج ٢ ص ٢٠٧)

٣٠٧ - قَالَ أَمِيرُ الْمُؤْمِنِينَ عَلَيْهِ السَّلَامُ : اَلْإِسْتِشَارَةُ عَيْنُ الْهِدَايَةِ.
(وسائل الشيعة ج ٢ ص ٢٠٧)

٣٠٨ - قَالَ الصَّادِقُ عَلَيْهِ السَّلَامُ : لَنْ يَهْلِكَ امْرُؤٌ عَنْ مَشُورَةٍ.
وسائل الشيعة ج ٢ ص ٢٠٧

٣٠٩ - قَالَ النَّبِيُّ صَلَّى اللهُ عَلَيْهِ وَآلِهِ : اَلْحَزْمُ أَنْ تَسْتَشِيرَ ذَا الرَّأْيِ وَتُطِيعَ أَمْرَهُ.
(بحار الانوار ج ١٥ كتاب العشرة ص ١٤٦)

٣١٠ - قَوْلُهُ تَعَالَى : وَشَاوِرْهُمْ فِي الْأَمْرِ فَإِذَا عَزَمْتَ فَتَوَكَّلْ عَلَى اللهِ.
(سورة آل عمران - آية ١٦٠)

٣١١ - قَوْلُهُ تَعَالَى : وَالَّذِينَ اسْتَجَابُوا لِرَبِّهِمْ وَأَقَامُوا الصَّلَاةَ وَأَمْرُهُمْ شُورَى بَيْنَهُمْ وَمِمَّا رَزَقْنَاهُمْ يُنْفِقُونَ.
(سورة شورى - آية ٣٨)

٣١٢ - قَالَ عَلِيٌّ عَلَيْهِ السَّلَامُ : وَمَنْ اسْتَبَدَّ بِرَأْيِهِ هَلَكَ وَمَنْ شَاوَرَ الرِّجَالَ شَارَكَهَا فِي عُقُولِهَا. (نهج البلاغة ص ١١٥٥)

٣١٣ - قَالَ الصَّادِقُ عَلَيْهِ السَّلَامُ : اَلْمُسْتَبِدُّ بِرَأْيِهِ مَوْقُوفٌ عَلَى مَدَاحِضِ الزَّلَلِ. (بحار الانوار ج ١٥ كتاب العشرة ص ١٤٦)

٣١٤ - فِي وَصِيَّةِ عَلِيٍّ عَلَيْهِ السَّلَامُ لِمُحَمَّدِ بْنِ حَنَفِيَّةَ قَالَ ... قَدْ خَاطَرَ بِنَفْسِهِ مَنِ اسْتَغْنَى بِرَأْيِهِ وَمَنِ اسْتَقْبَلَ وُجُوهَ الْآرَاءِ عَرَفَ مَوَاقِعَ الْخَطَاءِ. (وسائل الشيعة ج ٢ ص ٢٠٨)

٣١٥ - قَالَ الصَّادِقُ عَلَيْهِ السَّلَامُ : اِسْتَشِرْ فِي أَمْرِكَ الَّذِينَ يَخْشَوْنَ

رَبَّهُمْ.   (وسائل الشيعه ج ٢ ص ٢٠٧)

٣١٦- عَنْ سَلْمَانَ قَالَ سَمِعْتُ آبَا عَبْدِ اللهِ ﷺ يَقُولُ: اِسْتَشِرِ الْعَاقِلَ مِنَ الرِّجَالِ الْوَرِعَ فَإِنَّهُ لَا يَأْمُرُ إِلَّا بِخَيْرٍ وَإِيَّاكَ وَالْخِلَافَ فَإِنَّ مُخَالَفَةَ الْوَرِعِ الْعَاقِلِ مُفْسِدَةٌ فِي الدِّينِ وَالدُّنْيَا.   (وسائل الشيعه ج ٢ ص ٢٠٧)

٣١٧- قَالَ الصَّادِقُ ﷺ: إِنَّ الْمَشُورَةَ لَا تَكُونُ إِلَّا بِحُدُودِهَا فَمَنْ عَرَفَهَا بِحُدُودِهَا وَإِلَّا كَانَتْ مَضَرَّتُهَا عَلَى الْمُسْتَشِيرِ أَكْثَرَ مِنْ مَنْفَعَتِهَا لَهُ فَأَوَّلُهَا أَنْ يَكُونَ الَّذِي تُشَاوِرُهُ عَاقِلاً وَالثَّانِيَةُ أَنْ يَكُونَ حُرًّا مُتَدَيِّنًا وَالثَّالِثَةُ أَنْ يَكُونَ صَدِيقًا مُوَاخِيًا وَالرَّابِعَةُ أَنْ تُطْلِعَهُ عَلَى سِرِّكَ فَيَكُونَ عِلْمُهُ بِهِ كَعِلْمِكَ بِنَفْسِكَ ثُمَّ يُسِرُّ ذَلِكَ وَيَكْتُمُهُ فَإِنَّهُ إِذَا كَانَ عَاقِلاً اِنْتَفَعْتَ بِمَشُورَتِهِ وَإِذَا كَانَ حُرًّا مُتَدَيِّنًا أَجْهَدَ نَفْسَهُ فِي النَّصِيحَةِ لَكَ، وَإِذَا كَانَ صَدِيقًا مُوَاخِيًا كَتَمَ سِرَّكَ إِذَا اَطْلَعْتَهُ عَلَيْهِ وَإِذَا اَطْلَعْتَهُ عَلَى سِرِّكَ فَكَانَ عِلْمُهُ بِهِ كَعِلْمِكَ بِهِ تَمَّتِ الْمَشُورَةُ وَكَمَلَتِ النَّصِيحَةُ.

(وسائل الشيعة ج ٢ ص ٢٠٨)

٣١٨- قَالَ الصَّادِقُ ﷺ (فِي حَدِيثٍ): أَمَا إِنَّهُ إِذَا فَعَلَ ذَلِكَ لَمْ يَخْذُلْهُ اللهُ بَلْ يَرْفَعُهُ اللهُ وَرَمَاهُ بِخَيْرِ الْأُمُورِ وَأَقْرَبِهَا إِلَى اللهِ تَعَالَى .

(وسائل الشيعة ج ٢ ص ٢٠٨)

٣١٩- عَنْ أَبِى الْحَسَنِ الرِّضَا عَلَيْهِ السَّلامُ أَنَّهُ ذَكَرَ أَبَاهُ فَقَالَ: كَانَ عَقْلُهُ لَا تُوَازَنُ بِهِ الْعُقُولُ وَرُبَّمَا شَاوَرَ الْأَسْوَدَ مِنْ سُودَانِهِ فَقِيلَ لَهُ تُشَاوِرُ مِثْلَ هٰذَا؟ فَقَالَ إِنَّ اللّٰهَ تَبَارَكَ وَتَعَالَى رُبَّمَا فَتَحَ عَلَى لِسَانِهِ.

(وسائل الشيعه ج ٢ ص ٢٠٨)

٣٢٠- قَالَ رَسُولُ اللّٰهِ صَلَّى اللّٰهُ عَلَيْهِ وَآلِهِ: يَا عَلِيُّ لَا تُشَاوِرَنَّ جَبَاناً فَإِنَّهُ يُضَيِّقُ عَلَيْكَ الْمَخْرَجَ... وَلَا تُشَاوِرَنَّ حَرِيصاً فَإِنَّهُ يَزِيدُكَ شَرَّهَا. (وسائل الشيعه ج ٢ ص ٢٠٨)

٣٢١- قَالَ أَمِيرُ الْمُؤْمِنِينَ عَلَيْهِ السَّلَامُ: مَنْ غَشَّ الْمُسْلِمِينَ فِي مَشُورَةٍ فَقَدْ بَرِئْتُ مِنْهُ.

(بحارالانوار ج ١٥ كتاب العشرة ص ١٤٤)

٣٢٢- قَالَ أَمِيرُ الْمُؤْمِنِينَ عَلَيْهِ السَّلَامُ: اَلْمُسْتَشَارُ مُؤْتَمَنٌ...

(وسائل الشيعه ج ٢ ص ٢٠٨)

٣٢٣- قَالَ رَسُولُ اللّٰهِ صَلَّى اللّٰهُ عَلَيْهِ وَآلِهِ: سَافِرُوا تَصِحُّوا سَافِرُوا تَغْنَمُوا.

(بحارالانوار ج ١٦ ص ٥٧)

٣٢٤- قَالَ رَسُولُ اللّٰهِ صَلَّى اللّٰهُ عَلَيْهِ وَآلِهِ: أَلَا أُنَبِّئُكُمْ بِشَرِّ النَّاسِ؟ قَالُوا بَلَى يَا رَسُولَ اللّٰهِ. فَقَالَ: مَنْ سَافَرَ وَحْدَهُ وَمَنَعَ رِفْدَهُ وَضَرَبَ عَبْدَهُ.

(بحارالانوار ج ١٥ كتاب العشرة ص ١٤)

٣٢٥- قَالَ رَسُولُ اللّٰهِ صَلَّى اللّٰهُ عَلَيْهِ وَآلِهِ: مَا اسْتَخْلَفَ رَجُلٌ عَلَى أَهْلِهِ بِخِلَافَةٍ أَفْضَلَ مِنْ رَكْعَتَيْنِ يَرْكَعُهُمَا إِذَا أَرَادَ الْخُرُوجَ إِلَى سَفَرٍ

250

وَيَقُولُ: اَللّٰهُمَّ اِنِّى اَسْتَوْدِعُكَ نَفْسِى وَاَهْلِى وَمَالِى وَ ذُرِّيَّتِى وَدُنْيَاىَ وَاٰخِرَتِى وَاَمَانَتِى وَخَاتِمَةَ عَمَلِى فَمَا قَالَ ذٰلِكَ اَحَدٌ اِلَّا اَعْطَاهُ اللهُ عَزَّ وَجَلَّ مَا سَئَلَ.

(وسائل الشيعه ج ٢ ص ١٨٢)

٣٢٦- قَالَ الصَّادِقُ عَلَيْهِ السَّلَامُ: تَصَدَّقْ وَاخْرُجْ اَىَّ يَوْمٍ شِئْتَ.

(فروع كافى ج ١ ص ٢٤٤)

٣٢٧- عَنْ حَمَّادِ بْنِ عُثْمَانَ قَالَ: قُلْتُ لِاَبِى عَبْدِ اللهِ عَلَيْهِ السَّلَامُ: اَ يَكْرَهُ السَّفَرَ فِى شَىْءٍ مِنَ الْاَيَّامِ الْمَكْرُوهَةِ الْاَرْبِعَاءِ وَ غَيْرِهِ؟ فَقَالَ: اِفْتَتِحْ سَفَرَكَ بِالصَّدَقَةِ وَاقْرَأْ اٰيَةَ الْكُرْسِىِّ اِذَا بَدَالَكَ. (فروع كافى ج ١ ص ٢٤٤)

٣٢٨- عَنْ اَحَدِهِمَا عَلَيْهِ السَّلَامُ قَالَ: كَانَ اَبِى اِذَا خَرَجَ يَوْمَ الْاَرْبِعَاءِ مِنْ اٰخِرِ الشَّهْرِ وَفِى يَوْمٍ يَكْرَهُ النَّاسُ مِنْ مَحَاقٍّ اَوْ غَيْرِهِ تَصَدَّقَ بِصَدَقَةٍ ثُمَّ خَرَجَ.

(وسائل الشيعه ج ٢ ص ١٨٢)

٣٢٩- قَالَ رَسُولُ اللهِ صَلَّى اللهُ عَلَيْهِ وَاٰلِهِ: سِتٌّ مِنَ الْمُرُوَّةِ ثَلَاثٌ مِنْهَا فِى الْحَضَرِ وَثَلَاثٌ مِنْهَا فِى السَّفَرِ ... وَاَمَّا الَّتِى فِى السَّفَرِ فَبَذْلُ الزَّادِ وَحُسْنُ الْخُلُقِ وَالْمِزَاحُ فِى غَيْرِ الْمَعَاصِى.

(بحار الانوار ج ١٦ ص ٧٥)

٣٣٠- قَالَ الصَّادِقُ عَلَيْهِ السَّلَامُ: اَلْمُرُوَّةُ فِى السَّفَرِ كَثْرَةُ الزَّادِ وَطِيبُ وَبَذْلُهُ لِمَنْ كَانَ مَعَكَ وَكِتْمَانٌ عَلَى الْقَوْمِ سِرَّهُمْ بَعْدَ مُفَارَقَتِكَ اِيَّاهُمْ وَكَثْرَةُ الْمِزَاحِ فِى غَيْرِ مَا

251

يَسْخَطُ اللهُ عَزَّ وَجَلَّ. (بحارالانوار ج ١٦ ص ٧٥)

٣٣١- قَالَ رَسُولُ اللهِ ﷺ: مِنَ السُّنَّةِ إِذَا خَرَجَ الْقَوْمُ فِي سَفَرٍ أَنْ يُخْرِجُوا نَفَقَتَهُمْ فَإِنَّ ذَلِكَ أَطْيَبُ لِأَنْفُسِهِمْ وَأَحْسَنُ لِأَخْلَاقِهِمْ. (بحارالانوار ج ١٦ ص ٧٥)

٣٣٢- قَالَ رَسُولُ اللهِ ﷺ: مِنْ شَرَفِ الرَّجُلِ أَنْ يُطَيِّبَ زَادَهُ إِذَا خَرَجَ فِي سَفَرٍ. (بحارالانوار ج ١٦ ص ٧٦)

٣٣٣- قَالَ رَسُولُ اللهِ ﷺ: سَيِّدُ الْقَوْمِ خَادِمُهُمْ فِي السَّفَرِ. (بحارالانوار ج ١٦ ص ٧٧)

٣٣٤- رُوِيَ عَنِ النَّبِيِّ ﷺ أَنَّهُ أَمَرَ أَصْحَابَهُ بِذَبْحِ شَاةٍ فِي السَّفَرِ فَقَالَ رَجُلٌ مِنَ الْقَوْمِ: عَلَيَّ ذَبْحُهَا وَقَالَ الْآخَرُ: عَلَيَّ سَلْخُهَا. وَقَالَ آخَرُ: عَلَيَّ قَطْعُهَا وَقَالَ آخَرُ: عَلَيَّ طَبْخُهَا. فَقَالَ رَسُولُ اللهِ ﷺ: عَلَيَّ أَنْ أَلْقُطَ لَكُمُ الْحَطَبَ. فَقَالُوا يَا رَسُولَ اللهِ لَا تَتْعَبْ بِآبَائِنَا وَأُمَّهَاتِنَا أَنْتَ، نَحْنُ نَكْفِيكَ. قَالَ: عَرَفْتُ أَنَّكُمْ تَكْفُونِي وَلَكِنَّ اللهَ عَزَّ وَجَلَّ يَكْرَهُ مِنْ عَبْدِهِ إِذَا كَانَ مَعَ أَصْحَابِهِ أَنْ يَنْفَرِدَ بَيْنَهُمْ فَقَامَ يَلْقُطُ الْحَطَبَ لَهُمْ.

(بحارالانوار ج ١٦ ص ٧٧)

٣٣٥- كَانَ عَلِيُّ بْنُ الْحُسَيْنِ ﷺ: لَا يُسَافِرُ إِلَّا مَعَ رِفْقَةٍ لَا يَعْرِفُونَهُ وَيَشْتَرِطُ عَلَيْهِمْ أَنْ يَكُونَ مِنْ خُدَّامِ الرَّفْقَةِ فِيمَا يَحْتَاجُونَ إِلَيْهِ. فَسَافَرَ مَرَّةً مَعَ قَوْمٍ فَرَآهُ رَجُلٌ فَعَرَفَهُ فَقَالَ لَهُمْ: أَتَدْرُونَ مَنْ هَذَا؟ قَالُوا: لَا. قَالَ: لِهَذَا

عَلِيُّ بْنُ الْحُسَيْنِ. فَوثَبُوا إِلَيْهِ فَقَبَّلُوا يَدَيْهِ وَرِجْلَيْهِ فَقَالُوا يَا بْنَ رَسُولِ اللهِ أَرَدْتَ أَنْ تُصَلِّيَنَا نَارَجَهَنَّمَ لَوْ بَدَرَتْ إِلَيْكَ مِنَّا يَدٌ أَوْ لِسَانٌ أَمَاكُنَّا قَدْ هَلَكْنَا آخِرَ الدَّهْرِ فَمَا الَّذِي حَمَلَكَ عَلَى هَذَا؟ فَقَالَ إِنِّي كُنْتُ سَافَرْتُ مَعَ قَوْمٍ يَعْرِفُونِي فَأَعْطَوْنِي بِرَسُولِ اللهِ مَا لا أَسْتَحِقُّ فَأَخَافُ أَنْ تُعْطُونِي مِثْلَ ذَلِكَ فَصَارَ كِتْمَانُ أَمْرِي أَحَبَّ إِلَيَّ. (وسائل الشيعه ج ٢ ص ١٨٩)

٣٣٦ - قَالَ رَسُولُ اللهِ ﷺ: حَقُّ الْمُسَافِرِ أَنْ يُقِيمَ عَلَيْهِ أَصْحَابُهُ إِذَا مَرِضَ ثَلْثًا. (اصول کافی ص ٦٢٥)

٣٣٧ - عَنْ أَبِي عَبْدِاللهِ ﷺ عَنْ آبَائِهِ أَنَّ أَمِيرَ الْمُؤْمِنِينَ ﷺ صَاحَبَ رَجُلًا ذِمِّيًّا فَقَالَ لَهُ الذِّمِّيُّ أَيْنَ تُرِيدُ يَا أَبَا عَبْدِاللهِ؟ قَالَ أُرِيدُ الْكُوفَةَ. فَلَمَّا عَدَلَ الطَّرِيقُ بِالذِّمِّيِّ عَدَلَ مَعَهُ أَمِيرُ الْمُؤْمِنِينَ ﷺ فَقَالَ لَهُ الذِّمِّيُّ أَلَسْتَ زَعَمْتَ أَنَّكَ تُرِيدُ الْكُوفَةَ؟ فَقَالَ لَهُ بَلَى. فَقَالَ لَهُ الذِّمِّيُّ: فَقَدْ تَرَكْتَ الطَّرِيقَ. فَقَالَ لَهُ قَدْ عَلِمْتُ قَالَ: فَلِمَ عَدَلْتَ مَعِي وَ قَدْ عَلِمْتَ ذَلِكَ؟ فَقَالَ لَهُ أَمِيرُ الْمُؤْمِنِينَ ﷺ هَذَا مِنْ تَمَامِ حُسْنِ الصُّحْبَةِ أَنْ يُشَيِّعَ الرَّجُلُ صَاحِبَهُ هُنَيْئَةً إِذَا فَارَقَهُ وَكَذَلِكَ أَمَرَنَا نَبِيُّنَا ﷺ فَقَالَ لَهُ الذِّمِّيُّ هَكَذَا (قَالَ خ ل)؟ قَالَ: نَعَمْ. قَالَ الذِّمِّيُّ لَا جَرَمَ إِنَّمَا تَبِعَهُ مَنْ تَبِعَهُ لِأَفْعَالِهِ الْكَرِيمَةِ فَأَنَا أُشْهِدُكَ أَنِّي عَلَى دِينِكَ وَرَجَعَ الذِّمِّيُّ مَعَ أَمِيرِ الْمُؤْمِنِينَ ﷺ فَلَمَّا عَرَفَهُ

اَسْلَمَ .	(اصول كافى ص ٦٢٦)

٣٣٨ - قَالَ جَعْفَرُ بْنُ مُحَمَّدٍ عليه السلام : اِذَا سَافَرَ اَحَدُكُمْ فَقَدِمَ مِنْ سَفَرِهِ فَلْيَأْتِ اَهْلَهُ بِمَا تَيَسَّرَ لَهُ وَلَوْ بِحَجَرٍ ...

(وسائل الشيعه ج ٢ ص ١٩٣)

٣٣٩ - قَالَ عَلِيُّ بْنُ الْحُسَيْنِ عليه السلام : مَنْ خَلَفَ حَاجًّا فِى اَهْلِهِ وَمَالِهِ كَانَ لَهُ كَاَجْرِهِ حَتَّى كَاَنَّهُ يَسْتَلِمُ الْاَحْجَارَ .

(وسائل الشيعه ج ٢ ص ١٨٩)

٣٤٠ - كَانَ عَلِيُّ بْنُ الْحُسَيْنِ عليه السلام يَقُولُ : يَا مَعْشَرَ مَنْ لَمْ يَحُجَّ اِسْتَبْشِرُوا بِالْحَاجِّ وَصَافِحُوهُمْ وَعَظِّمُوهُمْ فَاِنَّ ذَلِكَ يَجِبُ عَلَيْكُمْ تُشَارِكُوهُمْ فِى الْاَجْرِ .

(وسائل الشيعه ج ٢ ص ١٩١)

٣٤١ - قَالَ الصَّادِقُ عليه السلام (فِى حَدِيثٍ) : وَاِذَا قَدِمَ الرَّجُلُ مِنَ السَّفَرِ وَدَخَلَ مَنْزِلَهُ يَنْبَغِى اَنْ لَا يَشْتَغِلَ بِشَىْءٍ حَتَّى يَصُبَّ عَلَى نَفْسِهِ الْمَاءَ وَيُصَلِّىَ رَكْعَتَيْنِ وَيَسْجُدَ وَيَشْكُرَ اللهَ مِائَةَ مَرَّةٍ ...

(بحار الانوار ج ١٥ ص ٨٠)

٣٤٢ - قَالَ عَلِىٌّ عليه السلام : فَرَضَ اللهُ .... وَالْجِهَادَ عِزًّا لِلْاِسْلَامِ .

(نهج البلاغه ص ١١/٨٧)

٣٤٣ - قَالَ رَسُولُ اللهِ صلى الله عليه وآله : اِغْزُوا تُوَرِّثُوا اَبْنَاءَكُمْ مَجْدًا .

(فروع كافى ج ١ ص ٣٢٩)

٣٤٤ - قَالَ رَسُولُ اللهِ صلى الله عليه وآله : اَلْخَيْرُ كُلُّهُ فِى السَّيْفِ وَتَحْتَ ظِلِّ السَّيْفِ وَلَا يُقِيمُ النَّاسَ اِلَّا بِالسَّيْفِ وَالسُّيُوفُ مَقَالِيدُ

اَلْجَنَّةُ وَالنَّارُ . (فروع كافى ج ١ ص ٣٢٧)

٣٤٥- قَالَ أَمِيرُ الْمُؤْمِنِينَ عليه السلام: إِنَّ اللهَ فَرَضَ الْجِهَادَ وَعَظَّمَهُ وَجَعَلَهُ نَصْرَهُ وَنَاصِرَهُ وَاللهِ مَاصَلَحَتْ دُنْيَا وَلَا دِينٌ اِلَّابِهِ . (فروع كافى ج ١ ص ٣٢٩)

٣٤٦- قَالَ رَسُولُ اللهِ صلى الله عليه وآله (فِى حَدِيثٍ): فَمَنْ تَرَكَ الْجِهَادَ اَلْبَسَهُ اللهُ ذُلًّا وَفَقْرًا فِى مَعِيشَتِهِ وَمُحقًّا فِى دِينِهِ ...
(فروع كافى ج ١ ص ٣٢٧)

٣٤٧- قَالَ أَمِيرُ الْمُؤْمِنِينَ عليه السلام : أَمَّا بَعْدُ : فَإِنَّ الْجِهَادَ بَابٌ مِنْ أَبْوَابِ الْجَنَّةِ فَتَحَهُ لِخَاصَّةِ أَوْلِيَائِهِ وَهُوَلِبَاسُ التَّقْوَى وَدِرْعُ اللهِ الْحَصِينَةُ وَجَنَّتُهُ الْوَثِيقَةُ فَمَنْ تَرَكَهُ رَغْبَةً عَنْهُ اَلْبَسَهُ اللهُ ثَوْبَ الذُّلِّ وَشَمْلَةَ الْبَلَاءِ وَدُيِّثَ بِالصَّغَارِ وَالْقَمَاءِ وَضُرِبَ عَلَى قَلْبِهِ بِالْاِسْهَابِ وَاُدِيلَ الْحَقُّ مِنْهُ بِتَضْيِيعِ الْجِهَادِ وَسِيمَ الْخَسْفِ وَمُنِعَ النَّصَفِ . (نهج البلاغة ص ٨٥)

٣٤٨- قَوْلُهُ تَعَالَى : وَلَا تَحْسَبَنَّ الَّذِينَ قُتِلُوا فِى سَبِيلِ اللهِ أَمْوَاتًا بَلْ أَحْيَاءٌ عِنْدَ رَبِّهِمْ يُرْزَقُونَ. فَرِحِينَ بِمَا آتَاهُمُ اللهُ مِنْ فَضْلِهِ وَيَسْتَبْشِرُونَ بِالَّذِينَ لَمْ يَلْحَقُوا بِهِمْ مِنْ خَلْفِهِمْ اَلَّا خَوْفٌ عَلَيْهِمْ وَلَاهُمْ يَحْزَنُونَ . يَسْتَبْشِرُونَ بِنِعْمَةٍ مِنَ اللهِ وَفَضْلٍ وَّأَنَّ اللهَ لَا يُضِيعُ أَجْرَ الْمُؤْمِنِينَ . (سوره آل عمران-آيت ١٧٠)

٣٤٩- قَالَ عَلِىُّ بْنُ الْحُسَيْنِ عليهما السلام: بَيْنَمَا عَلِىٌّ عليه السلام يَخْطُبُ

النَّاسَ وَيَحُضُّهُمْ عَلَى الْجِهَادِ، إِذْ قَامَ إِلَيْهِ شَابٌّ فَقَالَ يَا أَمِيرَ الْمُؤْمِنِينَ أَخْبِرْنِي عَنْ فَضْلِ الْغُزَاةِ فِي سَبِيلِ اللهِ. فَقَالَ عَلِيٌّ عَلَيْهِ السَّلَامُ: كُنْتُ رَدِيفَ رَسُولِ اللهِ ﷺ عَلَى نَاقَتِهِ الْعَضْبَاءِ وَنَحْنُ قَافِلُونَ مِنْ غَزْوَةِ ذَاتِ السَّلَاسِلِ فَسَأَلْتُهُ عَمَّا سَأَلْتَنِي عَنْهُ فَقَالَ ﷺ: اِنَّ الْغُزَاةَ إِذَا هَمُّوا بِالْغَزْوِ كَتَبَ اللهُ لَهُمْ بَرَاءَةً مِنَ النَّارِ فَإِذَا تَجَهَّزُوا لِغَزْوِهِمْ بَاهَى اللهُ تَعَالَى بِهِمُ الْمَلَائِكَةَ فَإِذَا وَدَّعَهُمْ أَهْلُوهُمْ بَكَتْ عَلَيْهِمُ الْحِيطَانُ وَالْبُيُوتُ وَيَخْرُجُونَ مِنْ ذُنُوبِهِمْ كَمَا تَخْرُجُ الْحَيَّةُ مِنْ سَلْخِهَا ...

(مستدرك الوسائل ج ٢ ص ٢٤٣)

٣٥٠ - .... (شرائع الإسلام ص ٨٧)

٣٥١ - قَالَ الصَّادِقُ عَلَيْهِ السَّلَامُ: ثَلَاثَةٌ دَعْوَتُهُمْ مُسْتَجَابَةٌ: أَحَدُهُمُ الْغَازِي فِي سَبِيلِ اللهِ فَانْظُرُوا كَيْفَ تَخْلُفُونَهُ.

(وسائل الشيعة ج ٢ ص ٤١٧)

٣٥٢ - قَالَ رَسُولُ اللهِ ﷺ: مَنْ بَلَّغَ رِسَالَةَ غَازٍ كَانَ كَمَنْ أَعْتَقَ رَقَبَةً وَهُوَ شَرِيكُهُ فِي ثَوَابِ غَزْوَتِهِ.

(وسائل الشيعة ج ٢ ص ٤١٧)

٣٥٣ - قَالَ رَسُولُ اللهِ ﷺ: مَنْ قَالَ لِغَازٍ مَرْحَبًا وَأَهْلًا حَيَّاهُ اللهُ يَوْمَ الْقِيَامَةِ وَاسْتَقْبَلَهُ الْمَلَائِكَةُ بِالتَّرْحِيبِ وَالتَّسْلِيمِ.

(مستدرك الوسائل ج ٢ ص ٢٤٥)

٣٥٤ - قَوْلُهُ تَعَالَى: وَقَاتِلُوا فِي سَبِيلِ اللهِ الَّذِينَ يُقَاتِلُونَكُمْ وَلَا

تَعْتَدُوا اِنَّ اللّٰهَ لَا يُحِبُّ الْمُعْتَدِينَ .

(سوره بقره ـ آيت ١٩٠)

٣٥٥ ـ قَوْلُهُ تَعَالىٰ : وَقَاتِلُوهُمْ حَتّٰى لَا تَكُونَ فِتْنَةٌ وَيَكُونَ الدِّينُ لِلّٰهِ فَاِنِ انْتَهَوْا فَلَا عُدْوَانَ اِلَّا عَلَى الظَّالِمِينَ.

(سوره بقره ـ آيت ١٩٣)

٣٥٦ ـ قَالَ اَمِيرُ الْمُؤْمِنِينَ عَلَيْهِ السَّلَامُ : بَعَثَنِى رَسُولُ اللّٰهِ صَلَّى اللّٰهُ عَلَيْهِ وَآلِهِ اِلَى الْيَمَنِ فَقَالَ يَا عَلِىُّ لَا تُقَاتِلَنَّ اَحَدًا حَتّٰى تَدْعُوهُ اِلَى الْاِسْلَامِ وَاَيْمُ اللّٰهِ لَاِنْ يَهْدِى اللّٰهُ عَزَّ وَجَلَّ عَلٰى يَدَيْكَ رَجُلًا خَيْرٌ لَّكَ مِمَّا طَلَعَتْ عَلَيْهِ الشَّمْسُ وَغَرَبَتْ وَلَكَ وَلَاؤُهُ يَا عَلِىُّ . (وسائل الشيعه ج ٢ ص ٤٢١)

٣٥٧ ـ قَالَ عَلِىٌّ عَلَيْهِ السَّلَامُ : اِنَّ رَسُولَ اللّٰهِ صَلَّى اللّٰهُ عَلَيْهِ وَآلِهِ اَمَرَ بِالشِّعَارِ قَبْلَ الْحَرْبِ وَقَالَ : وَلٰكِنْ فِى شِعَارِكُمُ اسْمٌ مِّنْ اَسْمَاءِ اللّٰهِ تَعَالىٰ . (مستدرك الوسائل ج ٢ ص ٢٦٥)

٣٥٨ ـ قَالَ النَّبِىُّ صَلَّى اللّٰهُ عَلَيْهِ وَآلِهِ : اُقْتُلُوا الْمُشْرِكِينَ وَاسْتَحْيُوا شُيُوخَهُمْ وَصِبْيَانَهُمْ . (وسائل الشيعه ج ٢ ص ٤٢٥)

٣٥٩ ـ قَالَ اَبُو عَبْدِ اللّٰهِ عَلَيْهِ السَّلَامُ : كَانَ رَسُولُ اللّٰهِ صَلَّى اللّٰهُ عَلَيْهِ وَآلِهِ اِذَا اَرَادَ اَنْ يَبْعَثَ سَرِيَّةً دَعَاهُمْ فَاَجْلَسَهُمْ بَيْنَ يَدَيْهِ ثُمَّ يَقُولُ: سِيرُوا بِسْمِ اللّٰهِ وَبِاللّٰهِ وَفِى سَبِيلِ اللّٰهِ وَعَلٰى مِلَّةِ رَسُولِ اللّٰهِ لَا تَغُلُّوا وَلَا تُمَثِّلُوا وَلَا تَغْدِرُوا وَلَا تَقْتُلُوا شَيْخًا فَانِيًا وَلَا صَبِيًّا وَّلَا امْرَاَةً وَلَا تَقْطَعُوا شَجَرًا اِلَّا اَنْ تَضْطَرُّوا اِلَيْهَا وَاَيَّمَا رَجُلٍ مِّنْ اَدْنَى الْمُسْلِمِينَ اَوْ

أَفْضَلِهِمْ نَظَرَ إِلَى أَحَدٍ مِنَ الْمُشْرِكِينَ فَهُوَ جَارٌ حَتَّى يَسْمَعَ كَلَامَ اللهِ فَإِنْ تَبِعَكُمْ فَأَخُوكُمْ فِي الدِّينِ وَإِنْ أَبَى فَأَبْلِغُوهُ مَأْمَنَهُ وَاسْتَعِينُوا بِاللهِ.

(وسائل الشيعه ج ٢ ص ٤٢٤)

٣٦٠ - قَالَ رَسُولُ اللهِ ﷺ: ذِمَّةُ الْمُسْلِمِينَ وَاحِدَةٌ يَسْعَى بِهَا أَدْنَاهُمْ.

(مستدرك الوسائل ج ٢ ص ٢٥٠)

٣٦١ - قَالَ السَّكُونِيُّ قُلْتُ لِأَبِي عَبْدِ اللهِ ﷺ: مَا مَعْنَى قَوْلِ النَّبِيِّ ﷺ يَسْعَى بِذِمَّتِهِمْ أَدْنَاهُمْ ؟ قَالَ: لَوْ أَنَّ جَيْشًا مِنَ الْمُسْلِمِينَ حَاصَرُوا قَوْمًا مِنَ الْمُشْرِكِينَ فَأَشْرَفَ رَجُلٌ فَقَالَ أَعْطُونِي الْأَمَانَ حَتَّى أَلْقَى صَاحِبَكُمْ وَأُنَاظِرَهُ فَأَعْطَاهُ أَدْنَاهُمُ الْأَمَانَ وَجَبَ عَلَى أَفْضَلِهِمُ الْوَفَاءُ بِهِ.

(وسائل الشيعه ج ٢ ص ٤٢٥)

٣٦٢ - قَالَ الصَّادِقُ ﷺ أَنَّ عَلِيًّا ﷺ أَجَازَ أَمَانَ مَمْلُوكٍ لِأَهْلِ حِصْنٍ مِنَ الْحُصُونِ وَقَالَ هُوَ مِنَ الْمُؤْمِنِينَ.

(وسائل الشيعه ج ٢ ص ٤٢٥)

٣٦٣ - قَالَ الصَّادِقُ ﷺ: لَوْ أَنَّ قَوْمًا حَاصَرُوا مَدِينَةً فَسَأَلُوهُمُ الْأَمَانَ فَقَالُوا: لَا. فَظَنُّوا أَنَّهُمْ قَالُوا: نَعَمْ. فَنَزَلُوا إِلَيْهِمْ كَانُوا آمِنِينَ. (وسائل الشيعه ج ٢ ص ٤٢٥)

٣٦٤ - قَالَ عَلِيٌّ ﷺ: إِيَّاكُمْ وَالْمِرَاءَ وَالْخُصُومَةَ فَإِنَّهُمَا يُمَرِّضَانِ الْقُلُوبَ عَلَى الْإِخْوَانِ وَيَنْبُتُ عَلَيْهِمَا النِّفَاقُ.

(اصول كافى ص ٤٥١)

258

٣٦٥ - قَالَ عَلِيٌّ عليه السلام: خَيْرُ النَّاسِ قُضَاةُ الْحَقِّ .
(بحار الانوار ج ٢٤ ص ٧)

٣٦٦ - فِي عَهْدِ عَلِيٍّ عليه السلام لِلْاَشْتَرِ: ثُمَّ اخْتَرْ لِلْحُكْمِ بَيْنَ النَّاسِ اَفْضَلَ رَعِيَّتِكَ فِي نَفْسِكَ مِمَّنْ لَا تَضِيقُ بِهِ الْاُمُورُ وَلَا تَمْحَكُهُ الْخُصُومُ وَلَا يَتَمَادَى فِي الزَّلَّةِ وَلَا يَحْصُرُ مِنَ الْفَيْءِ اِلَى الْحَقِّ اِذَا عَرَفَهُ وَلَا تُشْرِفُ نَفْسُهُ عَلَى طَمَعٍ وَلَا يَكْتَفِي بِاَدْنَى فَهْمٍ دُونَ اَقْصَاهُ، وَاَوْقَفَهُمْ فِي الشُّبُهَاتِ وَاَخَذَهُمْ بِالْحُجَجِ وَاَقَلَّهُمْ تَبَرُّماً بِمُرَاجَعَةِ الْخَصْمِ وَاَصْبَرَهُمْ عَلَى تَكَشُّفِ الْاُمُورِ وَاَصْرَمَهُمْ عِنْدَ اتِّضَاحِ الْحُكْمِ مِمَّنْ لَا يَزْدَهِيهِ اِطْرَاءٌ وَلَا يَسْتَمِيلُهُ اِغْرَاءٌ وَاُولَئِكَ قَلِيلٌ.
(نهج البلاغه ص ١٠٠)

٣٦٧ - قَالَ الْبَاقِرُ عليه السلام: اِنَّ الْمَرْاَةَ لَا تُوَلَّى الْقَضَاءَ وَلَا تُوَلَّى الْاِمَارَةَ.
(بحار الانوار ج ٢٤ ص ٩)

٣٦٨ - قَوْلُهُ تَعَالَى: وَمَنْ لَمْ يَحْكُمْ بِمَا اَنْزَلَ اللهُ فَاُولَئِكَ هُمُ الْفَاسِقُونَ.
(سوره مائده - آیت ٤٧)

٣٦٩ - قَوْلُهُ تَعَالَى: وَمَنْ لَمْ يَحْكُمْ بِمَا اَنْزَلَ اللهُ فَاُولَئِكَ هُمُ الظَّالِمُونَ .
(سوره مائده - آیت ٤٥)

٣٧٠ - قَوْلُهُ تَعَالَى: وَمَنْ لَمْ يَحْكُمْ بِمَا اَنْزَلَ اللهُ فَاُولَئِكَ هُمُ الْكَافِرُونَ .
(سوره مائده - آیت ٤٤)

٣٧١ - قَالَ الصَّادِقُ عليه السلام: مَنْ حَكَمَ فِي دِرْهَمَيْنِ بِغَيْرِ مَا اَنْزَلَ

اللهَ فَقَدْ كَفَرَ .   (بحار الانوار ج ٢٤ ص ٦)

٣٧٢ - قَالَ الصَّادِقُ عَلَيْهِ السَّلامُ (فِي حَدِيثٍ): وَاِذَا جَارَ الْحُكَّامُ فِي الْقَضَاءِ أَمْسَكَ الْقَطْرَ مِنَ السَّمَاءِ .

(بحار الانوار ج ٢٤ ص ٦)

٣٧٣ - قَالَ النَّبِيُّ صَلَّى اللهُ عَلَيْهِ وَآلِهِ: لِسَانُ الْقَاضِي بَيْنَ الْجَمْرَتَيْنِ مِنْ نَارٍ حَتَّى يَقْضِيَ بَيْنَ النَّاسِ فَاِمَّا اِلَى الْجَنَّةِ وَاِمَّا اِلَى النَّارِ .

(وسائل الشيعه ج ٣ ص ٣٩٦)

٣٧٤ - وَمِنْ عَهْدِ عَلِيٍّ عَلَيْهِ السَّلامُ اِلَى مُحَمَّدِ بْنِ اَبِي بَكْرٍ: فَاخْفِضْ لَهُمْ جَنَاحَكَ وَاَلِنْ لَهُمْ جَانِبَكَ وَابْسُطْ لَهُمْ وَجْهَكَ وَآسِ بَيْنَهُمْ فِي اللَّحْظَةِ وَالنَّظْرَةِ حَتَّى لَا يَطْمَعَ الْعُظَمَاءُ فِي حَيْفِكَ لَهُمْ وَلَا يَيْاَسَ الضُّعَفَاءُ مِنْ عَدْلِكَ عَلَيْهِمْ .

(نهج البلاغة ص ٨٧٧)

٣٧٥ - فِي النَّبَوِيِّ: مَنِ ابْتُلِيَ بِالْقَضَاءِ بَيْنَ الْمُسْلِمِينَ فَلْيَعْدِلْ بَيْنَهُمْ فِي لَحْظَتِهِ وَاِشَارَتِهِ وَمَعْقِدِهِ وَلَا يَرْفَعَنَّ صَوْتَهُ عَلَى اَحَدِهِمَا مَا لَا يَرْفَعُ عَلَى الْآخَرِ .

(جواهر كتاب القضاء)

٣٧٦ - رُوِيَ اَنَّ اَمِيرَ الْمُؤْمِنِينَ عَلَيْهِ السَّلامُ وَلَّى اَبَا الْاَسْوَدِ الدُّئَلِيَّ الْقَضَاءَ ثُمَّ عَزَلَهُ . فَقَالَ لِمَ عَزَلْتَنِي وَمَا خُنْتُ وَلَا جَنَيْتُ ؟ فَقَالَ اِنِّي رَاَيْتُ كَلَامَكَ يَعْلُو كَلَامَ خَصْمِكَ .

(مستدرك الوسائل ج ٣ ص ١٩٧)

٣٧٧- عَنْ رَسُولِ اللهِ ﷺ وَنَهَى عَنْ تَلْقِينِ الشُّهُودِ .

(مستدرك الوسائل ج٣ ص١٩٥)

٣٧٨- فِي النَّبَوِيِّ : مَنْ وُلِّيَ شَيْئاً مِنَ النَّاسِ فَاحْتَجَبَ دُونَ حَاجَتِهِمْ احْتَجَبَ اللهُ تَعَالَى دُونَ حَاجَتِهِ وَفَاقَتِهِ وَ فَقْرِهِ .
(جواهر كتاب القضاء)

٣٧٩- عَنْ عَلِيٍّ ﷺ أَنَّهُ بَلَغَهُ أَنَّ شُرَيْحاً يَقْضِي فِي بَيْتِهِ فَقَالَ يَا شُرَيْحُ اجْلِسْ فِي الْمَسْجِدِ فَإِنَّهُ أَعْدَلُ بَيْنَ النَّاسِ. فَإِنَّهُ وَهْنٌ بِالْقَاضِي أَنْ يَجْلِسَ فِي بَيْتِهِ .

(مستدرك الوسائل ج٣ ص١٩٧)

٣٨٠- عَنْ رَسُولِ اللهِ ﷺ أَنَّهُ نَهَى أَنْ يَقْضِيَ الْقَاضِي وَهُوَ غَضْبَانُ أَوْ جَائِعٌ أَوْ نَاعِسٌ .

(مستدرك الوسائل ج٣ ص١٩٥)

٣٨١- قَالَ عَلِيٌّ ﷺ ، مَا عَدَلَ وَالٍ اتَّجَرَ فِي رَعِيَّتِهِ أَبَداً.
(جواهر كتاب القضاء)

٣٨٢- عَنْ أَمِيرِ الْمُؤْمِنِينَ ﷺ أَنَّهُ أَتَى سُوقَ الْكَرَابِيسِ فَقَالَ يَا شَيْخُ أَحْسِنْ بَيْعِي فِي قَمِيصِي بِثَلَاثِ دَرَاهِمَ فَلَمَّا عَرَفَهُ لَمْ يَشْتَرِ مِنْهُ حَتَّى أَتَى غُلَاماً حَدَثاً فَاشْتَرَى مِنْهُ قَمِيصاً بِثَلَاثَةِ دَرَاهِمَ . (جواهر كتاب القضاء)

٣٨٣- إِنَّ رَجُلاً نَزَلَ بِأَمِيرِ الْمُؤْمِنِينَ ﷺ فَمَكَثَ عِنْدَهُ أَيَّاماً ثُمَّ تَقَدَّمَ إِلَيْهِ لِخُصُومَةٍ لَمْ يَذْكُرْهَا لِأَمِيرِ الْمُؤْمِنِينَ ﷺ فَقَالَ لَهُ: أَخَصْمٌ أَنْتَ ؟ قَالَ نَعَمْ. قَالَ تَحَوَّلْ عَنَّا فَإِنَّ

رَسُولُ اللهِ ﷺ نَهَى أَنْ يُضَافَ الْخَصْمُ إِلَّا وَمَعَهُ خَصْمُهُ.
(وسائل الشيعه ج ٣ ص ٣٩٥)

٣٨٤ - قَالَ الصَّادِقُ ﷷ: اَلرَّشَا فِي الْحُكْمِ هُوَ الْكُفْرُ بِاللهِ.
(بحار الانوار ج ٢٤ ص ٩)

٣٨٥ - قَالَ النَّبِيُّ ﷺ: لَعَنَ اللهُ الرَّاشِيَ وَالْمُرْتَشِيَ وَالْمَاشِيَ بَيْنَهُمَا.
(بحار الانوار ج ٢٤ ص ٩)

٣٨٦ - قَالَ النَّبِيُّ ﷺ: إِيَّاكُمْ وَالرِّشْوَةَ فَإِنَّهَا مَحْضُ الْكُفْرِ وَلَا يَشُمُّ صَاحِبُ الرِّشْوَةِ رِيحَ الْجَنَّةِ.
(بحار الانوار ج ٢٤ ص ٩)

٣٨٧ - عَنْ أَمِيرِ الْمُؤْمِنِينَ ﷷ فِيمَا كَتَبَهُ إِلَى الْأَشْتَرِ ثُمَّ الْكِثْرَ تَعَاهُدَ قَضَائِهِ وَافْسَحْ لَهُ فِي الْبَذْلِ مَا يُزِيلُ عِلَّتَهُ وَتَقِلُّ مَعَهُ حَاجَتُهُ إِلَى النَّاسِ وَأَعْطِهِ مِنَ الْمَنْزِلَةِ لَدَيْكَ مَا لَا يَطْمَعُ فِيهِ غَيْرُهُ ... (نهج البلاغه ص ١٠٠١)

٣٨٨ - قَالَ رَسُولُ اللهِ ﷺ: نِعْمَ الْعَوْنُ عَلَى تَقْوَى اللهِ الْغِنَى.
(من لا يحضره الفقيه ص ٣٥٣)

٣٨٩ - قَالَ الصَّادِقُ ﷷ: نِعْمَ الْعَوْنُ الدُّنْيَا عَلَى الْآخِرَةِ.
(من لا يحضره الفقيه ص ٣٥٣)

٣٩٠ - قَالَ رَسُولُ اللهِ ﷺ: مَلْعُونٌ مَنْ أَلْقَى كَلَّهُ عَلَى النَّاسِ.
(فروع كافى ج ١٥ ص ٣٤٧)

٣٩١ - قَالَ مُوسَى بْنُ جَعْفَرٍ ﷷ: إِنَّ اللهَ لَيُبْغِضُ الْعَبْدَ الْفَارِغَ.
(من لا يحضره الفقيه ص ٣٥٣)

٣٩٢- قَالَ الصَّادِقُ عليه السلام: ثَلَاثَةٌ لَا يُسْتَجَابُ لَهُمْ دَعْوَةٌ: ... وَرَجُلٌ جَلَسَ فِي بَيْتِهِ وَتَرَكَ الطَّلَبَ يَقُولُ: يَارَبِّ ارْزُقْنِي فَيَقُولُ الرَّبُّ: اَوَلَمْ اَجْعَلْ لَكَ السَّبِيلَ إِلَى الطَّلَبِ لِلرِّزْقِ.
(اثناعشریه طبع جدید قم ص ١٠٧)

٣٩٣- قَالَ الصَّادِقُ عليه السلام: لَا تَكْسُلُوا فِي طَلَبِ مَعَايِشِكُمْ فَإِنَّ آبَاءَنَا قَدْ كَانُوا يَرْكُضُونَ فِيهَا وَيَطْلُبُونَهَا.
(من لايحضره الفقيه ص ٣٥٣)

٣٩٤- قَالَ اَمِيرُ المُؤْمِنِينَ عليه السلام: إِنَّ اللّٰهَ يُحِبُّ المُتَحَرِّفَ الاَمِينَ.
(من لايحضره الفقيه ص ٣٥٣)

٣٩٥- عَنْ اَبِي الحَسَنِ مُوسَى عليه السلام: مَنْ طَلَبَ هٰذَا الرِّزْقَ مِنْ حِلِّهِ لِيَعُودَ عَلَى نَفْسِهِ وَعِيَالِهِ كَانَ كَالمُجَاهِدِ فِي سَبِيلِ اللّٰهِ.
(وسائل الشيعه ج ٢ ص ٥٢٩)

٣٩٦- قَالَ مُحَمَّدُ بْنُ مُنْكَدِرٍ: خَرَجْتُ إِلَى بَعْضِ نَوَاحِي المَدِينَةِ فِي سَاعَةٍ حَارَّةٍ فَلَقَانِي اَبُو جَعْفَرٍ مُحَمَّدُ بْنُ عَلِيٍّ عليه السلام وَكَانَ رَجُلًا بَادِنًا ثَقِيلًا وَهُوَ مُتَّكِئٌ عَلَى غُلَامَيْنِ اَسْوَدَيْنِ اَوْ مَوْلَيَيْنِ فَقُلْتُ فِي نَفْسِي سُبْحَانَ اللّٰهِ! شَيْخٌ مِنْ اَشْيَاخِ قُرَيْشٍ فِي هٰذِهِ السَّاعَةِ عَلَى مِثْلِ هٰذِهِ الحَالَةِ فِي طَلَبِ الدُّنْيَا! اَمَا اِنِّي لَاَعِظُهُ فَدَنَوْتُ مِنْهُ فَسَلَّمْتُ عَلَيْهِ فَرَدَّ عَلَيَّ بِنَهْرٍ (بَهْرٍ خ ل) وَهُوَ يَتَصَابُّ عَرَقًا. فَقُلْتُ: اَصْلَحَكَ اللّٰهُ شَيْخٌ مِنْ اَشْيَاخِ قُرَيْشٍ فِي هٰذِهِ السَّاعَةِ عَلَى هٰذِهِ الحَالَةِ فِي طَلَبِ الدُّنْيَا! اَرَاَيْتَ لَوْ جَاءَ اَجَلُكَ وَاَنْتَ عَلَى هٰذِهِ الحَالِ

فَقَالَ لَوْ جَاءَنِىَ الْمَوْتُ وَأَنَا عَلَى هَذِهِ الْحَالِ جَاءَنِى وَأَنَا فِى طَاعَةٍ مِنْ طَاعَةِ اللهِ وَأَكُفَّ بِهَا نَفْسِى وَعِيَالِى عَنْكَ وَعَنِ النَّاسِ ...

(وسائل الشيعه ج ٢ ص ٥٢٩)

٣٩٧- قَالَ الصَّادِقُ ﷺ: مَا فِى الْأَعْمَالِ شَىْءٌ أَحَبُّ إِلَى اللهِ مِنَ الزِّرَاعَةِ.

(بحار الانوار ج ٢٣ ص ٢٠)

٣٩٨- سيابه عَنْ أَبِى عَبْدِ اللهِ ﷺ سَأَلَهُ رَجُلٌ فَقَالَ جُعِلْتُ فِدَاكَ أَسْمَعُ قَوْماً يَقُولُونَ إِنَّ الزِّرَاعَةَ مَكْرُوهَةٌ فَقَالَ لَهُ: اِزْرَعُوا وَاغْرِسُوا فَلَا وَاللهِ مَا عَمِلَ النَّاسُ عَمَلاً أَحَبَّ وَلَا أَطْيَبَ مِنْهُ.

(فروع كافى ج ١ ص ٤٠٤)

٣٩٩- عَنِ الصَّادِقِ ﷺ عَنْ آبَائِهِ قَالَ: سُئِلَ رَسُولُ اللهِ ﷺ أَىُّ الْمَالِ خَيْرٌ؟ قَالَ ﷺ: زَرْعٌ زَرَعَهُ صَاحِبُهُ وَأَصْلَحَهُ وَأَدَّى حَقَّهُ يَوْمَ حَصَادِهِ ...

(بحار الانوار ج ٢٣ ص ١٩)

٤٠٠- عَنِ الْبَاقِرِ ﷺ قَالَ كَانَ أَمِيرُ الْمُؤْمِنِينَ ﷺ يَقُولُ: مَنْ وَجَدَ مَاءً وَتُرَاباً ثُمَّ افْتَقَرَ فَأَبْعَدَهُ اللهُ.

(بحار الانوار ج ٢٣ ص ١٩)

٤٠١- قَالَ النَّبِىُّ ﷺ لِعَمَّتِهِ: مَا يَمْنَعُكِ مِنْ أَنْ تَتَّخِذِى فِى بَيْتِكِ الْبَرَكَةَ فَقَالَتْ يَا رَسُولَ اللهِ مَا الْبَرَكَةُ؟ فَقَالَ ﷺ: شَاةٌ تُحْلَبُ فَإِنَّهُ مَنْ كَانَتْ فِى دَارِهِ شَاةٌ تُحْلَبُ أَوْ نَعْجَةٌ أَوْ بَقَرَةٌ فَبَرَكَاتٌ كُلُّهُنَّ.

(بحار الانوار ج ١٤ ص ٦٨٦)

٤٠٢ - قَالَ رَسُولُ اللهِ ﷺ: اَلشَّاةُ نِعْمَ الْمَالُ الشَّاةُ.

(بحارالانوار ج ١٤ ص ٧٨٦)

٤٠٣ - عَلَيْكُمْ بِالْغَنَمِ وَالْحَرْثِ فَاِنَّهُمَا يَرُوحَانِ بِخَيْرٍ وَّ يَغْدُوَانِ بِخَيْرٍ. (بحارالانوار ج ١٤ ص ٢٨٦)

٤٠٤ - قَالَ الصَّادِقُ ﷿: اِتَّخِذُوا الدَّابَّةَ فَاِنَّهَا زَيْنٌ وَتَقْضِىْ عَلَيْهَا الْحَوَائِجَ وَرِزْقُهَا عَلَى اللهِ.

(وسائل الشیعه ج ٢ ص ١٩٣)

٤٠٥ - قَالَ الصَّادِقُ ﷿: مِنْ سَعَادَةِ الْمُؤْمِنِ دَابَّةٌ يَرْكَبُهَا فِىْ حَوَائِجِهِ وَيَقْضِىْ عَلَيْهِ حُقُوْقَ اِخْوَانِهِ.

(وسائل الشیعه ج ٢ ص ١٩٣)

٤٠٦ - قَالَ رَسُولُ اللهِ ﷺ: اِنَّ مِنْ سَعَادَةِ الْمَرْءِ الْمُسْلِمِ اَنْ يَّشْبِهَهُ وَلَدُهُ وَالْمَرْاَةُ الْجَلَّاءُ ذَاتُ دِيْنٍ وَالْمَرْكَبُ الْهَنِيْءُ وَالْمَسْكَنُ الْوَاسِعُ.

(بحارالانوار ج ١٦ ص ٨٢)

٤٠٧ - قَوْلُهُ تَعَالَى: وَالَّذِىْ خَلَقَ الْاَزْوَاجَ كُلَّهَا وَجَعَلَ لَكُمْ مِّنَ الْفُلْكِ وَالْاَنْعَامِ مَا تَرْكَبُوْنَ. لِتَسْتَوُوْا عَلَى ظُهُوْرِهٖ ثُمَّ تَذْكُرُوْا نِعْمَةَ رَبِّكُمْ اِذَا اسْتَوَيْتُمْ عَلَيْهِ وَتَقُوْلُوْا سُبْحَانَ الَّذِىْ سَخَّرَ لَنَا هٰذَا وَمَا كُنَّا لَهٗ مُقْرِنِيْنَ. وَاِنَّا اِلَى رَبِّنَا لَمُنْقَلِبُوْنَ. (سوره زخرف - آيت ١٢-١٤)

٤٠٨ - قَالَ رَسُولُ اللهِ ﷺ: اَلْبَرَكَةُ عَشَرَةُ اَجْزَاءٍ تِسْعَةُ اَعْشَارِهَا فِى التِّجَارَةِ. (بحارالانوار ج ٢٣ ص ٥)

265

٤٠٩ - قَالَ رَسُولُ اللهِ ﷺ: اَلتَّاجِرُ الصَّدُوقُ يُحْشَرُ يَوْمَ الْقِيَامَةِ مَعَ الصِّدِّيقِينَ وَالشُّهَدَاءِ.

(احياء العلوم ج ٢ ص ٤٥)

٤١٠ - قَالَ الصَّادِقُ عليه السلام: ثَلَاثَةٌ يُدْخِلُهُمُ اللهُ الْجَنَّةَ بِغَيْرِ حِسَابٍ: اِمَامٌ عَادِلٌ وَتَاجِرٌ صَدُوقٌ وَشَيْخٌ اَفْنَى عُمْرَهُ فِي طَاعَةِ اللهِ عَزَّ وَجَلَّ.

(بحار الانوار ج ٢٣ ص ٥)

٤١١ - قَالَ عَلِيٌّ عليه السلام: تَعَرَّضُوا لِلتِّجَارَةِ فَاِنَّ لَكُمْ فِيهَا غِنًى عَمَّا فِي اَيْدِي النَّاسِ.   (فروع كافى ج ١ ص ٣٧٠)

٤١٢ - قَالَ الصَّادِقُ عليه السلام: اَلتِّجَارَةُ تَزِيدُ فِي الْعَقْلِ.

(فروع كافى ج ١ ص ٣٧٠)

٤١٣ - قَالَ الصَّادِقُ عليه السلام: تَرْكُ التِّجَارَةِ يَنْقُصُ الْعَقْلَ.

(فروع كافى ج ١ ص ٣٧٠)

٤١٤ - قَالَ الصَّادِقُ عليه السلام: (فِي حَدِيثٍ) لَا تَدَعُوا التِّجَارَةَ فَتَهُونُوا اِتَّجِرُوا بَارَكَ اللهُ لَكُمْ.   (فروع كافى ج ١ ص ٣٧٠)

٤١٥ - قَوْلُهُ تَعَالَى: رِجَالٌ لَا تُلْهِيهِمْ تِجَارَةٌ وَلَا بَيْعٌ عَنْ ذِكْرِ اللهِ...   (سوره نور - آیت ٣٧)

٤١٦ - فِقْهُ الرِّضَا: وَاِذَا كُنْتَ فِي تِجَارَتِكَ وَحَضَرَتِ الصَّلَوةُ فَلَا يَشْغَلْكَ عَنْهَا مَتْجَرُكَ فَاِنَّ اللهَ وَصَفَ قَوْمًا وَ مَدَحَهُمْ فَقَالَ: رِجَالٌ لَا تُلْهِيهِمْ تِجَارَةٌ وَلَا بَيْعٌ عَنْ ذِكْرِ اللهِ. وَكَانَ هٰؤُلَاءِ الْقَوْمُ يَتَّجِرُونَ فَاِذَا

حَضَرَتِ الصَّلٰوةُ تَرَكُوا تِجَارَتَهُمْ وَقَامُوا اِلٰى صَلاٰتِهِمْ وَكَانُوا اَعْظَمَ اَجْراً مِمَّنْ لاٰ يَتَّجِرُ فَيُصَلِّىْ.

(مستدرك الوسائل ج ٢ ص ٤٦٤)

٤١٧ ـ قَالَ عَلِىُّ بْنُ الْحُسَيْنِ عَلَيْهِ السَّلَامُ (فِى رِوَايَةٍ) : مِنْ سَعَادَةِ الْمَرْءِ اَنْ يَكُوْنَ مَتْجَرُهُ فِىْ بِلاَدِهِ وَيَكُوْنَ خُلَطَائُهُ صَالِحِيْنَ وَيَكُوْنَ لَهُ وَلَدٌ يَسْتَعِيْنُ بِهِ.

(بحارالانوار ج ٢٣ ص ٥)

٤١٨ ـ قَالَ اَمِيْرُ الْمُؤْمِنِيْنَ عَلَيْهِ السَّلَامُ : يَا مَعْشَرَ التُّجَّارِ اَلْفِقْهُ ثُمَّ الْمَتْجَرُ اَلْفِقْهُ ثُمَّ الْمَتْجَرُ اَلْفِقْهُ ثُمَّ الْمَتْجَرُ ...

(فروع كافى ج ١ ص ٣٧١)

٤١٩ ـ قَالَ اَمِيْرُ الْمُؤْمِنِيْنَ عَلَيْهِ السَّلَامُ: مَنِ اتَّجَرَ بِغَيْرِ عِلْمٍ اِرْتَطَمَ فِى الرِّبَا ثُمَّ ارْتَطَمَ.

(فروع كافى ج ١ ص ٣٧٢)

٤٢٠ ـ قَالَ رَسُوْلُ اللهِ صَلَّى اللهُ عَلَيْهِ وَآلِهِ: مَنْ بَاعَ وَاشْتَرَى فَلْيَحْفَظْ خَمْسَ خِصَالٍ وَاِلاَّ فَلاَ يَشْتَرِيَنَّ وَلاَ يَبِيْعَنَّ : اَلرِّبَا وَالْحَلْفَ وَكِتْمَانَ الْعَيْبِ وَالْحَمْدَ اِذَا بَاعَ وَالذَّمَّ اِذَا اشْتَرٰى.

(فروع كافى ج ١ ص ٣٧١)

٤٢١ ـ قَالَ اَمِيْرُ الْمُؤْمِنِيْنَ عَلَيْهِ السَّلَامُ: يَا اَهْلَ السُّوْقِ اِتَّقُوا اللهَ وَاِيَّاكُمْ وَالْحَلْفَ فَاِنَّهُ يُنْفِقُ السِّلْعَةَ وَيَمْحَقُ الْبَرَكَةَ.

(مستدرك الوسائل ج ٢ ص ٤٦٧)

٤٢٢ ـ قَالَ الصَّادِقُ عَلَيْهِ السَّلَامُ: اِذَا دَخَلْتَ سُوْقَكَ فَقُلْ : اَللّٰهُمَّ اِنِّىْ اَسْئَلُكَ خَيْرَهَا وَخَيْرَ اَهْلِهَا وَاَعُوْذُ بِكَ مِنْ شَرِّهَا

وَمِنْ شَرِّ اَهْلِهَا. اَللّٰهُمَّ اِنِّي اَعُوذُ بِكَ مِنْ اَنْ اَظْلِمَ اَوْ اُظْلَمَ اَوْ اَبْغِيَ اَوْ يُبْغىٰ عَلَيَّ اَوْ اَعْتَدِيَ اَوْ يُعْتَدىٰ عَلَيَّ اَللّٰهُمَّ اِنِّي اَعُوذُ بِكَ مِنْ شَرِّ اِبْلِيسَ وَجُنُودِهِ وَشَرِّ فَسَقَةِ الْعَرَبِ وَالْعَجَمِ وَحَسْبِىَ اللهُ لَا اِلٰهَ اِلَّا هُوَ عَلَيْهِ تَوَكَّلْتُ وَهُوَ رَبُّ الْعَرْشِ الْعَظِيْمِ.

(فروع كافى ج ١٤ ص ٣٧٣)

٤٢٣ - قَالَ اَبُوجَعْفَرٍ عَلَيْهِ السَّلَامُ (فِي حَدِيثٍ): اِنْ وُلِّيْتَ اَخَاكَ فَحَسِّنْ وَاِلَّا فَبِعْهُ بَيْعَ الْبَصِيرِ الْمُدَارِىْ.

(وسائل الشيعه ج ٢ ص ٥٧٦)

٤٢٤ - قَالَ اَبُوجَعْفَرٍ عَلَيْهِ السَّلَامُ: مَاكِسِ الْمُشْتَرِىَ فَاِنَّهُ اَطْيَبُ لِلنَّفْسِ وَاِنْ اَعْطىٰ الْجَزِيْلَ: فَاِنَّ الْمَغْبُونَ فِى بَيْعِهِ وَشِرَائِهِ غَيْرُ مَحْمُودٍ وَلَا مَاجُورٍ.

(وسائل الشيعه ج ٢ ص ٥٨٣)

٤٢٥ - قَالَ الصَّادِقُ عَلَيْهِ السَّلَامُ (فِي حَدِيثٍ): اَنَّ رَسُولَ اللهِ ﷺ نَهىٰ عَنِ الْاِسْتِحْطَاطِ بِالصَّفْقَةِ.

(وسائل الشيعه ج ٢ ص ٥٨٢)

٤٢٦ - قَالَ رَسُولُ اللهِ ﷺ: يَأْتِىٰ عَلَى النَّاسِ زَمَانٌ يَشْكُونَ فِيْهِ رَبَّهُمْ قُلْتُ وَكَيْفَ يَشْكُونَ فِيْهِ رَبَّهُمْ قَالَ ﷺ يَقُولُ الرَّجُلُ وَاللهِ مَا رَبِحْتُ شَيْئًا مُنْذُ كَذَا وَكَذَا وَلَا اَكُلُ وَلَا اَشْرَبُ اِلَّا مِنْ رَأْسِ مَالِىْ. وَيْحَكَ وَهَلْ اَصْلُ مَالِكَ وَذَرْوَتُهُ اِلَّا مِنْ رَبِّكَ. (وسائل الشيعه ج ٢ ص ٥٨٢)

٤٢٧ - قَالَ الصَّادِقُ عَلَيْهِ السَّلَامُ : اَيُّمَا عَبْدٍ اَقَالَ مُسْلِمًا فِي بَيْعٍ اَقَالَهُ اللهُ تَعَالَى عَثْرَتَهُ يَوْمَ الْقِيَامَةِ .

(فروع كافى ج ١ ص ٣٧٢)

٤٢٨ - قَالَ الصَّادِقُ عَلَيْهِ السَّلَامُ : وَنَهَى رَسُولُ اللهِ صَلَّى اللهُ عَلَيْهِ وَآلِهِ اَنْ يَدْخُلَ الرَّجُلُ فِي سَوْمِ اَخِيهِ الْمُسْلِمِ .

(وسائل الشيعه ج ٢ ص ٥٨٣)

٤٢٩ - قَالَ عَاصِمُ بْنُ حُمَيْدٍ قَالَ لِي اَبُوعَبْدِ اللهِ عَلَيْهِ السَّلَامُ : اَيَّ شَيْءٍ تُعَالِجُ ؟ قُلْتُ اَبِيعُ الطَّعَامَ : فَقَالَ عَلَيْهِ السَّلَامُ لِي : اِشْتَرِ الْجَيِّدَ وَبِعِ الْجَيِّدَ فَاِنَّ الْجَيِّدَ اِذَا اَبِعْتَهُ قِيلَ لَكَ بَارَكَ اللهُ فِيكَ وَفِيمَنْ بَاعَكَ . (فروع كافى ج ١ ص ٣٨٦)

٤٣٠ - قَالَ رَسُولُ اللهِ صَلَّى اللهُ عَلَيْهِ وَآلِهِ : اَيُّمَا رَجُلٍ اِشْتَرَى طَعَامًا فَكَبَسَهُ اَرْبَعِينَ صَبَاحًا يُرِيدُ بِهِ غِلَاءَ الْمُسْلِمِينَ ثُمَّ بَاعَهُ فَقَصَّدَ بِثَمَنِهِ لَمْ يَكُنْ لَهُ كَفَّارَةٌ لِمَا صَنَعَ .

(وسائل الشيعه ج ٢ ص ٥٧٩)

٤٣١ - دَعَا اَبُوعَبْدِاللهِ عَلَيْهِ السَّلَامُ مَوْلًى لَهُ يُقَالُ لَهُ "مُصَادِفْ" فَاَعْطَاهُ اَلْفَ دِينَارٍ قَالَ لَهُ تَجَهَّزْ حَتَّى تَخْرُجَ اِلَى مِصْرَ فَاِنَّ عَيَالِى قَدْ كَثُرُوا. قَالَ فَتَجَهَّزَ بِمَتَاعٍ وَخَرَجَ مَعَ التُّجَّارِ اِلَى مِصْرَ فَلَمَّا دَنَوْا مِنْ مِصْرَ اِسْتَقْبَلَتْهُمْ قَافِلَةٌ خَارِجَةٌ مِنْ مِصْرَ فَسَئَلُوهُمْ عَنِ الْمَتَاعِ الَّذِى مَعَهُمْ مَا حَالُهُ فِي الْمَدِينَةِ وَكَانَ مَتَاعُ الْعَامَّةِ فَاَخْبَرُوهُمْ اَنَّهُ لَيْسَ بِمِصْرَ مِنْهُ شَىْءٌ فَتَحَالَفُوا وَتَعَاقَدُوا عَلَى اَنْ لَا يَنْقُصُوا

269

مَتَاعَهُمْ مِنْ رِبْحِ الدِّينَارِ دِينَارًا فَلَمَّا قَبَضُوا أَمْوَالَهُمْ وَانْصَرَفُوا إِلَى الْمَدِينَةِ دَخَلَ مُصَادِفٌ إِلَى أَبِي عَبْدِ اللّٰهِ عَلَيْهِ السَّلاَمُ وَمَعَهُ كِيسَانِ فِي كُلِّ وَاحِدٍ أَلْفُ دِينَارٍ فَقَالَ جُعِلْتُ فِدَاكَ هٰذَا رَأْسُ الْمَالِ وَهٰذَا الْآخَرُ رِبْحٌ. فَقَالَ عَلَيْهِ السَّلاَمُ: إِنَّ هٰذَا الرِّبْحَ كَثِيرٌ وَلٰكِنْ مَا صَنَعْتُمْ فِي الْمَتَاعِ، فَحَدَّثَهُ كَيْفَ صَنَعُوا وَكَيْفَ تَحَالَفُوا فَقَالَ: سُبْحَانَ اللّٰهِ تَحْلِفُونَ عَلَى قَوْمٍ مُسْلِمِينَ أَلَّا تَبِيعُوهُمْ إِلَّا بِرِبْحِ الدِّينَارِ دِينَارًا ثُمَّ أَخَذَ عَلَيْهِ السَّلاَمُ أَحَدَ الْكِيسَيْنِ فَقَالَ عَلَيْهِ السَّلاَمُ: هٰذَا رَأْسُ مَالِي وَلاَ حَاجَةَ لَنَا فِي هٰذَا الرِّبْحِ ثُمَّ قَالَ: يَا مُصَادِفُ مُجَادَلَةُ السُّيُوفِ أَهْوَنُ مِنْ طَلَبِ الْحَلاَلِ.

(فروع كافي ج ١ ص ٣٧٤)

٤٣٢ ـ قَالَ أَبُو جَعْفَرٍ عَلَيْهِ السَّلاَمُ: كَانَ أَمِيرُ الْمُؤْمِنِينَ عَلَيْهِ السَّلاَمُ بِالْكُوفَةِ عِنْدَكُمْ يَغْتَدِي كُلَّ يَوْمٍ بُكْرَةً مِنَ الْقَصْرِ فَيَطُوفُ فِي أَسْوَاقِ الْكُوفَةِ سُوقًا سُوقًا وَمَعَهُ الدِّرَّةُ عَلَى عَاتِقِهِ وَكَانَ لَهَا طَرَفَانِ وَكَانَتْ تُسَمَّى السَّبِيبَةَ فَيَقِفُ عَلَى أَهْلِ كُلِّ سُوقٍ فَيُنَادِي: يَا مَعْشَرَ التُّجَّارِ اتَّقُوا اللّٰهَ عَزَّ وَجَلَّ ـ فَإِذَا سَمِعُوا صَوْتَهُ أَلْقَوْا مَا بِأَيْدِيهِمْ وَأَرْعَوْا إِلَيْهِ بِقُلُوبِهِمْ وَسَمِعُوا بِآذَانِهِمْ ـ فَيَقُولُ عَلَيْهِ السَّلاَمُ: قَدِّمُوا الْاِسْتِخَارَةَ وَتَبَرَّكُوا بِالسُّهُولَةِ وَاقْتَرِبُوا مِنَ الْمُبْتَاعِينَ وَتَزَيَّنُوا بِالْحِلْمِ وَتَنَاهَوْا عَنِ الْيَمِينِ وَجَانِبُوا الْكِذْبَ وَتَجَافُوا عَنِ الظُّلْمِ وَأَنْصِفُوا الْمَظْلُومِينَ وَلَا تَقْرَبُوا الرِّبَا

وَأَوْفُوا الْكَيْلَ وَالْمِيزَانَ وَلَا تَبْخَسُوا النَّاسَ أَشْيَاءَهُمْ وَلَا تَعْثَوْا فِى الْأَرْضِ مُفْسِدِينَ. فَيَطُوفُ عليه في جَمِيعِ أَسْوَاقِ الْكُوفَةِ ثُمَّ يَرْجِعُ فَيَقْعُدُ لِلنَّاسِ.

(فروع كافى ج ١ ص ٣٧١)

٤٣٣ - فى عَهْدِ عَلِىٍّ عليه الى الْأَشْتَرِ: ثُمَّ اسْتَوْصِ بِالتُّجَّارِ وَ ذَوِى الصِّنَاعَاتِ وَأَوْصِ بِهِمْ خَيْرًا: الْمُقِيمُ مِنْهُمْ وَالْمُضْطَرِبُ بِمَالِهِ وَالْمُتَرَفِّقُ بِبَدَنِهِ فَإِنَّهُمْ مَوَادُّ الْمَنَافِعِ وَأَسْبَابُ الْمَرَافِقِ وَجِلَّابُهَا مِنَ الْمَبَاعِدِ وَ الْمَطَارِحِ فِى بَرِّكَ وَبَحْرِكَ وَسَهْلِكَ وَجَبَلِكَ وَحَيْثُ لَا يَلْتَئِمُ النَّاسُ لِمَوَاضِعِهَا وَلَا يَجْتَرِئُونَ عَلَيْهَا فَإِنَّهُمْ سِلْمٌ لَا تَخَافُ بَائِقَتَهُ وَصُلْحٌ لَا تُغْشَى غَائِلَتُهُ وَتَفَقَّدْ أُمُورَهُمْ بِحَضْرَتِكَ وَفِى حَوَاشِى بِلَادِكَ. وَاعْلَمْ مَعَ ذَلِكَ أَنَّ فِى كَثِيرٍ مِنْهُمْ ضِيقًا فَاحِشًا وَشُحًّا قَبِيحًا وَاحْتِكَارًا لِلْمَنَافِعِ وَتَحَكُّمًا فِى الْبِيَاعَاتِ وَذَلِكَ مَضَرَّةٌ لِلْعَامَّةِ وَعَيْبٌ عَلَى الْوُلَاةِ فَامْنَعْ مِنَ الْاِحْتِكَارِ فَإِنَّ رَسُولَ اللهِ ﷺ مَنَعَ مِنْهُ وَلْيَكُنِ الْبَيْعُ بَيْعًا سَمْحًا بِمَوَازِينِ عَدْلٍ وَأَسْعَارٍ لَا تُجْحِفُ بِالْفَرِيقَيْنِ مِنَ الْبَائِعِ وَالْمُبْتَاعِ، فَمَنْ قَارَفَ حَكْرَةً بَعْدَ نَهْيِكَ إِيَّاهُ فَنَكِّلْ بِهِ وَعَاقِبْهُ فِى غَيْرِ إِسْرَافٍ.

(نهج البلاغه ص ١٠٠٨)

٤٣٤ - قَالَ رَسُولُ اللهِ ﷺ: رِذَالُ مَوْتَاكُمُ الْعُزَّابُ.

(وسائل الشيعه ج ٣ ص ٣)

٤٣٥ - قَالَ الصَّادِقُ علیه السلام : رَكْعَتَانِ يُصَلِّيهِمَا الْمُتَزَوِّجُ أَفْضَلُ مِنْ سَبْعِينَ رَكْعَةً يُصَلِّيهَا الْعَزَبُ .

(وسائل الشيعه ج ٣ ص ٢)

٤٣٦ - قَالَ رَسُولُ اللهِ صلى الله عليه وآله : مَنْ تَزَوَّجَ فَقَدْ أَحْرَزَ نِصْفَ دِينِهِ فَلْيَتَّقِ اللهَ فِى النِّصْفِ الْبَاقِى .

(سفينة البحار ج ١ ص ٥٦١)

٤٣٧ - قَالَ رَسُولُ اللهِ صلى الله عليه وآله (فِى حَدِيثٍ) لَمْ يُرْسِلْنِى اللهُ بِالرَّهْبَانِيَّةِ وَلكِنْ بَعَثَنِى بِالْحَنِيفِيَّةِ السَّمْحَةِ أَصُومُ وَأُصَلِّى وَأَلْمِسُ أَهْلِى فَمَنْ أَحَبَّ فِطْرَتِى فَلْيَسْتَنَّ بِسُنَّتِى وَمِنْ سُنَّتِىَ النِّكَاحُ .

(وسائل الشيعه ج ٣ ص ١٤)

٤٣٨ - قَوْلُهُ تَعَالَى : وَمِنْ آيَاتِهِ أَنْ خَلَقَ لَكُمْ مِنْ أَنْفُسِكُمْ أَزْوَاجًا لِتَسْكُنُوا إِلَيْهَا وَجَعَلَ بَيْنَكُمْ مَوَدَّةً وَرَحْمَةً .

(سوره روم - آيت ٢١)

٤٣٩ - قَالَ رَسُولُ اللهِ صلى الله عليه وآله : تَنَاكَحُوا وَتَنَاسَلُوا تَكْثُرُوا فَإِنِّى أُبَاهِى بِكُمُ الْأُمَمَ يَوْمَ الْقِيَامَةِ وَلَوْ بِالسِّقْطِ .

(سفينة البحار ج ١ ص ٥٦١)

٤٤٠ - قَالَ رَسُولُ اللهِ صلى الله عليه وآله : مَا يَمْنَعُ الْمُؤْمِنَ أَنْ يَتَّخِذَ أَهْلًا لَعَلَّ اللهَ أَنْ يَرْزُقَهُ نَسَمَةً تَثْقُلُ الْأَرْضَ بِلَا إِلهَ إِلَّا اللهُ .

(وسائل الشيعه ج ٣ ص ٢)

٤٤١ - قَالَ رَسُولُ اللهِ صلى الله عليه وآله : مَنْ تَرَكَ التَّزْوِيجَ مَخَافَةَ الْعَيْلَةِ

فَقَدْ سَاءَ ظَنُّهُ بِاللهِ عَزَّ وَجَلَّ إِنَّ اللهَ عَزَّ وَجَلَّ يَقُولُ: إِنْ يَكُونُوا فُقَرَاءَ يُغْنِهِمُ اللهُ مِنْ فَضْلِهِ

(وسائل الشيعه ج ٣ ص ٥)

٤٤٢ - قَالَ رَسُولُ اللهِ ﷺ: تَزَوَّجُوا الرِّزْقِ فَإِنَّ فِيهِنَّ الْبَرَكَةَ.

(من لا يحضره الفقيه ص ٤١٠)

٤٤٣ - قَالَ رَسُولُ اللهِ ﷺ: مَنْ عَمِلَ فِي تَزْوِيجٍ بَيْنَ مُؤْمِنَيْنِ حَتَّى يَجْمَعَ بَيْنَهُمَا زَوَّجَهُ اللهُ أَلْفَ امْرَأَةٍ مِنْ حُورٍ عِينٍ.

(سفينة البحار ج ١ ص ٥٦١)

٤٤٤ - قَالَ رَسُولُ اللهِ ﷺ مَنْ تَزَوَّجَ امْرَأَةً لَا يَتَزَوَّجُهَا إِلَّا لِجَمَالِهَا لَمْ يَرَ فِيهَا مَا يُحِبُّ وَمَنْ تَزَوَّجَهَا لِمَالِهَا لَا يَتَزَوَّجُهَا إِلَّا لَهُ وَكَّلَهُ اللهُ إِلَيْهِ فَعَلَيْكُمْ بِذَاتِ الدِّينِ.

(وسائل الشيعة ج ٣ ص ٦)

٤٤٥ - قَالَ الصَّادِقُ ﷺ: إِذَا تَزَوَّجَ الرَّجُلُ الْمَرْأَةَ لِجَمَالِهَا أَوْ لِمَالِهَا وُكِّلَ إِلَى ذَلِكَ وَإِذَا تَزَوَّجَهَا لِدِينِهَا رَزَقَهُ اللهُ الْمَالَ وَالْجَمَالَ. (وسائل الشيعه ج ٣ ص ٦)

٤٤٦ - قَالَ عَلِيٌّ ﷺ: إِيَّاكُمْ وَتَزْوِيجَ الْحُمَقَاءِ فَإِنَّ صُحْبَتَهَا بَلَاءٌ وَوَلَدُهَا ضَيَاعٌ. (وسائل الشيعه ج ٣ ص ٦)

٤٤٧ - عَنْ أَبِي يَعْفُورٍ عَنِ الصَّادِقِ ﷺ قَالَ: قُلْتُ لَهُ إِنِّي أُرِيدُ أَنْ أَتَزَوَّجَ امْرَأَةً وَإِنَّ أَبَوَيَّ أَرَادَا غَيْرَهَا. قَالَ ﷺ: تَزَوَّجِ الَّتِي هَوِيتَ وَدَعِ الَّتِي هَوِيَ أَبَوَاكَ.

(سفينة البحار ج ٢ ص ٥٨٦)

٤٤٨- قَوْلُهُ تَعَالى : وَإِنْ أَرَدْتُمُ اسْتِبْدَالَ زَوْجٍ مَكَانَ زَوْجٍ وَآتَيْتُمْ إِحْدَاهُنَّ قِنْطَارًا فَلَا تَأْخُذُوا مِنْهُ شَيْئًا أَتَأْخُذُونَهُ بُهْتَانًا وَإِثْمًا مُبِينًا.

(سوره نساء آيت ٢٤)

٤٤٩- قَالَ رَسُولُ اللهِ ﷺ : الشُؤْمُ فِي ثَلَاثَةِ أَشْيَاءَ : فِي الدَّابَّةِ وَالْمَرْأَةِ وَالدَّارِ فَأَمَّا الْمَرْأَةُ فَشُؤْمُهَا غَلَاءُ مَهْرٍ وَعُسْرُ وِلَادَتِهَا. (وسائل الشيعه ج ٣ ص ١٠٤)

٤٥٠- قَالَ رَسُولُ اللهِ ﷺ : أَفْضَلُ نِسَاءٍ أُمَّتِي أَصْبَحُهُنَّ وَجْهًا وَأَقَلُّهُنَّ مَهْرًا. (وسائل الشيعه ج ٣ ص ١٠٤)

٤٥١- قَالَ الصَّادِقُ ﷿ : مِنْ بَرَكَةِ الْمَرْأَةِ خِفَّةُ مُؤْنَتِهَا وَتَيَسُّرُ وِلَادَتِهَا، وَمِنْ شُؤْمِهَا شِدَّةُ مُؤْنَتِهَا وَتَعَسُّرُ وِلَادَتِهَا.

(وسائل الشيعه ج ٣ ص ١٠٤)

٤٥٢- قَالَ جَابِرُ بْنُ عَبْدِ اللهِ الْأَنْصَارِيُّ : كُنَّا عِنْدَ النَّبِيِّ ﷺ يَقُولُ : إِنَّ خَيْرَ نِسَائِكُمُ الْوَلُودُ الْوَدُودُ الْعَفِيفَةُ الْعَزِيزَةُ فِي أَهْلِهَا الذَّلِيلَةُ مَعَ بَعْلِهَا الْمُتَبَرِّجَةُ مَعَ زَوْجِهَا الْحَصَانُ عَلَى غَيْرِهِ الَّتِي تَسْمَعُ قَوْلَهُ وَتُطِيعُ أَمْرَهُ وَإِذَا خَلَا بِهَا بَذَلَتْ لَهُ مَا يُرِيدُ مِنْهَا وَلَمْ تَبَذَّلْ كَتَبَذُّلِ الرَّجُلِ.

(فروع كافى ج ٢ ص ٣)

٤٥٣- قَالَ رَسُولُ اللهِ ﷺ : مَا اسْتَفَادَ امْرُؤٌ فَائِدَةً بَعْدَ الْإِسْلَامِ أَفْضَلَ مِنْ زَوْجَةٍ مُسْلِمَةٍ تَسُرُّهُ إِذَا نَظَرَ إِلَيْهَا وَتُطِيعُهُ إِذَا أَمَرَهَا وَتَحْفَظُهُ إِذَا غَابَ عَنْهَا فِي نَفْسِهَا

وَمَالِهِ .	(فروع كافى ج ٢ ص ٤)

٤٥٤ - إِنَّ قَوْمًا أَتَوْا رَسُولَ اللهِ ﷺ فَقَالُوا : يَا رَسُولَ اللهِ إِنَّا رَأَيْنَا أُنَاسًا يَسْجُدُ بَعْضُهُمْ لِبَعْضٍ فَقَالَ رَسُولُ اللهِ ﷺ : لَوْ أَمَرْتُ أَحَدًا أَنْ يَسْجُدَ لِأَحَدٍ لَأَمَرْتُ الْمَرْأَةَ أَنْ تَسْجُدَ لِزَوْجِهَا .	(فروع كافى ج ٢ ص ٦٠)

٤٥٥ - قَالَ مُوسَى بْنُ جَعْفَرٍ عليه السلام : جِهَادُ الْمَرْأَةِ حُسْنُ التَّبَعُّلِ .
(فروع كافى ج ٢ ص ٦٠)

٤٥٦ - قَالَ رَسُولُ اللهِ ﷺ : لَا تُؤَدَّى الْمَرْأَةُ حَقَّ اللهِ عَزَّوَجَلَّ حَتَّى تُؤَدِّىَ حَقَّ زَوْجِهَا . (مكارم الاخلاق ص ٢٤٧)

٤٥٧ - قَالَ السَّجَّادُ عليه السلام : أَرْضَاكُمْ عِنْدَ اللهِ أَسْبَغُكُمْ عَلَى عِيَالِهِ .
(جامع السعادات ج ٢ ص ١٤١)

٤٥٨ - قَالَ رَسُولُ اللهِ ﷺ : خَيْرُكُمْ خَيْرُكُمْ لِأَهْلِهِ .
(جامع السعادات ج ٢ ص ١٣٩)

٤٥٩ - قَالَتْ خَوْلَةُ لِرَسُولِ اللهِ ﷺ : (فى حديث) فَمَا حَقِّى عَلَيْهِ قَالَ ﷺ حَقُّكِ عَلَيْهِ أَنْ يُطْعِمَكِ مِمَّا يَأْكُلُ وَيَكْسُوَكِ مِمَّا يَلْبَسُ وَلَا يَلْطِمُ وَلَا يَصِيحُ فِى وَجْهِكِ .
(مكارم الاخلاق ص ٢٥٠)

٤٦٠ - قَالَ الرِّضَا عليه السلام : يَنْبَغِى لِلرَّجُلِ أَنْ يُوَسِّعَ عَلَى عِيَالِهِ لِئَلَّا يَتَمَنَّوْا مَوْتَهُ . (جامع السعادات ج ٢ ص ١٤١)

٤٦١ - قَالَ الْبَاقِرُ عليه السلام : مَنْ كَانَتْ عِنْدَهُ امْرَأَةٌ فَلَمْ يَكْسُهَا مَا يُوَارِى عَوْرَتَهَا وَيُطْعِمُهَا مَا يُقِيمُ صُلْبَهَا كَانَ حَقًّا عَلَى الْإِمَامِ

اَنْ يُفَرِّقَ بَيْنَهُمَا. (مكارم الاخلاق ص ٢٤٩)

٤٦٢ - قَالَ السَّجَادُ عَلَيْهِ السَّلامُ: لَأَنْ أَدْخُلَ السُّوقَ وَمَعِي دَرَاهِمُ أَبْتَاعُ لِعِيَالِي لَحْمًا وَقَدْ قَرِمُوا إِلَيْهِ أَحَبُّ إِلَيَّ مِنْ أَنْ أُعْتِقَ نَسَمَةً.
(جامع السعادات ج ٢ ص ١٤١)

٤٦٣ - قَالَ رَسُولُ اللهِ صَلَّى اللهُ عَلَيْهِ وَآلِهِ لِأَمِيرِ الْمُؤْمِنِينَ عَلَيْهِ السَّلامُ بَعْدَ مَا رَآهُ فِي الْبَيْتِ يُنَقِّي الْعَدَسَ وَفَاطِمَةُ عَلَيْهَا السَّلامُ جَالِسَةٌ عِنْدَ الْقِدْرِ: اِسْمَعْ مِنِّي يَا أَبَا الْحَسَنِ وَمَا أَقُولُ إِلَّا مِنْ أَمْرِ رَبِّي! مَا مِنْ رَجُلٍ يُعِينُ امْرَأَتَهُ فِي بَيْتِهَا إِلَّا كَانَ لَهُ بِكُلِّ شَعْرَةٍ عَلَى بَدَنِهِ عِبَادَةُ سَنَةٍ صِيَامُ نَهَارِهَا وَقِيَامُ لَيْلِهَا ...

... يَا عَلِيُّ مَنْ لَمْ يَأْنَفْ مِنْ خِدْمَةِ الْعِيَالِ دَخَلَ الْجَنَّةَ بِغَيْرِ حِسَابٍ ...

... يَا عَلِيُّ لَا يَخْدِمُ الْعِيَالَ إِلَّا صِدِّيقٌ أَوْ شَهِيدٌ أَوْ رَجُلٌ يُرِيدُ اللهُ بِهِ خَيْرَ الدُّنْيَا وَالآخِرَةِ.
(جامع السعادات ج ٢ ص ١٤٠)

٤٦٤ - قَالَ رَسُولُ اللهِ صَلَّى اللهُ عَلَيْهِ وَآلِهِ: مَنْ صَبَرَ عَلَى سُوءِ خُلُقِ امْرَأَتِهِ أَعْطَاهُ اللهُ مِنَ الْأَجْرِ مَا أَعْطَى أَيُّوبَ عَلَيْهِ السَّلامُ عَلَى بَلَائِهِ وَمَنْ صَبَرَتْ عَلَى سُوءِ خُلُقِ زَوْجِهَا أَعْطَاهَا اللهُ مِثْلَ ثَوَابِ آسِيَةَ بِنْتِ مُزَاحِمٍ. (مكارم الاخلاق ص ٢٤٥)

٤٦٥ - قَالَ رَسُولُ اللهِ صَلَّى اللهُ عَلَيْهِ وَآلِهِ: خَيْرُ الرِّجَالِ مِنْ أُمَّتِي الَّذِينَ لَا يَتَطَاوَلُونَ عَلَى أَهْلِيهِمْ وَيُحْسِنُونَ عَلَيْهِمْ وَلَا يَظْلِمُونَهُمْ
(مكارم الاخلاق ص ٢٤٨)

٤٦٦ - قَالَ رَسُولُ اللهِ ﷺ ايَضْرِبُ اَحَدُكُمُ الْمَرْئَةَ ثُمَّ يَظَلُّ يُعَانِقُهَا.   (فروع كافى ج ٢ ص ٦١)

٤٦٧ - قَالَ رَسُولُ اللهِ ﷺ اَوْصَانِى جَبْرَئِيلُ بِالْمَرْئَةِ حَتَّى ظَنَنْتُ اَنَّهُ لَا يَنْبَغِى طَلَاقُهَا اِلَّا مِنْ فَاحِشَةٍ بَيِّنَةٍ.
(مكارم الاخلاق ص ٢٤١)

٤٦٨ - قَالَ رَسُولُ اللهِ ﷺ وَاِنَّ الرَّجُلَ لَيُوجَرُ فِى رَفْعِ اللُّقْمَةِ اِلَى فَمِ امْرَأَتِهِ.   (جامع السعادات ج ٢ ص ١٣٩)

٤٦٩ - قَالَ رَسُولُ اللهِ ﷺ اَيُّمَا امْرَأَةٍ لَمْ تَرْفُقْ بِزَوْجِهَا وَحَمَلَتْهُ عَلَى مَا لَا يَقْدِرُ عَلَيْهِ وَمَا لَا يُطِيقُ لَمْ تُقْبَلْ مِنْهَا حَسَنَةٌ وَتَلْقَى اللهَ وَهُوَ عَلَيْهَا غَضْبَانُ.
(مكارم الاخلاق ص ٢٤٦)

٤٧٠ - قَالَ رَسُولُ اللهِ ﷺ اَيُّمَا امْرَأَةٍ اَذَتْ زَوْجَهَا بِلِسَانِهَا لَمْ يَقْبَلِ اللهُ مِنْهَا صَرْفًا وَلَا عَدْلًا وَلَا حَسَنَةً مِنْ عَمَلِهَا حَتَّى تُرْضِيَهُ وَاِنْ صَامَتْ نَهَارَهَا وَقَامَتْ لَيْلَهَا وَاَعْتَقَتِ الرِّقَابَ وَحَمَلَتْ عَلَى جِيَادِ الْخَيْلِ فِى سَبِيلِ اللهِ فَكَانَتْ اَوَّلَ مَنْ يَرِدُ النَّارَ وَكَذَلِكَ الرَّجُلُ اِذَا كَانَ لَهَا ظَالِمًا.   (مكارم الاخلاق ص ٢٤٦)

٤٧١ - عَنْ اَحَدِهِمَا ﵇ وَسُئِلَ عَنْ حُلِىِّ الذَّهَبِ لِلنِّسَاءِ فَقَالَ ﷺ لَيْسَ بِهِ بَأْسٌ وَلَا يَنْبَغِى لِلْمَرْأَةِ اَنْ تُعَطِّلَ نَفْسَهَا وَلَوْ تُعَلِّقُ فِى رَقَبَتِهَا قِلَادَةً وَلَا يَنْبَغِى لَهَا اَنْ تَدَعَ يَدَهَا مِنَ الْخِضَابِ وَلَوْ اَنْ غِلَّ تَمَسَّهَا بِالْحِنَّاءِ مَسْحًا

وَلَوْ كَانَتْ مُسِنَّةً. (مكارم الاخلاق ص ١٠٧)

٤٧٢- قَالَ الرِّضَا عَلَيْهِ السَّلَامُ تَهْيِئَةُ الرَّجُلِ لِلْمَرْأَةِ مِمَّا تَزِيدُ فِي عِفَّتِهَا. (مكارم الاخلاق ص ١٠١)

٤٧٣- قَالَ حَسَنُ بْنُ جَهْمٍ قُلْتُ لِعَلِيِّ بْنِ مُوسَى عَلَيْهِ السَّلَامُ خَضَبْتَ؟ قَالَ عَلَيْهِ السَّلَامُ نَعَمْ بِالْحِنَّاءِ وَالْكَتَمِ. أَمَا عَلِمْتَ أَنَّ فِي ذَلِكَ لَأَجْرًا. إِنَّهَا تُحِبُّ أَنْ تَرَى مِنْكَ مِثْلَ الَّذِي تُحِبُّ أَنْ تَرَى مِنْهَا. (يَعْنِي الْمَرْأَةَ فِي التَّهَيُّئَةِ) وَلَقَدْ خَرَجْنَ نِسَاءٌ مِنَ الْعَفَافِ إِلَى الْفُجُورِ مَا أَخْرَجَهُنَّ إِلَّا قِلَّةُ تَهَيُّؤِ أَزْوَاجِهِنَّ. (مكارم الاخلاق ص ٩١)

٤٧٤- قَوْلُهُ تَعَالَى: وَجَعَلْنَا فِيهَا رَوَاسِيَ شَامِخَاتٍ وَأَسْقَيْنَاكُمْ مَاءً فُرَاتًا. (سوره مرسلات آيت ٢٧)

٤٧٥- قَالَ الصَّادِقُ عَلَيْهِ السَّلَامُ كَانَ النَّبِيُّ صَلَّى اللَّهُ عَلَيْهِ وَآلِهِ يُعْجِبُهُ أَنْ يَشْرَبَ فِي الْقَدَحِ الشَّامِيِّ وَكَانَ يَقُولُ: هِيَ مِنْ أَنْظَفِ آنِيَتِكُمْ. (وسائل الشيعه ج ٣ ص ٣١٠)

٤٧٦- قَالَ النَّبِيُّ صَلَّى اللَّهُ عَلَيْهِ وَآلِهِ أَنَّهُ نَهَى أَنْ يُتَنَفَّسَ فِي الْإِنَاءِ وَيُنْفَخَ فِيهِ. (مستدرك الوسائل ج ٢ ص ١٣١)

٤٧٧- قَالَ أَمِيرُ الْمُؤْمِنِينَ عَلَيْهِ السَّلَامُ لَا تَشْرَبُوا الْمَاءَ مِنْ ثُلْمَةِ الْإِنَاءِ وَلَا مِنْ عُرْوَتِهِ فَإِنَّ الشَّيْطَانَ يَقْعُدُ عَلَى الْعُرْوَةِ وَ الثُّلْمَةِ. (وسائل الشيعه ج ٣ ص ٣١٠)

٤٧٨- قَالَ رَسُولُ اللَّهِ صَلَّى اللَّهُ عَلَيْهِ وَآلِهِ وَلَا يَشْرَبَنَّ أَحَدُكُمُ الْمَاءَ مِنْ عِنْدِ عُرْوَةِ الْإِنَاءِ فَإِنَّهُ مُجْتَمَعُ الْوَسَخِ. (وسائل الشيعه ج ٣ ص ٣١٠)

٤٧٩ - قَالَ الصَّادِقُ عليه السلام: قَالَ أَبِي فِي حَدِيثٍ: وَلَا تَشْرَبْ مِنْ أُذُنِ الكُوزِ وَلَا مِنْ كَسْرٍ اِنْ كَانَ فِيهِ فَاِنَّهُ مَشْرَبُ الشَّيَاطِينِ.

(وسائل الشيعه ج ٣ ص ٣١٠)

٤٨٠ - قَالَ الصَّادِقُ عليه السلام: وَنَهَى (رَسُولُ اللهِ صلى الله عليه وآله) اَنْ يُشْرَبَ المَاءُ كَمَا تَشْرَبُ البَهَائِمُ قَالَ: وَقَالَ صلى الله عليه وآله: اِشْرَبُوا بِاَيْدِيكُمْ فَاِنَّهَا مِنْ خَيْرِ آنِيَتِكُمْ وَنَهَى عَنِ البُزَاقِ فِي البِئْرِ الَّتِي يُشْرَبُ مِنْهَا.

(من لا يحضره الفقيه ص ٤٦٧ حديث المناهي)

٤٨١ - قَالَ رَسُولُ اللهِ صلى الله عليه وآله: مَنْ تَوَضَّأَ قَبْلَ الطَّعَامِ عَاشَ فِي سَعَةٍ وَعُوفِيَ مِنْ بَلْوَى فِي جَسَدِهِ.

(مستدرك الوسائل ج ٣ ص ٩٠)

٤٨٢ - قَالَ رَسُولُ اللهِ صلى الله عليه وآله: الوُضُوءُ قَبْلَ الطَّعَامِ يَنْفِي الفَقْرَ وَبَعْدَهُ يَنْفِي الهَمَّ وَيَصِحُّ البَصَرَ.

(مستدرك الوسائل ج ٣ ص ٩٠)

٤٨٣ - قَالَ عَلِيٌّ عليه السلام: نِعْمَ البَيْتُ الحَمَّامُ يُذَكِّرُ النَّارَ وَيَذْهَبُ بِالدَّرَنِ.

(وسائل الشيعه ج ١ ص ٦٩)

٤٨٤ - قَالَ الصَّادِقُ عليه السلام (فِي حَدِيثٍ): وَاِنْ اَمْكَنَ اَنْ تَبْلَعَ مِنْهُ جُرْعَةً فَافْعَلْ.

(وسائل الشيعه ج ١ ص ٧١)

٤٨٥ - قَالَ الصَّادِقُ عليه السلام: غَسْلُ الرَّأْسِ بِالخِطْمِيِّ أَمَانٌ مِنَ الصُّدَاعِ وَبَرَاءَةٌ مِنَ الفَقْرِ وَطُهُورٌ لِلرَّأْسِ مِنَ الحَزَازِ.

(وسائل الشيعه ج ١ ص ٧٣)

٤٨٦ - قَالَ رَسُولُ اللهِ ﷺ: لَا يُطَوِّلَنَّ أَحَدُكُمْ شَارِبَهُ فَإِنَّ الشَّيْطَانَ يَتَّخِذُهُ مُخْبِئًا يَسْتَتِرُ بِهِ.
(وسائل الشيعه ج ١ ص ٨٣)

٤٨٧ - قَالَ رَسُولُ اللهِ ﷺ: لَا يُطَوِّلَنَّ أَحَدُكُمْ شَعْرًا بِطَيَّةً فَإِنَّ الشَّيْطَانَ يَتَّخِذُهُ مُخْبِئًا يَسْتَتِرُ بِهِ.
(وسائل الشيعه ج ١ ص ٨٣)

٤٨٨ - قَالَ عَلِيٌّ ﵇: نَطْفُ الْآبَاطِ يَنْفِي رَائِحَةَ الْمَكْرُوهَةِ وَهُوَ طَهُورٌ وَسُنَّةٌ مِمَّا أَمَرَ بِهِ الطِّيبَ.
(وسائل الشيعه ج ١ ص ٨٣)

٤٨٩ - قَالَ رَسُولُ اللهِ ﷺ لِلرِّجَالِ: قُصُّوا أَظَافِيرَكُمْ ...
(وسائل الشيعه ج ١ ص ٨٢)

٤٩٠ - قَالَ الصَّادِقُ ﵇: نَهَى رَسُولُ اللهِ ﷺ عَنْ تَقْلِيمِ الْأَظْفَارِ بِالْأَسْنَانِ.
(وسائل الشيعه ج ١ ص ٨٢)

٤٩١ - قَالَ أَبُو الْحَسَنِ ﵇: لَا يَنْبَغِي لِلرَّجُلِ أَنْ يَدَعَ الطِّيبَ فِي كُلِّ يَوْمٍ.
(وسائل الشيعه ج ١ ص ٨٤)

٤٩٢ - كَانَ النَّبِيُّ ﷺ يُحِبُّ الدُّهْنَ وَيَكْرَهُ الشَّعَثَ وَيَقُولُ: إِنَّ الدُّهْنَ يُذْهِبُ الْبُؤْسَ ...
(وسائل الشيعه ج ١ ص ٨٥)

٤٩٣ - قَالَ رَسُولُ اللهِ ﷺ: مَا زَالَ جِبْرَئِيلُ يُوصِينِي بِالسِّوَاكِ حَتَّى ظَنَنْتُ أَنَّهُ سَيَجْعَلُهُ فَرِيضَةً.
(وسائل الشيعه ج ١ ص ٦٦)

٤٩٤ - قَالَ رَسُولُ اللهِ ﷺ: لَوْلَا أَنْ أَشُقَّ عَلَى أُمَّتِي لَأَمَرْتُهُمْ بِالسِّوَاكِ مَعَ كُلِّ صَلَوةٍ. (وسائل الشيعه ج ١ ص ٦٨)

٤٩٥ - قَالَ الصَّادِقُ علیه السلام: اَلسِّوَاكُ مِنْ سُنَنِ الْمُرْسَلِينَ.
(وسائل الشيعه ج ١ ص ٦٦)

٤٩٦ - قَالَ عَلِيٌّ علیه السلام: وَالْمَضْمَضَةُ وَالْاِسْتِنْشَاقُ سُنَّةٌ وَطَهُورٌ لِلْفَمِ وَالْأَنْفِ. (وسائل الشيعه ج ١ ص ٥٨)

٤٩٧ - قَالَ رَسُولُ اللهِ ﷺ: مَنِ اتَّخَذَ ثَوْبًا فَلْيُنَظِّفْهُ.
(وسائل الشيعه ج ١ ص ٢٧٩)

٤٩٨ - قَالَ الصَّادِقُ علیه السلام: الثَّوْبُ النَّقِيُّ يَكْبِتُ الْعَدُوَّ.
(وسائل الشيعه ج ١ ص ٢٧٨)

٤٩٩ - قَالَ رَسُولُ اللهِ ﷺ: اِكْنِسُوا أَفْنِيَتَكُمْ وَلَا تَشَبَّهُوا بِالْيَهُودِ
(وسائل الشيعه ج ١ ص ٣١٩)

٥٠٠ - قَالَ أَبُو جَعْفَرٍ علیه السلام: كَنْسُ الْبُيُوتِ يَنْفِي الْفَقْرَ.
(وسائل الشيعه ج ١ ص ٣١٩)

٥٠١ - قَالَ عَلِيٌّ علیه السلام: نَظِّفُوا بُيُوتَكُمْ مِنْ خُيُوطِ الْعَنْكَبُوتِ فَإِنَّ تَرْكَهُ فِي الْبَيْتِ يُورِثُ الْفَقْرَ.
(وسائل الشيعه ج ١ ص ٣٢٠)

٥٠٢ - قَالَ رَسُولُ اللهِ ﷺ: مَنْ كَنَسَ الْمَسْجِدَ يَوْمَ الْخَمِيسِ لَيْلَةَ الْجُمُعَةِ فَأَخْرَجَ مِنْهُ مِنَ التُّرَابِ مَا يَذُرُّ فِي الْعَيْنِ غَفَرَ اللهُ لَهُ. (وسائل الشيعه ج ١ ص ٣٠٨)

٥٠٣ - قَالَ رَسُولُ اللهِ ﷺ: مَنْ قَمَّ مَسْجِدًا كَتَبَ اللهُ لَهُ

281

عِتْقَ رَقَبَةٍ ... (وسائل الشيعه ج ١ ص ٣٠٨)

٥٠٤ - قَالَ الصَّادِقُ ﷺ: نَهَى رَسُولُ اللهِ عَنِ التَّنَخُّعِ فِي الْمَسَاجِدِ
(وسائل الشيعه ج ١ ص ٣٠٧)

٥٠٥ - عَنِ الصَّادِقِ عَنْ أَبِيهِ عَنْ آبَائِهِ ﷺ قَالَ: مَنْ وَقَّرَ بِنُخَامَتِهِ الْمَسْجِدَ لَقِيَ اللهَ يَوْمَ الْقِيَامَةِ ضَاحِكًا قَدْ أُعْطِيَ كِتَابَهُ بِيَمِينِهِ. (وسائل الشيعه ج ١ ص ٣٠٧)

٥٠٦ - نَهَى رَسُولُ اللهِ ﷺ أَنْ يَّتَغَوَّطَ عَلَى شَفِيرِ بِئْرِ مَاءٍ يُسْتَعْذَبُ مِنْهَا أَوْ تَحْتَ شَجَرَةٍ فِيهَا ثَمَرَتُهَا.
(وسائل الشيعه ج ١ ص ٤٣)

٥٠٧ - قَالَ أَمِيرُ الْمُؤْمِنِينَ ﷺ: أَنَّهُ نَهَى أَنْ يَبُولَ الرَّجُلُ فِي الْمَاءِ الْجَارِي الَّا مِنْ ضَرُورَةٍ وَقَالَ إِنَّ لِلْمَاءِ أَهْلًا.
(وسائل الشيعه ج ١ ص ٤٥)

٥٠٨ - قَوْلُهُ تَعَالَى قُلْ مَنْ حَرَّمَ زِينَةَ اللهِ الَّتِي أَخْرَجَ لِعِبَادِهِ ...
(سوره اعراف آیت ٣٢)

٥٠٩ - قَالَ أَبُو عَبْدِ اللهِ ﷺ: اِلْبِسْ وَتَجَمَّلْ فَإِنَّ اللهَ جَمِيلٌ يُحِبُّ الْجَمَالَ وَلَكِنْ مِنْ حَلَالٍ.
(وسائل الشيعه ج ١ ص ٢٧٧)

٥١٠ - قَالَ أَبُو عَبْدِ اللهِ ﷺ: ثَلَاثَةُ أَشْيَاءَ لَا يُحَاسِبُ اللهُ عَلَيْهَا الْمُؤْمِنَ: طَعَامٌ يَأْكُلُهُ وَثَوْبٌ يَلْبَسُهُ وَزَوْجَةٌ صَالِحَةٌ تُعَاوِنُهُ وَيُحْصِنُ بِهَا فَرْجَهُ.
(وسائل الشيعة ج ١ ص ٢٧٧)

282

٥١١ - قَالَ اَمِيرُ الْمُؤْمِنِينَ عَلَيْهِ السَّلامُ : عَلَّمَنِى رَسُولُ اللهِ صَلَّى اللهُ عَلَيْهِ وَآلِهِ : اِذَا لَبِسْتَ ثَوْبًا جَدِيدًا اَنْ اَقُولَ : اَلْحَمْدُ لله الَّذِى كَسَانِى مِنَ اللِّبَاسِ مَا اَتَجَمَّلُ بِهِ فِى النَّاسِ . اَللّهُمَّ اجْعَلْهَا ثِيَابَ بَرَكَةٍ اَسْعَى فِيهَا لِمَرْضَاتِكَ وَاَعْمُرُ فِيهَا مَسَاجِدَكَ ...

(وسائل الشيعه ج ١ ص ٢٨٣)

٥١٢ - قَالَ اَبُو عَبْدِ اللهِ عَلَيْهِ السَّلامُ : اِذَا لَبِسْتَ ثَوْبًا فَقُلْ : اَللّهُمَّ اكْسُنِى لِبَاسَ الاِيمَانِ وَزَيِّنِّى بِالتَّقْوَى اَللّهُمَّ اجْعَلْهُ جَدِيدَهُ اَبْلِيهِ فِى طَاعَتِكَ وَطَاعَةِ رَسُولِكَ .

(وسائل الشيعه ج ١ ص ٢٨٤)

٥١٣ - قَالَ اَبُو عَبْدِ اللهِ عَلَيْهِ السَّلامُ : اِنَّ اللهَ جَمِيلٌ يُحِبُّ الْجَمَالَ وَالتَّجَمُّلَ وَيُبْغِضُ الْبُؤْسَ وَالتَّبَاؤُسَ فَاِنَّ اللهَ اِذَا اَنْعَمَ عَلَى عَبْدِهِ بِنِعْمَتِهِ اَحَبَّ اَنْ يَرَى عَلَيْهِ اَثَرَهَا . قَالَ : قِيلَ : كَيْفَ ذَلِكَ ؟ قَالَ : يُنَظِّفُ ثَوْبَهُ وَيُطَيِّبُ رِيحَهُ وَيُجَصِّصُ دَارَهُ وَيَكْنِسُ اَفْنِيَتَهُ حَتَّى اَنَّ السِّرَاجَ قَبْلَ مَغِيبِ الشَّمْسِ يَنْفِى الْفَقْرَ وَيَزِيدُ فِى الرِّزْقِ .

(وسائل الشيعه ج ١ ص ٢٧٨)

٥١٤ - قَالَ اَمِيرُ الْمُؤْمِنِينَ عَلَيْهِ السَّلامُ : اَلنَّظِيفُ مِنَ الثِّيَابِ يُذْهِبُ الْهَمَّ وَالْحُزْنَ ... (وسائل الشيعه ج ١ ص ٢٧٨)

٥١٥ - قَالَ عَلِيٌّ عَلَيْهِ السَّلامُ : عَلَيْكُمْ بِالصَّفِيقِ مِنَ الثِّيَابِ فَاِنَّ مَنْ رَقَّ ثَوْبُهُ رَقَّ دِينُهُ ، ... (وسائل الشيعه ج ١ ص ٢٨١)

٥١٦ - قَالَ عَلِىُّ بْنُ الْحُسَيْنِ عَلَيْهِ السَّلامُ : اِنَّ الْجَسَدَ اِذَا لَبِسَ الثَّوْبَ

اللَّيِّنَ طَغَى . (وسائل الشيعه ج١ ص٢٨٢)

٥١٧ - قَالَ رَسُولُ اللهِ ﷺ (فِي حَدِيثٍ): يَا أَبَاذَرِّ الْبَسِ الْخَشِنَ مِنَ اللِّبَاسِ وَالصَّفِيقَ مِنَ الثِّيَابِ لِئَلَّا تَجِدَ الْفَخْرَ فِيكَ مَسْلَكَهُ . (وسائل الشيعه ج١ ص٢٨٤)

٥١٨ - قَالَ عَلِيُّ بْنُ الْحُسَيْنِ ﷻ: مَنْ لَبِسَ ثَوْباً يُشْهِرُهُ كَسَاهُ اللهُ يَوْمَ الْقِيَامَةِ ثَوْباً مِنَ النَّارِ .
(وسائل الشيعه ج١ ص٢٨٠)

٥١٩ - قَالَ حَمَّادُ بْنُ عُثْمَانَ : كُنْتُ حَاضِراً لِأَبِي عَبْدِ اللهِ ﷻ إِذْ قَالَ لَهُ رَجُلٌ : أَصْلَحَكَ اللهُ ذَكَرْتَ أَنَّ عَلِيَّ بْنَ أَبِي طَالِبٍ ﷻ كَانَ يَلْبَسُ الْخَشِنَ، يَلْبَسُ الْقَمِيصَ بِأَرْبَعَةِ دَرَاهِمَ وَمَا أَشْبَهَ ذَلِكَ وَنَرَى عَلَيْكَ اللِّبَاسَ الْجَيِّدَ . قَالَ : فَقَالَ ﷻ : إِنَّ عَلِيَّ بْنَ أَبِي طَالِبٍ صَلَوَاتُ اللهِ عَلَيْهِ كَانَ يَلْبَسُ ذَلِكَ فِي زَمَانٍ لَا يُنْكَرُ وَلَوْ لَبِسَ مِثْلَ ذَلِكَ الْيَوْمَ شُهِرَ بِهِ، فَخَيْرُ لِبَاسِ كُلِّ زَمَانٍ لِبَاسُ أَهْلِهِ غَيْرَ أَنَّ قَائِمَنَا ﷻ إِذَا قَامَ لَبِسَ لِبَاسَ عَلِيٍّ ﷻ وَسَارَ بِسِيرَتِهِ . (وسائل الشيعه ج١ ص٢٧٩)

٥٢٠ - قَالَ رَسُولُ اللهِ ﷺ فِي وَصِيَّتِهِ لِأَبِي ذَرٍّ : يَا أَبَاذَرِّ ! يَكُونُ فِي آخِرِ الزَّمَانِ قَوْمٌ يَلْبَسُونَ الصُّوفَ فِي صَيْفِهِمْ وَشِتَائِهِمْ يَرَوْنَ أَنَّ لَهُمُ الْفَضْلَ بِذَلِكَ عَلَى غَيْرِهِمْ أُولَئِكَ يَلْعَنُهُمْ أَهْلُ السَّمَوَاتِ وَالْأَرْضِ .
(وسائل الشيعه ج١ ص٢٨١)

٥٢١ - قَالَ رَسُولُ اللهِ ﷺ (فِي اخِرِ خُطْبَةِ خَطَبَهَا) : وَمَنْ لَبِسَ ثَوْبًا فَاخْتَالَ فِيهِ خَسَفَ اللهُ بِهِ مِنْ شَفِيرِ جَهَنَّمَ يَتَخَلْخَلُ فِيهَا مَا دَامَتِ السَّمَوَاتُ وَالْأَرْضُ .

(وسائل الشيعه ج ١ ص ٢٨٣)

٥٢٢ - قَالَ سَلَمَةُ بَيَّاعُ الْقَلَانِسِ : كُنْتُ عِنْدَ أَبِي جَعْفَرٍ ﷷ إِذْ دَخَلَ عَلَيْهِ أَبُوعَبْدِ اللهِ ﷷ فَقَالَ أَبُوجَعْفَرٍ ﷷ : يَا بُنَيَّ أَلَا تُطَهِّرُ قَمِيصَكَ ؟ فَذَهَبَ فَظَنَنَّا أَنَّ ثَوْبَهُ قَدْ أَصَابَهُ شَيْءٌ فَرَجَعَ فَقَالَ اِنِّي لَهَكَذَا فَقُلْنَا : جُعِلْنَا فِدَاكَ مَا الْقَمِيصَةُ ؟ قَالَ : كَانَ قَمِيصُهُ طَوِيلًا فَأَمَرْتُهُ أَنْ يُقَصِّرَهُ اِنَّ اللهَ عَزَّ وَجَلَّ يَقُولُ : وَثِيَابَكَ فَطَهِّرْ .

(وسائل الشيعه ج ١ ص ٢٨٢)

٥٢٣ - قَالَ أَبُوعَبْدِ اللهِ ﷷ كَانَ رَسُولُ اللهِ ﷺ يَزْجُرُ الرَّجُلَ أَنْ يَتَشَبَّهَ بِالنِّسَاءِ وَيَنْهَى الْمَرْأَةَ أَنْ تَتَشَبَّهَ بِالرِّجَالِ فِي لِبَاسِهَا . (وسائل الشيعه ج ١ ص ٢٨٠)

٥٢٤ - قَوْلُهُ تَعَالَى : وَآتِ ذَا الْقُرْبَى حَقَّهُ وَالْمِسْكِينَ وَابْنَ السَّبِيلِ وَلَا تُبَذِّرْ تَبْذِيرًا . (سوره اسراء آيت ٢٦)

٥٢٥ - قَوْلُهُ تَعَالَى : فَآتِ ذَا الْقُرْبَى حَقَّهُ وَالْمِسْكِينَ وَابْنَ السَّبِيلِ ذَلِكَ خَيْرٌ لِلَّذِينَ يُرِيدُونَ وَجْهَ اللهِ وَأُولَئِكَ هُمُ الْمُفْلِحُونَ . (سوره روم - آيت ٣٨)

٥٢٦ - قَالَ أَبُو الْحَسَنِ الرِّضَا ﷷ يَكُونُ الرَّجُلُ يَصِلُ رَحِمَهُ فَيَكُونُ قَدْ بَقِيَ مِنْ عُمُرِهِ ثَلَاثُ سِنِينَ فَيُصَيِّرُهَا اللهُ

ثَلاثِينَ سَنَةً وَيَفْعَلُ اللهُ مَايَشَاءُ.

(اصول كافى ص ٣٨٣)

٥٢٧ - قَالَ اَبُوالْحَسَنِ الرِّضَا ﷺ: قَالَ اَبُوعَبْدِاللهِ ﷺ صِلْ رَحِمَكَ وَلَوْ بِشُرْبَةٍ مِنْ مَاءٍ. وَاَفْضَلُ مَا تُوصَلُ بِهِ الرَّحِمَ كَفُّ الْاَذى عَنْهَا. وَصِلَةُ الرَّحِمِ مَنْسَأَةٌ فِى الْاَجَلِ مَحَبَّةٌ فِى الْاَهْلِ. (اصول كافى ص ٣٨٤)

٥٢٨ - قَالَ اَبُوجَعْفَرٍ ﷺ: صِلَةُ الْاَرْحَامِ تُزَكِّى الْاَعْمَالَ وَ تَدْفَعُ الْبَلْوى وَتُنْمِى الْاَمْوَالَ وَتُنْسِئُ لَهُ فِى عُمْرِهِ وَتُوَسِّعُ فِى رِزْقِهِ وَتُحَبِّبُ فِى اَهْلِ بَيْتِهِ. فَلْيَتَّقِ اللهَ وَلْيَصِلْ رَحِمَهُ. (اصول كافى ص ٣٨٤)

٥٢٩ - قَالَ اَمِيرُ الْمُؤْمِنِينَ ﷺ: وَاَكْرِمْ عَشِيرَتَكَ فَاِنَّهُمْ جَنَاحُكَ الَّذِى بِهِ تَطِيرُ وَاَصْلُكَ الَّذِى اِلَيْهِ تَصِيرُ وَيَدُكَ الَّتِى بِهَا تَصُولُ... (نهج البلاغه ص ٩٣٠)

٥٣٠ - عَنِ النَّبِىِّ ﷺ اَنَّهُ قَالَ: لَا يَدْخُلُ الْجَنَّةَ قَاطِعُ رَحِمٍ.

(بحارالانوار ج ١٥ كتاب العشره ص ٢٧)

٥٣١ - عَنِ الْجَهْمِ بْنِ حُمَيْدٍ قَالَ: قُلْتُ لِاَبِى عَبْدِاللهِ ﷺ: تَكُونُ لِىَ الْقَرَابَةُ عَلى غَيْرِ اَمْرِى اَلَهُمْ عَلَىَّ حَقٌّ؟ قَالَ نَعَمْ، حَقُّ الرَّحِمِ لَا يَقْطَعُهُ شَىْءٌ وَاِذَا كَانُوا عَلَى اَمْرِكَ كَانَ لَهُمْ حَقَّانِ: حَقُّ الرَّحِمِ وَحَقُّ الْاِسْلامِ.

(اصول كافى ص ٣٨٦)

٥٣٢ - عَنْ اَبِى عَبْدِاللهِ ﷺ اَنَّ رَجُلًا اَتَى النَّبِىَّ ﷺ فَقَالَ:

يَا رَسُولَ اللهِ اَهْلِ بَيْتِي اَبَوْا اِلَّا تَوَثُّبَاً عَلَيَّ وَقَطِيعَةً لِي وَشَتِيمَةً فَاَرْفَضَهُمْ. قَالَ: اِذاً يَرْفُضَكُمُ اللهُ جَمِيعاً قَالَ: فَكَيْفَ اَصْنَعُ؟ قَالَ: تَصِلُ مَنْ قَطَعَكَ وَتُعْطِي مَنْ حَرَمَكَ وَتَعْفُو عَمَّنْ ظَلَمَكَ فَاِنَّكَ اِذَا فَعَلْتَ ذَلِكَ كَانَ لَكَ مِنَ اللهِ عَلَيْهِمْ ظَهِيرٌ. (اصول كافي ص ٣٨٣)

٥٣٣- قَالَ اَبُو عَبْدِ اللهِ عَلَيْهِ السَّلَامُ: مَا مِنْ مُؤْمِنٍ يَدْخُلُ بَيْتَهُ مُؤْمِنَيْنِ فَيُطْعِمُهُمَا شِبَعَهُمَا اِلَّا اَفْضَلُ مِنْ عِتْقِ نَسَمَةٍ.

(بحار الانوار ج ١٥ كتاب العشرة ص ٢٤٢)

٥٣٤- قَالَ اَبُو جَعْفَرٍ عَلَيْهِ السَّلَامُ: شِبَعُ اَرْبَعٍ مِنَ الْمُسْلِمِينَ يَعْدِلُ عِتْقَ رَقَبَةٍ مِنْ وُلْدِ اِسْمَعِيلَ عَلَيْهِ السَّلَامُ.

(بحار الانوار ج ١٥ كتاب العشرة ص ٢٤٢)

٥٣٥- قَالَ رَسُولُ اللهِ صَلَّى اللهُ عَلَيْهِ وَآلِهِ: اَلضَّيْفُ دَلِيلُ الْجَنَّةِ.

(بحار الانوار ج ١٥ كتاب العشرة ص ٢٤٢)

٥٣٦- قَالَ رَسُولُ اللهِ صَلَّى اللهُ عَلَيْهِ وَآلِهِ: اِذَا اَرَادَ اللهُ بِقَوْمٍ خَيْراً اَهْدَى اِلَيْهِمْ هَدِيَّةً قَالُوا: وَمَا تِلْكَ الْهَدِيَّةُ؟ قَالَ: اَلضَّيْفُ يَنْزِلُ بِرِزْقِهِ وَيَرْتَحِلُ بِذُنُوبِ اَهْلِ الْبَيْتِ.

(بحار الانوار ج ١٥ كتاب العشرة ص ٢٤٢)

٥٣٧- قَالَ رَسُولُ اللهِ صَلَّى اللهُ عَلَيْهِ وَآلِهِ (في حديث) وَمَا مِنْ ضَيْفٍ حَلَّ بِقَوْمٍ اِلَّا وَرِزْقُهُ مَعَهُ.

(بحار الانوار ج ١٥ كتاب العشرة ص ٢٤١)

٥٣٨- قَالَ اَمِيرُ الْمُؤْمِنِينَ عَلَيْهِ السَّلَامُ: مَا مِنْ مُؤْمِنٍ يُحِبُّ الضَّيْفَ اِلَّا

وَيَقُومُ مِنْ قَبْرِهِ وَوَجْهُهُ كَالْقَمَرِ لَيْلَةَ الْبَدْرِ فَيَنْظُرُ اَهْلُ الْجَمْعِ فَيَقُولُونَ: مَا هذَا اِلاّ نَبِيٌّ مُرْسَلٌ. فَيَقُولُ مَلَكٌ: لا هذَا مُؤْمِنٌ يُحِبُّ الضَّيْفَ وَيُكْرِمُ الضَّيْفَ وَلاَ سَبِيلَ لَهُ اِلاَّ اَنْ اُدْخِلَ الْجَنَّةَ.

(بحار الانوار ج ١٥ كتاب العشرة ص ٢٤٢)

٥٣٩ـ قَالَ الصَّادِقُ عَلَيْهِ السَّلامُ: اُتِيَ رَسُولُ اللهِ صَلَّى اللهُ عَلَيْهِ وَآلِهِ بِاَسَارَى فَقَدَّمَ رَجُلاً مِنْهُمْ لِيُضْرَبَ عُنُقُهُ فَقَالَ لَهُ جِبْرَئِيلُ: اَخِّرْ هذَا الْيَوْمَ يَا مُحَمَّدُ صَلَّى اللهُ عَلَيْهِ وَآلِهِ! فَرَدَّهُ وَاَخْرَجَ غَيْرَهُ حَتَّى كَانَ هُوَ آخِرَهُمْ فَدَعَا بِهِ لِيُضْرَبَ عُنُقُهُ فَقَالَ لَهُ جِبْرَئِيلُ يَا مُحَمَّدُ رَبُّكَ يُقْرِئُكَ السَّلاَمَ وَيَقُولُ لَكَ اَنَّ اَسِيرَكَ هذَا يُطْعِمُ الطَّعَامَ الضَّيْفَ وَيَصْبِرُ عَلَى النَّائِبَةِ وَيَحْمِلُ الْحَمَالاَتِ. فَقَالَ لَهُ النَّبِيُّ صَلَّى اللهُ عَلَيْهِ وَآلِهِ: اِنَّ جِبْرَئِيلَ اَخْبَرَنِي فِيكَ مِنَ اللهِ عَزَّ وَجَلَّ بِكَذَا وَكَذَا وَقَدْ اَعْتَقْتُكَ فَقَالَ لَهُ: وَاِنَّ رَبَّكَ لَيُحِبُّ هذَا ، فَقَالَ صَلَّى اللهُ عَلَيْهِ وَآلِهِ نَعَمْ. فَقَالَ: اَشْهَدُ اَنْ لاَ اِلهَ اِلاَّ اللهُ وَاَنَّكَ رَسُولُ اللهِ. وَالَّذِي بَعَثَكَ بِالْحَقِّ لاَ رَدَدْتُ عَنْ مَالِي اَحَداً اَبَداً.

(فروع كافي ج ١ ص ١٧٦)

٥٤٠ـ قَالَ الصَّادِقُ عَلَيْهِ السَّلامُ: اِذَا اَتَاكَ اَخُوكَ فَأْتِهِ بِمَا عِنْدَكَ وَاِذَا دَعَوْتَهُ فَتَكَلَّفْ.

(بحار الانوار ج ١٥ كتاب العشرة ص ٢٤٠)

٥٤١ـ قَالَ رَسُولُ اللهِ صَلَّى اللهُ عَلَيْهِ وَآلِهِ: صَاحِبُ الرَّحْلِ يَشْرَبُ اَوَّلَ الْقَوْمِ

وَيَتَوَضَّأُ آخِرُهُمْ .

(بحارالانوار ج١٥ كتاب العشرة ص ٢٤٠)

٥٤٢ - قَالَ رَسُولُ اللهِ ﷺ: مِنْ حَقِّ الضَّيْفِ اَنْ تَمْشِيَ مَعَهُ فَتُخْرِجَهُ مِنْ حَرِيمِكَ اِلَى البَابِ .

(بحارالانوار ج١٥ كتاب العشرة ص ٢٤٠)

٥٤٣ - نَزَلَ عَلَى اَبِي عَبْدِ اللهِ الصَّادِقِ ﷷ قَوْمٌ مِنْ جُهَيْنَةَ فَاَضَافَهُمْ فَلَمَّا اَرَادُوا الرِّحْلَةَ زَوَّدَهُمْ وَصَّلَهُمْ وَاَعْطَاهُمْ . ثُمَّ قَالَ لِغِلْمَانِهِ تَنَحَّوْا لَا تُعِينُوهُمْ فَلَمَّا فَرَغُوا جَاءُوا لِيُوَدِّعُوهُ فَقَالُوا لَهُ : يَا بْنَ رَسُولِ اللهِ فَقَدْ اَضَفْتَ فَاَحْسَنْتَ الضِّيَافَةَ وَاَعْطَيْتَ فَاَجْزَلْتَ العَطِيَّةَ، ثُمَّ اَمَرْتَ لِغِلْمَانِكَ اَنْ لَا يُعِينُونَا عَلَى الرِّحْلَةِ فَقَالَ ﷷ : اِنَّا اَهْلُ بَيْتٍ لَا نُعِينُ اَضْيَافَنَا عَلَى الرِّحْلَةِ مِنْ عِنْدِنَا . (بحارالانوار ج١٥ كتاب العشرة ص ٢٤٠)

٥٤٤ - قَالَ النَّبِيُّ ﷺ: مَنْ كَانَ يُؤْمِنُ بِاللهِ وَاليَوْمِ الآخِرِ فَلْيُكْرِمْ ضَيْفَهُ وَالضِّيَافَةُ ثَلَاثَةُ اَيَّامٍ وَلَيَالِيهِنَّ فَمَا فَوْقَ ذَلِكَ فَهُوَ صَدَقَةٌ . (بحارالانوار ج١٥ كتاب العشرة ص ٢٤٢)

٥٤٥ - قَالَ رَسُولُ اللهِ ﷺ: اِنَّ مِنْ حَقِّ الضَّيْفِ اَنْ يُعَدَّ لَهُ الخِلَالَ . (بحارالانوار ج١٥ كتاب العشرة ص ٢٤١)

٥٤٦ - عَنِ الصَّادِقِ ﷷ عَنْ اَبِيهِ قَالَ : اِذَا دَخَلَ اَحَدُكُمْ عَلَى اَخِيهِ فِي رَحْلِهِ فَلْيَقْعُدْ حَيْثُ يُؤْمَرُ صَاحِبُ الرَّحْلِ فَاِنَّ صَاحِبَ الرَّحْلِ اَعْرَفُ بِعَوْرَةِ بَيْتِهِ مِنَ الدَّاخِلِ

289

عَلَيْهِ. (بحارالانوار ج١٥ كتاب العشرة ص ٢٤١)

٥٤٧- عَنِ الرِّضَا عَنْ اَبَائِهِ ﷺ قَالَ: دَعَى رَجُلٌ اَمِيْرَ الْمُؤْمِنِيْنَ ﷺ فَقَالَ لَهُ قَدْ اَجَبْتُكَ عَلَى اَنْ تَضْمَنَ لِيْ ثَلَاثَ خِصَالٍ: قَالَ وَمَاهُنَّ يَا اَمِيْرَ الْمُؤْمِنِيْنَ قَالَ: لَا تُدْخِلْ عَلَىَّ شَيْئًا مِنْ خَارِجٍ وَلَا تَدَّخِرْ عَنِّيْ شَيْئًا فِى الْبَيْتِ وَلَا تَجْحَفْ بِالْعِيَالِ. قَالَ: ذٰلِكَ لَكَ. فَاَجَابَهُ اَمِيْرُ الْمُؤْمِنِيْنَ ﷺ.

(بحارالانوار ج١٥ كتاب العشرة ص ٢٤٠)

٥٤٨- قَوْلُهُ تَعَالٰى: وَيَسْئَلُوْنَكَ عَنِ الْيَتَامٰى قُلْ اِصْلَاحٌ لَهُمْ خَيْرٌ وَاِنْ تُخَالِطُوْهُمْ فَاِخْوَانُكُمْ وَاللهُ يَعْلَمُ الْمُفْسِدَ مِنَ الْمُصْلِحِ. (سورهٔ بقره - آیت ٢٢٠)

٥٤٩- عَنِ الصَّادِقِ عَنْ اَبَائِهِ ﷺ عَنْ رَسُوْلِ اللهِ ﷺ مَنْ عَالَ يَتِيْمًا حَتّٰى يَسْتَغْنِىَ عَنْهُ اَوْجَبَ اللهُ عَزَّوَجَلَّ لَهُ بِذٰلِكَ الْجَنَّةَ كَمَا اَوْجَبَ لِاٰكِلِ مَالِ الْيَتِيْمِ النَّارَ.

(بحارالانوار ج١٥ كتاب العشرة ص ١٢٠)

٥٥٠- عَنْ اَبِىْ عَبْدِاللهِ ﷺ قَالَ: مَا مِنْ عَبْدٍ يَمْسَحُ يَدَهُ عَلٰى رَأْسِ يَتِيْمٍ رَحْمَةً لَهُ اِلَّا اَعْطَاهُ اللهُ بِكُلِّ شَعْرَةٍ نُوْرًا يَّوْمَ الْقِيَامَةِ.

(بحارالانوار ج١٥ كتاب العشرة ص ١٢٠)

٥٥١- قَالَ عَلِىٌّ ﷺ فِىْ وَصِيَّتِهِ لِابْنِهِ: اَللهَ اَللهَ فِى الْاَيْتَامِ فَلَا تَغُبُّوْا اَفْوَاهَهُمْ وَلَا يَضِيْعُوْا بِحَضْرَتِكُمْ. (نهج البلاغه ط ٩٦)

٥٥٢- قَالَ رَسُولُ اللهِ ﷺ: مَرَّ عِيسَى بْنُ مَرْيَمَ ﷺ بِقَبْرٍ يُعَذَّبُ صَاحِبُهُ ثُمَّ مَرَّ بِهِ مِنْ قَابِلٍ فَإِذَا هُوَ لَيْسَ يُعَذَّبُ. فَقَالَ يَا رَبِّ مَرَرْتُ بِهٰذَا الْقَبْرِ عَامَ أَوَّلَ فَكَانَ صَاحِبُهُ يُعَذَّبُ ثُمَّ مَرَرْتُ بِهِ الْعَامَ فَإِذَا هُوَ لَيْسَ يُعَذَّبُ فَأَوْحَى اللهُ عَزَّ وَجَلَّ إِلَيْهِ يَا رُوحَ اللهِ إِنَّهُ أَدْرَكَ لَهُ وَلَدٌ صَالِحٌ فَأَصْلَحَ طَرِيقًا وَآوَى يَتِيمًا فَغَفَرْتُ لَهُ بِمَا عَمِلَ ابْنُهُ.

(بحار الانوار ج ١٥ كتاب العشره ص ١١٩)

٥٥٣- قَالَ رَسُولُ اللهِ ﷺ: مَنْ كَفَلَ يَتِيمًا وَكَفَلَ نَفَقَتَهُ كُنْتُ أَنَا وَهُوَ فِي الْجَنَّةِ كَهَاتَيْنِ (وَقَرَنَ بَيْنَ اِصْبَعَيْهِ الْمُسَبِّحَةِ وَالْوُسْطَى).

(بحار الانوار ج ١٥ كتاب العشره ص ١١٩)

٥٥٤- قَالَ ﷺ: حُرْمَةُ الْمُسْلِمِ مَيِّتًا كَحُرْمَتِهِ حَيًّا.

(مصباح الفقيه ج١ ص ٨٠٦)

٥٥٥- قَالَ النَّبِيُّ ﷺ: فُرِضَ عَلَى أُمَّتِي غُسْلُ مَوْتَاهَا وَالصَّلوٰةُ عَلَيْهَا. (مستدرك الوسائل ج١ ص ١١٧)

٥٥٦- قَالَ الصَّادِقُ ﷺ: وَغُسْلُ الْمَيِّتِ وَاجِبٌ.

(وسائل الشيعه ج٢ ص ١٢٨)

٥٥٧- عَنْ أَبِي عَبْدِاللهِ ﷺ أَنَّهُ سُئِلَ عَنِ الْمَرْأَةِ تَمُوتُ فِي السَّفَرِ وَلَيْسَ مَعَهَا ذُو رَحِمٍ وَلَا نِسَاءٌ. قَالَ ﷺ: كَمَا هِيَ بِثِيَابِهَا. وَعَنِ الرَّجُلِ يَمُوتُ وَلَيْسَ مَعَهُ إِلَّا

النِّسَاءُ لَيْسَ مَعَهُنَّ رَجُلٌ. قَالَ عليه: يُدْفَنُ كَمَا هُوَ بِثِيَابِهِ. (وسائل الشيعه ج ١ ص ١٣٤)

٥٥٨- قَالَ أَبُوذَرٍّ: قَالَ لِي رَسُولُ اللهِ ﷺ: وَصَلِّ عَلَى الْجَنَائِزِ لَعَلَّ ذَلِكَ يُحْزِنُكَ فَإِنَّ الْحَزِنَ فِي أَمْرِ اللهِ يُعَوَّضُ خَيْرًا (مستدرك الوسائل ج ١ ص ١١١)

٥٥٩- قَالَ رَسُولُ اللهِ ﷺ: كَرَامَةُ الْمَيِّتِ تَعْجِيلُهُ. (وسائل الشيعه ج ١ ص ١٢٨)

٥٦٠- قَالَ رَسُولُ اللهِ ﷺ: عُودُوا الْمَرْضَى وَاتَّبِعُوا الْجَنَائِزَ يُذَكِّرْكُمُ الْآخِرَةَ. (مستدرك الوسائل ج ١ ص ١١٩)

٥٦١- قَالَ الرِّضَا عليه: ..... مَنْ شَيَّعَ جَنَازَةَ وَلِيٍّ مِنْ أَوْلِيَائِنَا خَرَجَ مِنْ ذُنُوبِهِ كَيَوْمٍ وَلَدَتْهُ أُمُّهُ لَا ذَنْبَ عَلَيْهِ... (مستدرك الوسائل ج ١ ص ١١٩)

٥٦٢- قَالَ النَّبِيُّ ﷺ: يَا أَبَاذَرٍّ! إِذَا اتَّبَعْتَ جَنَازَةً فَلْيَكُنْ عَمَلُكَ فِيهَا التَّفَكُّرَ وَالْخُشُوعَ وَاعْلَمْ أَنَّكَ لَاحِقٌ بِهِ (مستدرك الوسائل ج ١ ص ١٣١)

٥٦٣- رُوِيَ أَنَّ رَسُولَ اللهِ ﷺ خَرَجَ فِي جَنَازَةٍ فَقَالَ رَجُلٌ: هَذِهِ جَنَازَةٌ صَالِحٌ. فَقَالَ آخَرُ مِثْلَ ذَلِكَ. فَقَالَ مِثْلَهُ الثَّالِثُ. فَقَالَ ﷺ: وَجَبَتِ الْجَنَّةُ - وَرَبِّ الْكَعْبَةِ - لِأَنَّ الْمُؤْمِنِينَ شُهَدَاءُ اللهِ وَاللهُ لَا يَرُدُّ شَهَادَتَهُمْ. (مستدرك الوسائل ج ١ ص ١٣٧)

٥٦٤- قَالَ رَسُولُ اللهِ ﷺ: مَا مِنْ عَبْدٍ مُسْلِمٍ غَسَّلَ أَخَاهُ

مُسْلِمًا فَلَمْ يَقْذِرْهُ وَلَمْ يَنْظُرْ اِلَى عَوْرَتِهِ وَلَمْ يَذْكُرْ مِنْهُ سُوءًا ثُمَّ شَيَّعَهُ وَصَلَّى عَلَيْهِ ثُمَّ جَلَسَ حَتَّى يُوَارَى فِي قَبْرِهِ الاَّ خَرَجَ عَطِلًا مِنْ ذُنُوْبِهِ .

(مستدرك الوسائل ج ١ ص ٩٩)

٥٦٥ - قَالَ النَّبِيُّ ﷺ: لَاَنْ اَطَأَ عَلَى جَمْرَةٍ اَوْ سَيْفٍ اَحَبُّ اِلَيَّ مِنْ اَنْ اَطَأَ عَلَى قَبْرِ مُسْلِمٍ .

(مستدرك الوسائل ج ١ ص ١٣٢)

٥٦٦ - فِي وَصِيَّةِ النَّبِيِّ ﷺ لِعَلِيٍّ ﷷ: يَا عَلِيُّ! كَرِهَ اللهُ عَزَّوَجَلَّ لِاُمَّتِيَ الْعَبَثَ فِي الصَّلَوةِ وَالْمَنَّ فِي الصَّدَقَةِ وَاِتْيَانَ الْمَسَاجِدِ جُنُبًا وَّالضَّحِكَ بَيْنَ الْقُبُوْرِ .

(من لا يحضره الفقيه ص ٥٧٣)

٥٦٧ - قَالَ الصَّادِقُ ﷷ: مِنْ حَقِّ الْمُؤْمِنِ عَلَى الْمُؤْمِنِ ... وَاِذَا مَاتَ فَالزِّيَارَةُ لَهُ اِلَى قَبْرِهِ .

(مستدرك الوسائل ج ١ ص ١٢٩)

٥٦٨ - قَالَ رَسُوْلُ اللهِ ﷺ: لِلدَّابَّةِ عَلَى صَاحِبِهَا خِصَالٌ: يَبْدَأُ بِعَلِفِهَا اِذَا نَزَلَ وَيَعْرِضُ عَلَيْهَا الْمَاءَ اِذَا اَمَرَّ بِهِ وَلَا يَضْرِبُ وَجْهَهَا فَاِنَّهَا يُسَبِّحُ بِحَمْدِ رَبِّهَا وَلَا يَقِفُ عَلَى ظَهْرِهَا اِلَّا فِي سَبِيْلِ اللهِ وَلَا يَحْمِلُهَا فَوْقَ طَاقَتِهَا وَلَا يُكَلِّفُهَا مِنَ الْمَشْيِ اِلَّا مَا تُطِيْقُ . (من لا يحضره الفقيه ص ٢٢٨)

٥٦٩ - قَالَ اَبُو الْحَسَنِ ﷷ: مِنْ مُرُوَّةِ الرَّجُلِ اَنْ يَكُوْنَ دَوَابُّهُ سِمَانًا .

(وسائل الشيعه ج ٢ ص ١٩٤)

٥٧٠ - اِنَّ عَلِيًّا عَلَيْهِ السَّلامُ كَانَ يَسْهُمُ لِلْفَارِسِ ثَلَاثَةَ اَسْهُمٍ: سَهْمَيْنِ لِفَرَسَيْهِ وَسَهْمًا لَهُ. وَيَجْعَلُ لِلرَّاجِلِ سَهْمًا.

(وسائل الشيعه ج ٢ ص ٤٣٣)

٥٧١ - قَالَ الْبَاقِرُ عَلَيْهِ السَّلامُ: اِنَّ اللهَ تَعَالَى يُحِبُّ اِبْرَادَ الْكَبِدِ الْحَرَّاءِ وَمَنْ سَقَى كَبِدًا حَرَّاءَ مِنْ بَهِيمَةٍ وَّغَيْرِهَا اَظَلَّهُ اللهُ يَوْمَ لَا ظِلَّ اِلَّا ظِلُّهُ. (وسائل الشيعه ج ٢ ص ٥٠)

٥٧٢ - قَالَ الصَّادِقُ عَلَيْهِ السَّلامُ: اِنَّ لِكُلِّ شَيْءٍ حُرْمَةٌ وَحُرْمَةُ الْبَهَائِمِ فِي وُجُوهِهَا. (وسائل الشيعه ج ٢ ص ١٩٦)

٥٧٣ - قَالَ رَسُولُ اللهِ صَلَّى اللهُ عَلَيْهِ وَآلِهِ: لَا تَتَوَرَّكُوا عَلَى الدَّوَابِّ وَلَا تَتَّخِذُوا ظُهُورَهَا مَجَالِسَ. (من لا يحضره الفقيه ص ٢٢٨)

٥٧٤ - قَالَ رَسُولُ اللهِ صَلَّى اللهُ عَلَيْهِ وَآلِهِ: لَا يَرْتَدِفُ ثَلَاثَةٌ عَلَى دَابَّةٍ فَاِنَّ اَحَدَهُمْ مَلْعُونٌ. (وسائل الشيعه ج ٢ ص ١٩٧)

٥٧٥ - قَالَ رَسُولُ اللهِ صَلَّى اللهُ عَلَيْهِ وَآلِهِ: اِنَّ اللهَ تَبَارَكَ وَتَعَالَى يُحِبُّ الرِّفْقَ وَيُعِينُ عَلَيْهِ، فَاِذَا رَكِبْتُمُ الدَّوَابَّ الْعِجَافَ فَاَنْزِلُوهَا مَنَازِلَهَا فَاِنْ كَانَتِ الْاَرْضُ مُجْدَبَةً فَانْجُوا عَلَيْهَا فَاِنْ كَانَتْ مُخْصِبَةً فَاَنْزِلُوهَا مَنَازِلَهَا.

(من لا يحضره الفقيه ص ٢٢٩)

٥٧٦ - قَالَ اَبُو جَعْفَرٍ عَلَيْهِ السَّلامُ: اِذَا سِرْتَ فِي اَرْضٍ خَصِبَةٍ فَارْفُقْ بِالسَّيْرِ وَاِذَا سِرْتَ فِي اَرْضٍ مُجْدَبَةٍ فَعَجِّلْ بِالسَّيْرِ.

(من لا يحضره الفقيه ص ٢٢٩)

٥٧٧ - عَنْ اَبِي عَبْدِ اللهِ عَلَيْهِ السَّلامُ اَنَّ اَبَا جَعْفَرٍ عَلَيْهِ السَّلامُ قَالَ: لَا تُقْبَلُ

شَهَادَةُ سَابِقِ الْحَاجِّ لِأَنَّهُ قَتَلَ رَاحِلَتَهُ.....

(وسائل الشيعه ج ٣ ص ٤١٥)

٥٧٨- قَالَ رَسُولُ اللهِ ﷺ: اضْرِبُوهَا عَلَى النِّفَارِ وَلَاتَضْرِبُوهَا عَلَى الْعِثَارِ. (فروع كافى ج ٢ ص ٢٣٠)

٥٧٩- قَالَ رَسُولُ اللهِ ﷺ: مَنْ قَتَلَ عُصْفُوراً عَبَثاً جَاءَ يَوْمَ الْقِيَامَةِ وَلَهُ صُرَاخٌ حَوْلَ الْعَرْشِ يَقُولُ: رَبِّ سَلْ هذَا فِيمَ قَتَلَنِي مِنْ غَيْرِ مَنْفَعَةٍ.

(مستدرك الوسائل ج ٣ ص ٥٨)

٥٨٠- قَالَ الصَّادِقُ ﷺ: إِنَّ امْرَأَةً عُذِّبَتْ فِي هِرَّةٍ رَبَطَتْهَا حَتَّى مَاتَتْ عَطَشاً. (وسائل الشيعه ج ٢ ص ٢٠٣)

٥٨١- إِنَّ أَمِيرَ الْمُؤْمِنِينَ ﷺ قَالَ: لَا تُذْبَحُ الشَّاةُ عِنْدَ الشَّاةِ وَلَا الْجَزُورُ عِنْدَ الْجَزُورِ وَهُوَ يَنْظُرُ إِلَيْهِ.

(وسائل الشيعه ج ٣ ص ٢٣٩)

٥٨٢- عَنْ مُحَمَّدِ بْنِ الْفُضَيْلِ عَنْ أَبِي الْحَسَنِ الرِّضَا ﷺ قَالَ: قُلْتُ لَهُ: كَانَ عِنْدِي كَبْشٌ سَنَةً لِأُضَحِّيَ بِهِ فَلَمَّا أَخَذْتُهُ وَأَضْجَعْتُهُ نَظَرَ إِلَيَّ فَرَحِمْتُهُ وَرَقَقْتُ لَهُ ثُمَّ إِنِّي ذَبَحْتُهُ قَالَ فَقَالَ ﷺ: مَا كُنْتُ أُحِبُّ لَكَ أَنْ تَفْعَلَ لَا تُرَبِّيَنَّ شَيْئاً مِنْ هَذَا ثُمَّ تَذْبَحُهُ.

(وسائل الشيعه ج ٣ ص ٢٤٧)

✡

الخوئي الخيريّة

AL-KHOEI